Man of the Year

For Emily,

Man
of the Year

Lou Cove

Enjoy the ride!

Lou

FLATIRON
BOOKS
NEW YORK

www.flatironbooks.com

Lyrics from "Song of the Soul" used by permission. Courtesy of Cris Williamson.

The Library of Congress Cataloging-in-Publication Data is available upon request.

ISBN 978-1-250-12396-1 (hardcover)
ISBN 978-1-250-12397-8 (e-book)

Our books may be purchased in bulk for promotional, educational, or business use. Please contact your local bookseller or the Macmillan Corporate and Premium Sales Department at 1-800-221-7945, extension 5442, or by e-mail at MacmillanSpecialMarkets@macmillan.com.

First Edition: May 2017

10 9 8 7 6 5 4 3 2 1

For Dana, who made me promise
to just do my best.

And for Sam and Sylvie.
You're just as old as we were then,
but you're too young to read this book.

Howie and me, 1978

It contributes greatly towards a man's moral and intellectual health, to be brought into habits of companionship with individuals unlike himself, who care little for his pursuits, and whose sphere and abilities he must go out of himself to appreciate . . . There was one man, especially, the observation of whose character gave me a new idea of talent.

—*Nathaniel Hawthorne*

If I'm going to be Starsky, then you're going to have to be my Hutch.

—*Howie Gordon*

Part I

Cover
Story

At Home in Salem

What the hell are we doing in Salem? The town famous for torching neighbors who seemed anything other than Puritan. We're not just strangers, we're Jews! Sure, we're unobservant, noncomformist, freethinking New York Jews in paisley-patched dungarees—but still, we're so very Other, and so very wandering. Nice to meet you, Salem, Massachusetts. We'll be gone soon.

It's our eighth move in twelve years, but none of the first seven were nearly as bleak. Everything about Salem is different than Manhattan, right from the break of day. No noise. No cars. No life until the Salem dads emerge from their front doors, suited up and shuffling to the train for the slow weekday ride to Boston. They are followed by the sockless, Docksider-wearing sea-captain wannabes, unshaven and still bleary from the rum scrum of the night before. They buy fresh bread and weak coffee at the Athens Bakery, drag on long brown cigarettes on their way to their boats or their private painting studios, avoiding the gaze of the dudes cruising rusty Camaros and booming Jethro Tull and Black Sabbath, gunning for their morning dog's hair at the Pig's Eye.

But on Sunday mornings these streets are empty. I ride alone.

I deliver papers, and not that well. At six thirty each Sunday my alarm buzzes and a fresh pile of *North Shore Sunday*s, bound with wire and wrapped in plastic, waits for me on the front steps.

I grab a T-shirt, the striped jeans I wore yesterday, a Marblehead zip sweatshirt and my canvas paper bag. Atjeh, our dog, is still settled by the foot of my bed in the same Sunday rhythm reserved for the rest of the Cove family. Her black lids rise wearily when I open the door, ice-blue eyes indifferent.

The *North Shore Sunday* has just enough original content to merit being called a newspaper, but it's otherwise filled with advertisements for the butcher sale at the A&P, marine supplies, and cordwood delivery. People don't pay for it—the only person who seems to care if it shows up is Mr. Getchell, my route supervisor—but I still try to get tips for delivering it when I can.

Outside, it looks as if the cold mist might give way. I snip the rigid newspaper bindings with the wire-cutter crotch of my pliers. The news of the week is a mix of global import and local fluff. The Vatican denies foul play but refuses to conduct an autopsy on Pope John Paul I. The Marblehead Squirts hockey team made the cover after a visit to Quebec. Peter Frampton is still recovering from his car accident. I fill the stiff paperboy bag with my burden. I hate this. Every part of it. Waking up early, balancing as I ride, the sack cutting into my shoulder like a claw, rolling through the haunted streets alone, forced into neighborhoods that smell like damp ashtrays. I rarely finish the job, and now towers of undelivered papers teeter in my closet and sop up rabbit tinkle in Bunny Yabba's wooden crate in the center of my room. The first few weeks, I threw maybe twenty or thirty copies in there. Just the last couple of streets' worth. As the weather got colder I started quitting the route three-quarters of the way in. Then halfway.

I shamble out back, where my Apollo waits by a rosebush. It's a Ross, five-speed, stout, rugged tires, whitewalls, chrome fenders, banana seat, and Easy Rider handlebars. The saving grace of any paper route morning.

This is the eighth time I've had to move. Eighth! Mama and Papa keep trying to convince us that moving to Salem is a great achievement, the realization of a long-held dream to return to the place of their youth, the North Shore of Massachusetts—and to do so in spectacular fashion. Mama—who grew up nearby in Lynn, Lynn, the city of sin, you never come out the way you went in—spent months shopping for a house in Marblehead. That's the next town over from Salem, where Papa grew up and where his parents, Grandma Wini and Grandpa Sam, still live. We've ended up just a few miles away from them, and that's really the only good thing I can say about leaving our apartment on West End Avenue in New York.

"It needs to be something historical. Something old," Mama had said over the phone to the Realtor, who couldn't produce anything close to my parents' price range in the dense clapboard cluster of houses along Marblehead's sparkling harbor.

"Would you consider living in Salem?" the Realtor had asked as Mama calculated mortgage rates on a piece of pink scrap paper.

"There's only one street I would consider living on in Salem and that's Chestnut Street," she answered, believing this wasn't an option.

"Well, then you better come and see this house."

"It's the most beautiful street in America," Mama told us. "And I'm not the only one who feels that way."

Apparently it was true because Papa had said the same thing over the phone to me when he heard that Mama was going to look at 31 Chestnut. "It's the most beautiful street in America," he said cheerily. "Magazine worthy. You'll see."

"Who says that?" I asked Mama, wondering what was so bad

about the first street we lived on. Or the fourth. Or the seventh. "Who says it's the most beautiful? And why do we need to live somewhere beautiful? Riverside Park is beautiful." So was Washington, D.C. And Westport, Connecticut. And New York the first time around.

"It is," said Mama, "and it smells like someone peed all over it. This is a better place to grow up. You'll see."

Our house is one of three brick homes pressed into one, side by side—a gift from a Salem sea merchant to his three daughters. Our part, the left third of the manor, has three sprawling floors, all of which show their age. "Seventy-three-hundred square feet!" Papa never tires of proclaiming, whatever that means. There are seven bedrooms, five bathrooms, a haunted attic, and an entire apartment hidden behind an unlocked swinging door in the disproportionately small galley kitchen.

My sister, Amanda, and I run the length of the house when we first arrive, through not one but two living rooms, craning to see the dust bunnies and dead flies caught in the cobwebs dangling from the impossibly high ceilings. There are fireplaces in nearly every room, and a gigantic basement, once the servants' kitchen, with a wooden dumbwaiter at one end. It could still be used to transport toys and snacks ("but NO kids!") to the little kitchen above by way of a thick, oily rope worn smooth by decades of calloused hands sending dishes and meals up and down. Every room shows its age, wallpaper drooping and bubbled, signs of water recently dribbled from under the crown moldings and ceiling medallions, and fractures in all the wood floors which promise legendary splinters.

The truth is, my father didn't want to leave New York. He loved the hustle, distraction, and music of the streets. He delighted in discovering the next cheese, cigar, smoked-fish, or magic-trick shop. He lived for the museums, the movie theaters, and his work. His enthusiasm for life and that city was infectious.

My mother shared no such feelings. The only way he was able to convince her to move back to New York (the city of my birth) was to promise the eventual return to shtetl life in one of the seaside towns on the North Shore. "Two years in the city," he told her. "That's all I need to reach the next level." It took three, but she prevailed.

From the outside our new home suggests a great triumph, but wealthy as we may appear to the tourists who goggle at the towering manors of Chestnut Street, they can't see the leaky ceilings and exposed horsehair plaster from the outside. And they can't see the apartment we need to rent to Frank, our spectacularly hairy and exultantly gay tenant, who was Papa's fraternity brother in college. "This little bit of neglect is how we could afford to buy it," Mama said. "And the rent is how we'll afford to keep it." Their relief was evident when Frank, a blast from Papa's past, answered the ad in the *Salem Evening News*.

I sling the bag over my shoulder, roll the bike back along the brick walkway, and saddle up on an empty Chestnut Street. Rolling east, up Flint and across Essex, knocking off the scarier sections by Route 107 before the weirdos over there wake up.

"Grandpa Sam had a paper route when he was a boy," Grandma Wini told me when I got mine. "He always tried to stay one step behind the milkman, who also made deliveries before dawn. My Sammy would get to the stoop and open up those fresh bottles of milk so he could sip the cream off the top. If it was too cold out, the cream would freeze and he was out of luck. If that happened, he would go to the homes that got their rolls delivered from the bakery. Can you imagine him? Poor, hungry *faygele*."

"He's not gay," I say, confused.

"Oy! *Faygele*, silly! It's Yiddish for *little bird*. Where do you hear such things?"

Gramps never told me about his paper route or the cream thing himself, but Gramps never tells me much besides what's for supper and what's in the *TV Guide*. "There's a new show on next Sunday, Big Lou. It's about a fellow with bionic arms and legs and eyes. Why don't you come over and watch with me?"

I deliver most of the papers and start to close the loop of my route, led by my nose toward the yeasty smell of Athens Bakery's bread wafting through the neighborhood. I stop pedaling at the corner of Botts and Essex, one house away from Gretchen's. She's the only girl in this new neighborhood who's willing to talk to me. Willing, but not necessarily wanted. Gretchen: always showing up unexpectedly. Usually sitting too close for comfort. She's twelve, too, but instead of attending my school, Oliver, she goes to some experimental place on the other side of town. "Fuh cool kids," she boasted once. "They might let yuh in."

I could turn home now and avoid her altogether, but before I can decide, I see her face flash in an upstairs window and I know she's been waiting for me.

Gretchen motions frantically to stay put so I wait out front. She's talking before the door even slams behind her.

"Didja finish yah route?"

I shake my head. "Just taking a break."

It's not warm enough for shorts today, but she's wearing them anyway. She sits on the brick path to her little house and motions for me to join. When she crosses her legs I can see the top of her thigh, all milk, slipping away into a darker fold of her khakis.

"See the *Love Boat* last night?" she asks. I shake my head again and she flaps her legs like a bird, and there it is: the yellow cotton panel of her panties, revealing skin more ginger-pink than the flesh of her leg.

"Ahnold was on it."

"From *Happy Days*?"

"Yup," she nods knowingly, looks down between her legs, then back at me. "Get a good look?"

I feel a spring of panic, and quickly look away from her crotch to the Witch House in the distance. They call it that, as if it were the home of Tituba or Sarah Good, but Mama says it is actually the house of a wealthy Puritan judge who participated at their infamous trials. Papa says everyone in Salem has an angle.

I look back and Gretchen is smiling, dropping her knees a little farther so the cuff of her khaki short gives an additional, breathtaking quarter of an inch or more. And then she slides a finger to her panties and moves the yellow fabric aside.

Shame vies with thrill. I want to see. I don't want to know. I stand up, certain a Puritan judge is rounding the corner with a thorny switch. "Gotta finish the route."

"I don't caih, yuh know. If yuh wanna look, I mean."

"I know," I nod, straddling the Apollo. "I just have to . . . Have to go."

I make a few more deliveries, pop out the north side of the cemetery, and catch the smell of the ocean breeze, skipped like a stone off the wharf toward Gallows Hill, carrying all those damp Salem odors.

Papa's asleep when I return. Mama's tinkering in the basement. I enter quietly, softly walking the steps to my room. I stash the overflow in the closet, drop a few pellets of food in between the pellets of poop in Bunny Yabba's crate, and return to the top bunk for a visit with Barbi Benton. If Gramps noticed the missing Barbi issues from his *Playboy* collection in his downstairs bathroom, he never hinted at it. Here, she's looking over her shoulder at me. Looking up from her poolside sunbathing. Turning away from her stained glass window to meet my eyes. Rising up from her bed of furs. The brunette Breck girl, but naked. Barbara Gordon minus her shiny purple Batgirl cowl.

May '72 is Barbi at her best, auburn hair and bangs taking up the entire cover, those incredible eyes, black but exploding with sparks of slate blue and white light, flawless Chiclet teeth that flash a smile, girl next door but more. Entertainment for Men. One dollar.

Barbi. So perfect. So flawless. Not like Gretchen. She's too . . . real.

I pull Bunny Yabba out of his stinking crate and take him to breakfast with me, checking the closet once more to make sure the door is shut and latched and the papers aren't spilling out. Atjeh scrambles ahead of me, flying down the stairs.

"Oh, don't bring him down here, honey," Mama says when she sees the rabbit tucked in the crook of my arm. "He'll just poop everywhere."

"He doesn't poop anywhere but his crate," says Papa, shuffling to the table, plaid nightshirt unbuttoned, chest bared. "He's the world's first house-trained rabbit." Mama rolls her eyes.

Papa doesn't eat breakfast anymore. "Stopped in 1962. Single most important thing I ever did for my health. That and running." Hard to imagine, given how skinny he is now, but his brown-and-white wedding photos prove he was once a porky Peter. Between that and his asthma, the chubby 1950s Jewish kid who wanted to play basketball like Bob Cousy had to reinvent himself.

"But Cousy's six-one!" Gramps told him. "You're five-six."

"But I *feel* like I'm seven-one. *Swish!*"

The brass knocker clacks from the end of the hall and Amanda bounces on her skinny legs from the table to answer it.

"Ugh! That's not Nusselballs, is it?" Mr. Nusselblatt is my Hebrew teacher. I call him Nusselballs. He looks like one of those old, black-hat New York rabbis, and he has the whitefish, horseradish, half-sour breath to match, but he's actually a twenty-two-year old student from Salem State.

"No, Hebrew lessons are Tuesday evenings. At the rate you're going you should be doing them three times a week," Mama warns. I collapse in my chair. First they move me to a city with no Jewish people, then they want me to do a bar mitzvah? Why don't they just take a picture of my circumcised penis and post it all over town?

"If we're so Jewish, why do we have a Christmas tree every year?" I protest.

"Because we're Americans," Papa says firmly from behind his newspaper. "Because we're free. Because it makes the house smell good."

Mama, daughter of the best kosher butcher on the North Shore, grimaces. For her, this is what you do. Tradition. For Papa, it's as much about the nose-to-the-grindstone act of achieving *something* as it is about becoming a man. I don't think he gives a crap if I bar mitzvah or I belly up to the bar. I'll be a man when he says I'm a man.

Amanda returns with the uninvited guest. It's Gretchen. She catches my eye, half smiles. I return the greeting halfheartedly, grateful to be the object of attention but wishing the subject were someone else.

"Bagel?" Mama offers, passing a basket of sesame, egg, and everything.

"These rolls?" Gretchen asks, which gets Papa's attention. "Rolls? Bagels. Come here, Gretchen," Papa says loudly, grabbing the basket and pulling out a sesame bagel. "We'll show you how this is done." He spreads a huge glob of chive cream cheese on a half, then piles red onions, tomato slices, lox, and capers.

"You'll need a little mouthwash after this," Mama says. "But you'll love it."

Papa finishes the project, slides a plate across the table to Gretchen, who sits down next to me, and everyone watches as she bites tentatively into the Sunday breakfast of choice in the Cove household.

"It tastes . . . a little . . . weeahd . . ." She pulls a thread of lox from under her tongue.

"Lox. Smoked salmon," Mama says. Gretchen stares quizzically at her. "Fish, darling. Smoked fish." Gretchen's face goes queasy.

Papa scoops up the Arts section now that Mama has moved on to Op-Ed. Amanda and our younger brother David divide the *Boston Globe* funnies.

We all sit in silence for a bit, reading. David hums softly to himself. "Listen to this," Papa says. "There's a new album by a band called the Sex Pistols. Great name! And it's called *Never Mind the Bollocks*. Hysterical."

"What's bollocks?" I ask.

"Testicles. It's the British way of saying balls."

Gretchen looks up, giggles, then blushes pink across her lily skin.

"Did someone say balls?" Frank sweeps into our dining room, a scruffy dumpling in a silk kimono. "And I thought I was just coming for a bagel!"

"God save the queen," Papa murmurs.

"All the queens," Frank chuckles, grabbing a bagel. He is the hairiest person I ever met. Like, *Planet of the Apes* hairy: short and round with black chest hair so thick you can't see his nipples or make out whether he has a bellybutton.

"I was in a tree on the field in front of my high school kissing my first crush," he told me one night when he was babysitting and Amanda and David had gone to bed. "Fell twenty-two feet. I was in a body cast for eight months and they shaved me from head to toe before they put me in. When I came out, I looked like this. Eat your heart out, Burt Reynolds! But those were the worst months of my life. I felt prickers and itches all over and I couldn't move. My sister would sit by the side of my bed and slide a ruler under the cast to scratch but it didn't help. My father said it was *volontà di Dio*—God's wrath for kissing a boy. He didn't say any-thing to me ever again after that."

"Do you miss your dad?" I'd asked.

"Every day, *ragazzino*. Every day. Cherish that Papa of yours."

"By the way, got a call last night," Papa says as Frank heads back to his apartment. "Special guests coming to stay with us for a while. They'll be here later today."

"Ooh," Frank says and stops at the door to inquire: "Boys or girls?"

"Who? You didn't tell us that," I say, ticked at Papa's typical last-minute surprise.

"Well, I'm telling you now," Papa says. "Remember our friends Howie and Carly? They just got married."

"Married boys?" Frank skitters back over, wraps an arm around Papa.

"Not Carl, Carly. Sorry, Charlie. They're on their honeymoon. Cross-country road trip, from Berkeley to Salem. They called from Philly. We're the last stop before they go back again. They'll stay for a week. Maybe two."

"Salem would make anyone turn around and go home," I grumble.

"Hey," Papa says in his *straighten-up* tone. "You've got Grandma Wini and Grandpa Sam here. You never complained about com-ing for holidays or summer vacations in the past. Plus your Aunt Leslie, Uncle Rick, and Cousin Greg live in Marblehead, too . . ."

"And Grandma Charlotte and Uncle Morris," Mama adds her side of the family.

"And them," Papa admits, no fan of his mother-in-law but always happy for a bourbon and a cigar with old Mo. "You've got your whole family. And now you'll have some very cool roommates for a couple of weeks."

My father met Howie at Antioch College in 1969. Papa was

ten years older, in from D.C. looking for interns to help fight the war on poverty. Howie was a junior assigned to tour him around campus. Instead of choosing any of the applicants, Papa asked Howie to come back with him. "He was smart, and he made me laugh, a real star. So I ended up hiring him. We had a hell of a time."

"Is he the hippie?" I ask.

"He's . . . a free spirit."

The name conjures vague memories, positive ones, but another disruption in our lives? "I don't want them to come," I say petulantly. "I don't want anyone to stay with us." A glance from Gretchen confirms that I'm acting like a little kid. "I mean, because we're still getting used to a new city. And now we have to get used to more strangers?"

"Friends are a part of life," Papa says. "The best part. If you don't spend real time with friends, you're not living life."

"Aren't *we* living?" Amanda asks.

He shakes his head. "Only if we do certain things. How do you really know if you're alive? Hm? How do you know?" he says to me.

"Your heart beats," I say flatly.

"Mechanics." Papa's voice rises. "Did you wake up ready to go today?" he asks, looking me in the eye, making sure I'm listening. "Did you play music today? Did you have sex today? Did you sweat? See a friend? Cook something delicious? Did you help someone today? *That's* how you know you had a good day. *That's* when you know you're alive."

Papa's enthusiasm for living is infectious. He has a way of rallying us like troops, a natural leadership that I envy.

Gretchen giggles again, squirms in her seat. Then she gives me a look that screams *let's go*.

"What's up?" I ask as we climb the stairs to my room.

"How come ya parents ah always talking about that kinda stuff?"

"What kind of stuff?" I reply, knowing full well it's Papa's plain-spoken style that's rattled her. But I don't care. I like it, and I wish he'd speak that way with me all the time.

"Sex and stuff."

"Well, he wasn't really talking about sex, he just said the word."

"And balls."

I shrug.

"My parents would kill me. Especially on a Sunday. And how come ya all read at the table?"

"That's what we do on Sunday mornings."

"Don't ya go to chuhch?"

"Jews don't go to church."

"But they go to a temple or something, right?"

"I guess. But we don't." Which is a fair point, now that I think about it. Where would my bar mitzvah be, anyway? In the back-yard?

"Then what's so Jewish about you? And that weahd guy who lives out back. I think he might be a fag."

"He's gay, if that's what you mean."

Gretchen frowns. I don't need her to tell me how different we are from everybody else in this stupid city. That was clear from the moment we sat on the front steps that first Saturday on Chestnut Street and got the stink eye from our neighbor Glovey Butler. The gray matriarch of Salem society is our most formidable neighbor, installed right next door with a houseful of familial ghosts and a very-much-alive grandson named Johnny. Our neighbors live in fear of crossing her path. Papa lives for winning her approval.

The Salemites don't quite know what to do with a family like ours.

Mama is brilliant: a computer programmer taking a break to stay home with my baby brother but never not working. She's comfortable around a jigsaw, handy with a slide rule. In other words, she's not your average Chestnut Street lady.

My father is purposefully anti-average: sporting a dandy bow tie, a carefully waxed handlebar mustache, and hair almost to his shoulders, he turns heads. I have no idea what the welfare recipients or the physically and mentally disabled folks he gets jobs for think of him, but I know he spends the majority of his days thinking and working on their behalf.

As for me, I haven't developed Papa's social conscience or his taste for ties, but I do wear my hair long, in tribute. I still have a bit of a lisp, and I like the Mets, not the Red Sox, so I'm primed for pummeling by the townies.

I picked my room based on how far it is from everyone else: third floor, end of the hall, glossy green paint on old wood floorboards, deep closet to hide stuff, and a marble fireplace. Two windows face east, toward the metal peak of the neighbors' widow's walk. I can't help but picture leagues of ashen old Glovey Butlers wearily looking out to sea for the husbands who will never return. How many of them have hopped the fencing meant to contain the grief-stricken and landed in these thorny piles of chestnuts below us?

I open the door and Gretchen's hand flies to her face.

"Ugh! What is that stink?" she screeches.

"Bunny Yabba's crate. I need to change it. Just follow me." I open the back window, and lead Gretchen to my private hideout—a long flat roof, still wet under the late September morning sky.

"Aw, wicked!" she says as she takes in the view. I gaze up at the peaked roof where I sometimes climb to be alone. It's my "Secure Position" and I consider showing Gretchen, then think better of it.

Maybe she senses my hackles rising. Or maybe she just wants

to show me that different, like me, is good in her mind. Exotic. Sidling up next to me on the flat copper ledge, Gretchen Pelletier puts her face right up to mine and says, "Kiss me."

We touch lips, mouths searching for the right angle, eyes open. It's my first time with a girl who didn't have the bottle spin her way. I reach for her forearms, pebbled into gooseflesh. Her white-blonde hair, pale lips, golden freckles, and the memory of those little blond wisps at the edge of those yellow panties collide in my mind. My lungs collapse around the crazy *bong-bong, bong-bong* of my heart.

The tip of her tongue tastes like smoked salmon, spearmint Dentyne, and . . . ash?

"Did you smoke something?" I ask, pulling away.

Gretchen frowns. "Yeah. I pinched some Salem Lights from my ma's purse. So?" She pulls a crumpled pack from her back pocket and holds it out to me. "Want one?"

"I think I . . . Let's try again, instead?" Gretchen nods and closes her eyes this time. I taste her again and move to put a hand on the soft new bump on her chest.

"Bring that filthy behavior indoors!" Glovey Butler caws from her third-floor rear window, bath mat still dripping dust and debris as she shakes it weakly. "This is a neighborhood, not a cowshed. And you, boy! Leave that poor girl alone. I'll be sure to let her mother know just what kind of a gentleman you are not."

We scramble back inside and fall on the bottom bunk, laughing. Her willowy throat rises and swells. Atjeh scrapes at the corner of my latched door and I let her in.

"Can't kiss in front of a dog," Gretchen smirks.

"I know. That's why we came inside." She guffaws, moves to me to kiss again but I pull back, reach for my comics pile by the bed. "You like Morbius?" Gretchen sits up on her elbows, looking confused. "Morbius. The Living Vampire?" I say.

"Is that . . . like . . . a movie or sumthin'?"

"Comic book character. You know. 'Mystery. Mood. Menace. In the fearful tradition of Dracula'?"

We sit quietly for a minute or two. I can tell she wants to fool around some more but I can't find my way back. She's pretty enough. She's funny. Annoying, but funny. And she keeps sitting closer to me until I can feel the warmth of her leg through my jeans.

"You want another bagel?" I ask. Gretchen twists up her face and holds her hands out, exasperated, like I just missed the easiest catch ever thrown.

The Best Way to Come Together

An hour later, Amanda and I are camped on the front steps of the house, waiting for Howie and Carly. The granite is still morning-cold but this October Sunday has warmed to T-shirt weather. Atjeh bays from the backyard. She nipped at a baby in a stroller on the morning walk with Papa, and ended up tied to the shedding Seckel pear tree.

I guess we're getting used to this. The eighth house. The Salem house. When we moved in, Papa and Mama unveiled a freshly polished brass plaque engraved in deep, all-cap letters: THE COVES, and screwed it so firmly to the front door that its face started curving in, like it was vacuum sealed to the house, as if to say, after seven houses in twelve years, this will be the true home.

"New Yorkers think of Salem as a backwater," my father said. "A cultural and intellectual wasteland. I am here to tell you that we are creating a new reality in the City of Salem. These streets, once populated by small minds, shall be expanded with new ideas, new ways of thinking. We will wage the war on poverty from this port. And if the lid on the coffin of sanctimony and moralizing needs one final nail in it, let us be the ones to hammer it in. Welcome home, family."

Then he handed me his Canon.

"Get closer. Frame the shot! Wait . . ."

My parents stood straight, smiled. Mama laughed, sticking out her topographical tongue—that deeply textured part of her we never see—and Papa curled the long whiskers of his handlebar.

We have arrived, they say with their eyes. *We have settled.*

"Now!" The camera clicks and whirrs.

Amanda fills the time waiting for our guests with speculation about them, pondering the baby girls they may have one day. "I could babysit," she says dreamily.

"Maybe triplets," I suggest, trapped beside my lifetime companion whose focus is limited to cute things and stuffed things. "Maybe all boys, all the same age, and all the youngest black belts ever." She scowls, then drifts off, considering an alternate universe for the imaginary family these people we don't even know are yet to have, sucking her fingers and watching the passing clouds.

"Remember when Mama made the strawberry shortcake in the tent in the Everglades?" she asks, randomly segueing to a moment I remember well. "How did she do it?"

"I don't know," I confess. It was Amanda's birthday, and we were camping, partway into a three-month cross-country drive from Marblehead to Mexico. The trip was intended to be a break between selling the latest house and all our frivolous possessions and buying some land in the country where my parents planned to begin a new life homesteading. But two and a half months into the drive, Papa reconsidered, and, renewing his dedication to fighting urban poverty, turned tail in Mexico and headed for New York. But in the back of the Jeep Wagoneer, drowned out by the Cat Stevens and Neil Young eight-tracks, my sister and I were blissfully unaware of our changing fortunes.

Amanda turned four in the Everglades. I was six and a half. Papa took us for a walk to look for alligators and when we came back, there was Mama, emerging from the big canvas tent with a double-decker strawberry shortcake. Whipped cream and berries on top. Even candles. No sign of an oven. No campsite refrigerator. But that was Mama, always creating something from nothing.

"That was amazing," Amanda says through the fingers in her mouth.

"That was," I say.

A caw beside us shatters the shared memory, "Idle hands!" Glovey Butler, the Old Mother Hubbard lookalike, materializes without a sound. We stare at her, not certain how to reply. ". . . are the devil's playground," she completes the adage, frowning with yet more disappointment, if that is possible. "Why are you just sitting there? Don't you go to school?"

"It's Sunday," I remind her.

"It's Sunday, Mrs. Butler," she corrects.

"It's Sunday, Mrs. Butler." I sigh.

"I didn't spend a decade of my life working to put Chestnut Street on the Commonwealth's Register of Historic Places just so a child of the Lower East Side or wherever it is you immigrated from could scamp up the place. And you," she lowers a withering glance my way, "neighborhood molester of young women? I've got my eye out."

"Hello, Glovey," Mama says, behind us. "Actually, we're from the Upper West Side." She hands us each a plate with a peanut butter, honey, and banana sandwich and potato chips.

"Mrs. Cove," Mrs. Butler replies coolly, and turns her back on my mother, slipping into the dark foyer of her own home.

"We're still hoping you'll come for dinner sometime soon," Mama calls after her before Glovey can completely shut us out.

"A formal response will follow a formal invitation," says Mrs. Butler.

"I understand. Just you wait. I have a new recipe for Moroccan game hen."

The old crow slams her door. Mama turns her attention back to us. "Guys? I am as excited as you are. More so, probably. But we don't know when Howie and Carly are going to arrive," she says gently.

"I'm not excited," I tell her, "I'm bored."

"Hmmmmm. Well, you might want to play or do something else while you're waiting, don't you think? It could take a long time."

She's interrupted by the high nasal honk of a powder-blue Volkswagen minibus gliding freely from one side of Chestnut Street's extra-wide, brick-lined expanse to the other.

Amanda leaps up and runs to the street, ignoring Mama's "Wait! Here!"

I stay put, watching. The sound of that bus, the color, the daring weave through this registered historic place . . . A spaceship is approaching 31 Chestnut Street, only without the mashed potato mountains or mysterious electrical outages to warn us in advance.

Behind the glint from the submarine windows there are smiling faces, and on the front of the bus is a sticker of Minnie Mouse, hands behind her back, skirt in swing, eyelashes batting.

"Hello, bambinos!" the woman who must be Carly calls from the passenger window, her long, straight black hair flapping against the side of the bus as it jerks to a stop in front of our house.

"Hi! Hi!" Amanda is a flurry of giddy words, wobbling on her oversized Stride Rite clogs. "Mama said you weren't morning people and that it's six hours from Philadelphia if you don't stop and that you might not even be here until DINNER! And we're not even done with LUNCH!"

Carly opens her door and leaps out. Kneeling down, she looks us in the eyes and says, "We are NOT morning people unless we're coming to see you, but we're YOUR people. So today, we are morning people because we are so excited to visit!" She opens her arms and Amanda immediately steps forward into them. I hold back, but Carly extends an arm and waves me into the soft embrace. The way she hugs—but doesn't squish—us makes me melt against her. In a flash, this stranger becomes the object of my desire, her softer skin, her greener grass, her unconditional affection, palpable, fragrant. Oh, I am desperate for it.

"Oooooooohhhh!" She sighs happily, eyes scrunched tight. "You are delicious little dumplings made by the Hunan Princess herself!"

"Who?" I ask.

A low-voiced reply comes from the other side of the bus as Howie strides around and toward us, "The Hunan Princess is your sweet, sublime, beautiful, light-ray mamapajama, hombre." His arms are outstretched for a hug and the sun makes his hair glow copper, falling in long waves below his ears, upside-down swells curling to frame his square jaw. Strands fall from the top of his head into his eyes, which search my own with what seems to be an honest desire to know me. His smile is infectious, his dashiki completely out of place, as are his brilliant orange silk pants, speckled with white and green Japanese flowers. A riot of color and spirit, he moves toward us, gallant smile turned up, chin pulled down, head cocked to the side. The most handsome man I have ever seen.

I hope Glovey Butler is watching.

Amanda and I swallow a long list of follow-up questions as Howie picks Mama off her feet and spins her until the flowers of his drawstring pants dissolve in a blur and our mother—our soft-spoken, impassive mother—begins to laugh. Uncontrollable, head-back laughter, long straight brown hair set loose in rolling crests, looking straight at the gray autumn sky that hangs skeptically over Chestnut Street.

I've never seen her so helplessly happy. Carly grabs my hand, and we begin to spin, all of us a tightening gyre on the front lawn.

"Now," Howie pulls away, returning my mother gently to earth, and looking at me, "where the hell's your old man?"

Pa's in the kitchen. It's a tiny *L*-shaped room, cramped compared to the rest of this dilapidated mansion. Originally a staging area for meals, this little space off the massive dining room was designed to receive meals via the dumbwaiter from the *real* kitchen in the basement. But for my father, cooking is performance art. He's not going to do it in the basement.

"El Jefe!" Howie calls, squeezing his way into the kitchen to hug his old friend and take in the view: every open surface covered with spices, knives, bottles of wine and oils, a bronze mortar and pestle, mustard seeds, fresh horseradish, oranges, figs, and a whole fish, head and scales still on. "All hail the chief!"

"Boobie! You made it. And in record time, too." Papa wraps his arms around his friend, hugging him firmly but keeping his hands at a slight angle to avoid getting whatever's dripping from them on Howie's dashiki. "Jesus, where the hell did you get those pants?"

"That's my lovely bride's handiwork," Howie says happily. Papa grabs a long wooden spoon in one hand, the handle of a small saucepan in the other, and stirs whatever has started to boil over. "Well, you look like a fucking geisha girl."

"Feel even better than that. There's freedom in the flow. You'll see."

"Well, you look good otherwise. Working out?"

"Breaking concrete with a sledgehammer."

"Make an honest hippie out of you."

"So what's for dinner?" Howie reaches for the saucepan, turns it his way, and dips a finger.

"Little Polish thing from the Old Country. *Ryba* with *galarecie*. Cold fish in aspic, carrot rings, hardboiled eggs, and lemon slices . . . Watch the handle," he adds, turning the saucepan around so the handle faces the back of the stove. "Kids."

"You're living the life, Jefe." Howie pats my father on the back. "I always knew you'd make good."

"Thanks for the vote of confidence, boychik."

Howie's admiration of Papa sparks an unfamiliar feeling: pride. Something I've never really felt about my father. But there it is. His open respect for my father is something I can't remember other men expressing. Uncle Ricky? Always quick with the comeback. Gramps? He seems to regard his son with a mixture of amusement and a *where did* you *come from?* confusion. And Papa's friends seem more likely to compete with him than to compliment him. And he with them. It's the one-upsmanship of men. I thought they all did it.

But not this man.

"Are you the same age as Papa?" I ask.

"Not quite, *hermanito*. He's like my big brother. Ten years older and a hundred years wiser."

Later, after our dinner—fish heads and eggs for the adults, jelly omelets, thank God, for us—Howie hangs a sheet on the family room wall and breaks out a box of Kodachrome slides. Mama wraps David in her arms. Amanda sits by her. Papa and Carly talk politics.

"Jerry Brown—" Carly implores.

"Fuck Jerry Brown! He lost last time. What's the point of trying again? Besides, we have a Democrat in the White House. Everybody needs to stick with Carter. Come on. Jerry Brown . . . Shit," Papa says.

"What do you think, Louis?" Carly asks, raven's-wing hair draping over her shoulder.

"Dunno," I shrug.

"No? Iran's gonna be an albatross for old Jimmy. I bet you have an opinion on this politics thing," Howie says, locking the carousel into place. "I remember you at that party when your folks lived in Georgetown."

"I was *two*," I say softly.

"Yeah, but you knew your stuff. You kept running around the party saying 'Nixon is a doodie! Nixon is a doodie!' And you were right, little man. You were SO right."

"You were there for that?"

Howie nods. "I've had my eye on you since you were a wee tumbleweed, Little Big Man."

"I like your minibus," I say, eager to keep up the conversation.

"I do, too," Howie says, transitioning smoothly along with me. "Want to drive it?"

"One day. One day," Papa says, cupping my face in his hand like I'm two instead of twelve. I pull away, and grimace.

Howie kneels down to Carly, kisses her the way people kiss in movies, not at home. I avert my eyes. She is beautiful, and he may be the most striking man I have ever met. Overwhelmed, I stare absentmindedly at the paperback spines on the shelf so no one will notice me blush. Kazantzakis. Nabokov. Roth. *The Joy of Sex*. David is asleep now, on the floor beside me.

"We should move to San Francisco," Papa muses.

"Please don't make us move again," I groan.

"We're not going anywhere," Mama assures us.

"But the freedom. Think about it," my father presses.

"Don't idealize, Jefe," Howie cautions. "I came to San Francisco the spring *after* the Summer of Love. Six months is all it took for *that* dream to curdle. The real hippies literally carried a coffin down the center of the streets of Haight-Ashbury, crying 'It's dead! It's over!' Now it's just people spare-changing on the streets and selling hippie shit, making money off it."

"Who died?" Amanda sits up, alarmed.

"The innocence," Howie says, standing.

Carly elbows him playfully. "Oh, Howie. It's still totally alive. You just went down a dark rabbit hole for no good reason."

"You're right. Back to business. It's showtime!" he shouts, flipping off the light switch by the door, futzing with the projector so that the image fills the wrinkled bedsheet.

"Where's that?" Mama asks as the first photo—a picture of Howie in a bathrobe, laughing with a small group of people—comes into focus.

"Our backyard. Just before the wedding. I'm laughing because if I don't laugh I'll probably cry my fucking eyes out and go running."

"Don't be silly," Mama chides. "You look happy. Really happy."

"It's a world of illusion!" Howie says with a Doug Henning bucktooth flourish. Finally, a reference I recognize.

The slides continue, tracking the moments leading up to a wedding that resembles none I've ever seen before.

"When do you put on your tuxedo and dress?" Amanda asks, sucking as usual at her ring and middle fingers.

Howie chuckles warmly. "It's not that kind of wedding, Sweet Tush." Carly snuggles against him, squeezing his arm and smiling as if to say: we know something you don't, but if you're very lucky, we might tell you.

"What do you mean?" Amanda asks, incredulous. "Everybody wears a tuxeee . . . doh?"

The image on the sheet switches from a slide of Howie and Carly facing each other in bathrobes to a slide with the robes lying at their feet, the bride and groom smiling those we-know-something-wonderful smiles. They are very, very naked.

The moment is immense. I have never seen breasts like that. Not in the ladies' locker room at the Y when I was still young enough to go with Mama. Not in Gramps's bathroom *Playboys*. Howie's penis is small and difficult to find in all that hair. Carly's boobs, though, are right there. And the two of them, naked on the screen, are sitting right beside us.

Amanda and I say nothing.

"You didn't!" Mama finally squeals. "You didn't! Did you?"

"Come on!" Papa says, leaning forward.

"Like the day we were born," Howie murmurs, as if recalling the greatest moment of his life. And maybe he is.

Gretchen isn't wrong about my parents being different. They keep *The Joy of Sex* and *Delta of Venus* alongside *Ulysses* and the big *American Heritage Dictionary* with the blue leather cover and silver embossed lettering on the bookshelf behind us. They went to Woodstock and saw Dylan turn electric at Newport. They smoke pot sometimes, occasionally in front of us.

But they aren't *this* different.

The slides continue. Howie and Carly, standing naked. Looking up. Raising arms. Shouting something as a rope attached to a giant wooden bucket above them is tugged by some kind of groomsman, showering them with steaming water. They reach forward, embracing so tightly it's hard to tell them apart, just a mass of skin and dripping hair. Everyone around them claps, laughs, smiles, shouts. Silent, but so noisy in my head.

"I don't . . ." Mama says.

"Far out . . ." Papa says.

"It was the best way we could think of to come together," Carly whispers, still clutching Howie's arm and looking at the photo of herself pressed into her new husband, naked, with nothing between them.

"Was that real?" Amanda asks.

"Oh, honey," Carly slides back over to my sister and wraps her in her arms, "that was as real as it gets."

I look at my father, then at Howie. Any man who gets girls to marry him naked deserves to be projected on a screen.

The heat on the side of my head pulls me out of my sudden

fixation. It is coming from the glare of Papa's gaze. Turning to face him, I know that he has sensed, with uncanny accuracy and speed, the germ of a betrayal.

We all have friends, his eyes telegraph in radioactive Morse code, *but there's only one* man *you should be taking your cues from here.*

Message received. No decoder ring necessary.

Howie clicks ahead a few slides. People eating party food. Guests departing. Carly brushing her teeth. Howie in bed. A picture maybe taken by Howie of his knees, his hairy legs, white tube socks with yellow stripes at the top, and Carly sitting at the end of the bed. And then one of Carly, eyes closed, face down. Eating something?

"What's that in your mouth?" Amanda asks the question I am wondering.

"It's Howie's penis," Carly says matter-of-factly.

"OH-KAY," Mama chirps loudly. She jumps up and flips on the lights. "Time for bed!"

High Over Salem

"My parents don't know I climb the slate roof above my room all the way to the top," I tell Howie through bites of an Elvis sandwich: bacon, banana, and peanut butter. "It's four stories. Probably the highest spot in the neighborhood."

"Well it's *there*. Isn't that the point, Mallory?" he asks.

I nod, feeling trusting enough after eight days with him to reveal my Secure Position—the roof ledge four stories over Chestnut Street that only I know how to get to.

We finish lunch and head up to my room and slip out the south-facing window to the flat roof where Gretchen and I kissed. But I plan to take Howie higher: just to our right, sitting in the open air, a segment of the upper roof hangs precariously, begging to be summited. You just have to jump to get to it. And if you can make it, you can climb to the Secure Position, balance on its forty-foot peak atop a single line of copper, and see the entire city.

"You have to jump," I explain, pointing to the edge of roof just out of reach.

"Jump? You're more rebel than I gave you credit for, son of Jefe. That's a fucking fall."

"Do you want to try it?"

"Hell, yeah," he says, slipping off his sneakers, leaping nimbly on bare feet to the slanted section and starting the crawl up to the peak.

I keep my Pumas on and follow. We position ourselves unsteadily at the center of the copper casing where the back and front roofs join. Turning to the north, we look down at the quiet expanse of Chestnut Street. Falling back the way we had come would probably be survivable—we'd just tumble over the edge and drop to the pebble roof outside my window. But one wrong move forward and there's nothing between us, the bricks of the walkway below, and the emerald moss growing thick between them, but not thick enough to cushion our crash.

"Look over there." I point to the harbor. Howie shifts on the edge, drawing a rectangular Sucrets tin from his pocket, snapping open the lid, and slipping a half-smoked joint and a book of matches from within.

"That is fucking *beautiful*. Look at that. The Atlantic."

We stare silently at the whitecap ripples of Salem Harbor. Sailboats bob and pitch between the power plant and the rocky split lip of Marblehead.

"Maybe this is the view that made Melville conjure his great white whale. His unattainable demon dream. You know, while he was shacking up with old Hawthorne here? Hard to believe that this beautiful scene inspired Melville to write the most boring book I ever read in my life. But I'll never forget how they made oil from blubber now, will I? Poor old sperm whale."

"Sperm whale." I look away, hiding a twelve-year-old's grin.

"I never understood that myself. First of all, it's in the *head* of the whale, not the dick. Second, it's supposed to have the consistency of wax, so it's more like smegma than jizz."

"Smegma?"

"A bummer for the goyim. You and I are exempt, son of Israel. One painful snip, one get-out-of-smegma-free-for-life card."

"Then what's jizz?"

"Nectar of the gods. Fruit of my loins. Pancake syrup for the pussy."

"I . . ."

"It's sperm, little Jefe. Just a fancy handle."

"I never had any," I confess.

"Oh! Yeah, well, it's coming, just hold on. There's plenty in your future." He takes a hit and speaks while holding his breath, eyes starting to water. "I promise."

We could just as easily be talking about movies or comic books. It doesn't seem any different when Howie brings sex up. Papa tries every once in a while, just to see if I "Have any questions?" but I always answer "No." One rainy Sunday afternoon my father came down from a short "nap" and joined me on the front steps. We sat together, not speaking for a few minutes. And then he said, "You know, you're too young to have sex right now, but when you can, you're going to *love* it." Gah!

Howie loses his balance for a moment and laughs, grabbing my shoulder and steadying himself. "I'm catching up on my Hawthorne. Salem tourist and all. You know what he said about this place? He said all sinners that weren't worthy of hanging should be sent on a pilgrimage to Salem and forced to spend time here."

"Guess I'm a sinner, then."

"Ha! I'm no literary genius. I just read that last night in the introduction to *The Scarlet Letter*. Hysterical. I think Hawthorne was all about the seduction of life. He didn't like it here because everyone was so goddamned puritanical. Very 1950s. Very McCarthyesque. So he did what any great artist should do: flipped the townies the bird. You know what that book is about, right?"

I shake my head.

"A minister diddles a hot local lady, and then they try to keep it a secret. She's married to a geezer who she thinks is lost at sea. She's all alone and she ends up having the minister's baby and no one knows who the father is but they know it can't be the old man, so they make her wear a red letter *A* on her chest. *A* for adulteress. And Hawthorne understood how fucked up this prude shit is. Plus, he had some personal history with prejudice—his ancestors, two sisters, had to sit in the town meetinghouse and wear forehead bands because they were lesbians."

"The sisters?" I can barely keep up.

"Yup. With each other. Those headbands were supposed to let everyone know that they had had incestuous relations. You can't make this shit up," he snorts. "Hawthorne would have been so free love if he were alive today. As soon as he got rich, he was out of here."

"I don't blame him. I mean, I'm kind of getting used to it. It's better with you guys here." Howie smiles warmly at this. "What was your high school like?" I ask him.

"Two years of hell. Then two years of happiness, mostly because of Mary Beth Scanlon."

"Who?"

"Shiksa goddess. Magical mystery tour of fantabulousness and first vagina I was ever permitted to touch."

"Was she mad?"

"With lust. Such a bad girl! I mean, not bad, but she was willing to do things the other girls weren't. And she was good at it." *Like Gretchen.* "I didn't play well with the good girls back then. I was a tubby sperm whale, you know. Big enough to have boobs. It's not a good thing. Especially in high school. So stay trim, young fellow. Stay trim."

"You're skinny now."

Howie lies back against the slate, exhales deeply, looks out at the big sky. His flat, barely hairy belly rises and falls. Exposed. Rugged. Ridged by muscle. He rubs it lovingly. "This? This didn't just happen. I worked my ass off. And took two months off of school to do it."

"Your parents let you leave school for two months?"

"It was that, or buy a bra. I didn't give them a choice."

Fat Howie. It's like saying Fat Fonzie. And this other part. *I didn't give them a choice.* How does that work? I get a choice between muesli and Grape-Nuts and that's about it.

I roll to him and stare.

"You have to kick the shit out of your demons," he says. "This one I beat into submission. That one . . ." he points to the swelling Atlantic, "that one still needs work."

"What do you mean?"

"I love to look at that ocean, you know? But I still can't go out on it. Not since my first trip at sea."

"Were you a sailor?"

"Well, first I was a crewman for *Mister Rogers' Neighborhood.* You believe that? Me! I got a girl pregnant, she needed an abortion, so I got a job at the Pittsburgh public television station working on a kids show. They call that irony, amigo."

How many questions can I ask, just about that sentence? "How old were you?"

"Second year college dropout."

"You dropped out of school twice?"

"Well, one was a voluntary leave of absence. It's a blur. But I was working in *Mister Rogers' Neighborhood* and my college roommate called. He'd been canoeing the Miami river and met a guy who asked him to crew a forty-nine-foot yacht for a retired Russian millionaire going from Nassau to the Galapagos Islands. My roommate was from Utah and knew *bupkes* about sailing. But we both knew *Adventures in Paradise.* You know that TV show?"

I shake my head, trying to stay aboard his train of thought.

"Adam Troy, handsome, dumb, on a schooner with seven gorgeous women sailing the South Pacific searching for adventure. So I said 'Let's go!' And I'm on the plane heading down to meet them, reading about jib, stern, all that sailing stuff. I grew up in Pittsburgh, for Christ's sake. Near the Monongahela River. It was a fire hazard that your parents told you to stay the hell away from. *That* was as close as I got to sailing. It was NOT *Mahblehead*. Believe me. But then I'm there and it's *Adventures in Paradise.* We dove in the harbor the minute we got there and everyone on the dock was laughing at us because that was where the ships dumped their bilges. But we were just happy. Until . . ." He shakes his head and swallows like he'd rather spit. "On the seventh day we hit the open sea for the first time. No more harbor to harbor. And there's nowhere to drop anchor, so it's just like a roller coaster. UPHILL. DOWNHILL." Howie leans back, eyes popping, then lurches forward toward the street below. "That's when I start puking."

"Oh no," I laugh, trying to imagine it. The ocean has never been anything but an inviting playground for me. Preston Beach, down the road from Grandma Wini's house with its soft waves and rich tidal pools of anemone and starfish. The endless sandy stretches of Plum Island and the warm rivulets that last until the sea returns to wash them away.

"You don't know puking until you've done it for two days straight. You don't care if you live or die. And then, on the third day, a storm kicked up in the middle of the night. No sky, just clouds and darkness, and the wind's blowing and it's three in morning. I'm at the wheel and the old Russian comes up screaming, 'Why didn't you call me? Climb the mast! Fix the sails!' "

Howie's hand shoots skyward, as if the mast is right before us and he looks to the top and shakes his head, *no.* "The Russian's getting panicky, which was a clue to me and my roommate that the shit was hitting the fan. He starts wailing at us, 'We're going to hit the reef! We're going to hit the reef!' I look and I realize he's right. We ARE going hit the fucking reef and miss the channel." Howie stands and staggers, feigning a loss of balance but the act of doing it, so high up here, brings the terror and the risk of his story to life for me.

And then, taking a deep breath and closing his eyes, he extends his left arm forward, draws the right back and strikes a perfect, balanced pose on the copper ridge of the roof. The wind lifts his hair gently and his nostrils flare as he inhales deeply, a beautiful California surfer catching the 31 Chestnut swell.

"There was this accident of life," he whispers. "We caught a wave and surfed over the reef and landed in the harbor, completely safe."

"That's. So. Pissah."

"That's one word for it," Howie shrugs, sitting back next to me and putting a hand on my shoulder. "I was so terrified of the idea that I could have fallen off that boat and fallen off the face of life and no one would know what happened to me. Me. Class president!"

"You were class president?" I ask, but he stares silently out to sea, adorned in clothes only a man of great confidence could wear, meditating on thoughts only a man of expansive mind (with mind-expanding accessories) could imagine. Whatever he sees out there, it is big. I haven't yet found a friend in this city, but I have found my hero, flying high over the streets of Salem not with a cape, but with an amazing pair of silk pants.

"I never felt so weak. But when forces so much greater than you step in—Mother Nature, Father Time, Brother Death in his black hood—you can't blame yourself for being scared. But I did. I did," he confesses. "It took me a long time to be able to tell this story, hombre."

Howie spits in the palm of his hand, extinguishes the joint with a faint sizzle, and returns what was left of it to the Sucrets tin. He looks back at the ocean, raises his arms over his head, and shouts at the top of his lungs: "NICE WORK, YAHWEH! KEEP IT UP!" Then he turns back to me: "Let's go see your *mamacita*." He throws his legs out in front of him, inches his butt forward, and slips down the warm slate shingle slide, taking the ride I've only dreamed of and disappearing over the edge. A moment later I hear a gravelly thud on the flat roof below. "All good!" he calls. "Hit it. I'll catch you."

I look down the long, gray stretch of roof, waiting. "I can't see you," I call.

"If I back up, I won't be able to catch you, now will I?"

I shiver pleasantly at the prospect of sliding full speed, but the idea of missing him altogether is unnerving. Usually, I shimmy carefully on my butt, hang off the edge, and drop to the flat roof. But I've always wanted to let go and ride that wicked slope. If I do it right I'll land feetfirst on the newly minted makeout zone outside my bedroom window, like Howie just did. But if I misjudge or slip too far to the left I'll miss the flat roof altogether and it's *Ding dong! Road pizza delivery for Frank!*

"Can you see my hands?" Howie yells. He jumps and I see his fingertips appear briefly at the end of the roof then disappear as he lands back on the gravel below, out of sight.

"Yes!"

"Aim for them. Come on! I gotta pee."

"OK," I answer, letting myself slide slowly forward, the rubber of my heels dragging at the slate but doing little to slow me once I really start moving. I lift my feet and abandon my fear as the speed fills my chest with a warm rush that makes me feel I can fly. I shout the first word that comes to mind, the curious word Howie had uttered at the top of our little world just a minute before:

"YAHWEH!" as the soles of my Pumas plow into his face. My palms break part of my fall, ripping open in a half dozen spots as the pebbles dig into the skin.

"You mutherfuckinglittlecocksuckingfuckeryoufuck! FUCK YOU!"

Dinner that night is beef bourguignon, zucchini potato pancakes, and Brussels sprouts. I hate Brussels sprouts. Papa calls to let us know he's still at the office. Mama shrugs and starts to serve.

Frank joins us, a jolly replacement for Papa with his rounder frame and shorter moustache. He takes my father's place at the head of the table and offers a word of thanks for the meal, and for his landlord family.

Howie, face swollen and woozy, makes fun of me for not eating the sprouts, taking some from my plate and filling his cheeks with them.

"Baby, you are the most handsome chipmunk I have ever seen," Carly says, scratching under his chin as he rolls his eyes in satisfaction.

"Looks more like W. C. Fields with that shnoz," Mama giggles.

There it is again. I know my mother as serious, attentive, self-sufficient, and super smart. But silly is a new one.

"Oy! These zucchini pancaketh!" Howie says, his mouth full of them. "You are a miracle worker. You are!" he yells. Mama shakes her head and blushes. "You are a miracle worker and I am Helen Keller. You're Anne Bancroft and I'm Patty Duke."

"Howie, you're ridiculous," Mama says. "It's zucchini pancakes."

Howie looks thoughtfully at her. "Maybe you're Anne Bancroft and I'm Dustin Hoffman."

Carly smacks him. I am lost. Again.

As dinner concludes, I roll a greasy sprout off my plate and let it drop into my lap, then flick the big spongy marble under the table to a panting Atjeh. It lands with a faint thump and is followed by the gobble of the wolf dog.

"Did you just waste a Brussels sprout?" Howie asks.

"No," I say, shooting him a *don't snitch on me* look that he should understand.

"A beautiful Brussels sprout made by the Hunan Princess?"

"*No*," I repeat hotly.

"Eat it," Howie points at my plate. "You haven't had any. You must try, *niño*."

"I'm eating," I object angrily.

"Man can't live on beef bourguignon alone. Try this," says Howie holding the green sprout in front of my face and shaking it. I want to barf. "This is good. This is good for you. Try it."

"Howie," Frank says softly, recognizing my discomfort. "Let the boy be fickle. It's better than being bitter. He looks up to you."

Carly smiles at this and rubs Howie's back.

"Whoa," Howie says, visibly blanching. "Did I just pull a big brother?"

"You kinda did, lover," Carly says with a firm tenderness.

"He would do it to me," Amanda says, not looking my way. "He deserves it."

"No one deserves it," Howie declares, standing. "Fuck. Fuck, fuck, fuck. That may be a part of me, that kind of macho-man, bully bullshit. That's some *old* shit. I don't know why it cropped up but I AM SORRY, *niño*. Will you accept my apology? It's true."

I look at Frank, who nods, a glow rising under his five o'clock shadow.

"Sure," I say, realizing that this is the first time a man has ever apologized to me for anything. The ones I know don't do it. But Howie just did.

"Let's-a play-a some music," says Frank, adopting a *Godfather* accent. "The whole-a-family's together."

Carly puts a new album on the record player. She, Amanda, and Mama start swirling around the dining room together, pulling me and Frank in as Cris Williamson and a choir of women's voices grow stronger and louder.

> *Love of my life I am crying,*
> *I am not dying,*
> *I am dancing.*

Howie joins and we all whirl through the house, music following us on Papa's multi-room sound system, voices rising as we master the chorus together. The idea that you could be crying for joy instead of sadness suddenly seems right. It is the first time I have ever danced in this house.

The song ends with the full-throated choir promising, *"And we will sing for a long, long time!"*

Everyone is flushed, a little winded, laughing. I think, *Maybe we'll stay here, like this, together after all.*

The next morning, I wake to the hum of warm and easy voices coming down the hall. It's an exotic sound for a Tuesday morning on Chestnut Street, usually marked by Mama's ritual shriek from the first floor to the third, calling for a timely departure for school that never happens.

I swing off the bunk, pull on a sweatshirt, and wander down to Howie and Carly's room, only to find everyone gathered in the bathroom. Amanda is perched on the toilet. Mama, Carly, and Howie have squeezed into the tub, each holding a personal pot of paint and a dribbling brush.

"Where's Papa?" I ask.

"Work," Mama says. "You slept late. Look what Howie did." She points to a painting just above the edge of the tub. It's a brownish bird—a cross between a hawk and a robin?—assuming a protective stance on a rock beside the recipe for Mama's zucchini potato pancakes which Howie has carefully transcribed in black and pink oils. "Yield: Six to Eight Servings."

"I couldn't sleep," Howie explains. The gauze is gone and the swelling's down, but his eyes are black and blue. His *S*'s have returned.

"Can he do that?" Amanda asks.

"I think he just did," Mama says, smiling. A fait accompli instead of a cause for concern. Instead of a highly organized, paint-by-numbers project there is a spontaneous, splattered, rainbow-infused mural on the wall of our guest bathroom and Mama is laughing, not fretting. She's kissing Carly on the cheek. Hugging Howie. They're all hugging. Again. "I'm so glad you're here," Mama smiles.

"So are we," they say in unison.

We fill the wall with as many creations as we can before we eat breakfast. Amanda paints a portrait of Bunny Yabba. David draws a stick figure of Mama. I make a vampire flying over the zucchini potato pancake recipe with blood dripping from his fangs and two bats on either side of him. Mama paints a list of her top five mystery novels, then joins forces with Carly to paint a garden of flowers with a fountain at the center. We're going to be late for school, but I don't say anything. You don't bother the Hunan Princess when she's happy.

Getting Whacked

Halloween comes, and with it a most intense observance by the locals. Back in New York we rode our apartment building's elevator up and down, knocked on a dozen doors, and went home with a little paper sack of candy, our faces damp with the condensation that accumulated on the insides of our sharp plastic masks. But in Salem, city of witches, the number of doors we knock on is endless, and the elaborate handmade or professional-grade costumes worn by children and adults in equal measure are genuinely frightening.

I lead Amanda on a trek through the neighborhood that does not end until our pillowcases are overflowing and her tears begin to spurt—partly from exhaustion and partly from a kid with a dangly eyeball and an axe in his forehead who jumped out of the bushes on Flint Street and made her pee a little in her Laura Ingalls Wilder pantaloons. I share some sugar loot with Howie and Carly and fall asleep on the edge of their bed as they whisper stories about commune living in Berkeley and the naked beach near Pacifica.

Howie and Carly's stay goes from one week to two, then to three, and still shows no signs of abating. They are the unexpected jackpot in the Salem lottery. In a town where you expect the locals to stone you to death when you pick the wrong slip, I've found a true prize: honest, loving adults who renounce social divisions, bring *everyone* to the table, and then dump everything on it. The more time I spend fluttering around the edges of their blissful life the more I want to lose myself in its sensuous anarchy. It was clear when the light hit the sheet that first evening: innuendo is over. Everything is explicit.

So, perhaps this is the place I will grow up, after all.

In contrast to the magical mystery tour under way at home, my school, Oliver, is just holding me back. Assignments aren't hard for me, but paying attention is. They don't reward smarts at Oliver. They reward compliance. But the real reward, I am learning, is in breaking the rules. One day, I absentmindedly tear the erasers off Mrs. Biegelbock's pencils while waiting at her desk to turn in a paper. She yells at me in front of the class, and that's it. But a few days later when I crush her empty Styrofoam coffee cup in a similar manner, she has the principal call my mother. And that is the last straw.

When Howie comes down the next morning, I am sorting candy. Mama is sorting her tools—a sledgehammer, gloves, a shovel—in preparation for demolishing a wall in the basement.

"I can't *believe* how much you take on, Princess. All work, never a complaint, just sleeves up, head down. And Lou, what? No school?" I nod as he pats my head lightly on his way to the kitchen and a fresh pot of coffee. I like what he said about Mama. I like how much he likes her. And I can see how, in her own quiet way, she enjoys being liked.

Still, the work ethic Howie appreciates in my mother is the same drive to *do* that keeps her from me. There's a joy and spark to her now that wasn't there before. At least not in New York. But it shines brightest for our guests, not for me.

"I'm pulling him from Oliver and sending him to another school," Mama says, wiping her brow and smiling at Howie. "They gave him a D on a spelling test even though he got every word right. In New York, he was top of the class. Without trying, I might add," she says, directing this last bit at me.

"I didn't set up the margins the right way, and my lines came out crooked," I grouse.

"But it's a spelling test," he reappears with a mug and a banana.

"And then he destroyed a Styrofoam cup. Oy! What a delinquent," she says in her most sarcastic Jewish-mother voice. "That's why he's going to the Alternative School," Mama concludes. I beam, proudly.

"Alternative School," Howie repeats as Mama lifts the sledgehammer to her shoulder. "I like the sound of that. And look at you, Hunan Princess. Who got in your way today?"

"Little renovation downstairs. Carving out space for a framing studio. It's an old hobby, and maybe even a way to make a little extra money around here, since I can't go back to work right now."

"Well ain't that just like the daughter of a Kosher butcher? Grab a tool and carve. I love it. So let me help," Howie offers. "I want to get dirty with you."

"I would love to," she laughs, "but I actually have to run some errands first, and what would really help me is if you could spend some time with Lou. I don't want him sitting around eating candy all day."

An alternative to candy never sounded so good.

"OK, but don't use that sledgehammer without me. I'm starting to get soft with all this easy living around here." And then, to me: "So, hombre, how 'bout we go visit your dad in the city today? Let's see how El Jefe spends his days."

"Why aren't we driving?" I ask, as we pass the blue and white mini-bus, beckoning like a yellow submarine.

"Well, I'm high, for starters."

The train to Boston is nothing like the subways in New York, where there are too many people too close together and the doors shut too suddenly. Once Mama pushed Amanda and me off a subway car ahead of her, then started to follow just as the doors began to close on her huge pregnant stomach. She screamed and I thought the baby would explode out onto the platform. David didn't appear for another few weeks, but I never forgot the terror in my mother's voice, rising above the cries of the few passengers who pleaded angrily with the conductor to *"Open the fucking doors!"*

The memories of New York have already started to blur. But the ugly ones stay sharp: brighter stars in a receding constellation. Why not the good ones? Why not the best?

Thirty-three minutes later, on soft seats in a half-full compartment, we roll into North Station.

"Naht station next. Naht station," the conductor calls out as he pulls ticket stubs from the seat backs. Howie doesn't move.

"I think this is it," I say.

"What? No. He said 'Naht Station.'"

"That's the way they say it. North Station."

We walk through Government Center, a complex of modern concrete structures that could have been the setting for Caesar's simian revolution at the end of *Conquest of the Planet of the Apes*. The buildings turn from concrete to brick as we make our way through a downtown crossing.

Howie stops at the outskirts of the Combat Zone, that infamous corner of Boston where all the girlie shows, strip clubs, and violence are on display. I zero in on the faint flicker of peep show bulbs and marquees that promise NUDE, NAKED, and ADULT while he checks Papa's office address on a slip of paper.

"Chez Jefe!" he says, motioning to a less seductive office building. "This is where the war on poverty meets the private sector petri dish. And your dad is the mad scientist. A little welfare reform here, a little capitalist efficiency there. Your Papa's gonna outsmart the Washington bureaucrats and actually get people jobs. Might even make a little dinero in the process." It doesn't make perfect sense to me, but somehow I understand my father's mission in life better than I ever have.

The elevator moves so slowly I can't tell if it's actually moving. My heart slams until, with a groan, the doors release. "You have a claustrophobia thing?" Howie whispers, noting my silent anxiety on the ride up. "Possession by the devil's my phobia thing . . . Hi! We're here to see Peter Cove."

The woman at the desk stares curiously at us, a grown man in flowered drawstring pants and a twelve-year-old boy with shoulder-length hair. "May I tell him who is calling?"

"Butch Cassidy and the Sundance Kid," Howie smiles. "And you must be Maid Marian."

"Joyce," the woman at the desk corrects, lifting the telephone to her ear.

"Joy to meet you, Joyce," he says. Her cheeks redden when he says her name. She looks away, Howie looks at me, and Joyce looks back at him. Looks away. Looks back again, up and down, catches a quick breath and shuts her eyes as if she's trying to go back to sleep. Howie gives me a jumpy brow wiggle and points back at Joyce with his eyes as if to say *Did you see her?* He doesn't notice that Joyce has seen *him*.

Beyond the reception desk there's a room full of people, mostly black, mostly women, filling out forms, speaking with staff.

"Ever see *The Exorcist*?" Howie asks. "My friends said, 'Hey! Movie night! Let's take some sugar cubes and ride.' And I'm thinking John Wayne. I'm thinking *Hondo*. I'm thinking *Rio Bravo*. I didn't know anything about this movie. Nobody knew anything about this movie."

"It's a horror movie, right?"

"That's one way to put it. I'm a *Frankenstein/Dracula* kind of guy. I loved *The Tingler* . . . You see *The Tingler*, Joyce?" Joyce, on the phone now, shakes her head. "Vibrators in the seats! Revolution in filmmaking. They should do that in porn films . . ." He pauses, making a mental note of the idea.

"Mr. Cove is just wrapping up a meeting," Joyce says, hanging up. "You can take a seat." She points to a sofa against the wall behind us, but we stay standing, continuing our conversation as if it was just the two of us alone on the roof.

"Anyway, *The Exorcist* isn't like those old movies. It's just totally real and fucking horrifying. The acid probably didn't help. But somewhere in there I just lost the ability to discern fiction from reality and I walked out of there thinking, whether it's the raging sea or the Devil himself, the universe *will* break you eventually. You're going to get whacked, one way or the other."

If Papa's ever been petrified of anything, he never mentioned it. Fear of failure, maybe, but his universe is meant for conquering. My universe feels indomitable, and Howie just confirmed what the experience of unexpected moves and perpetual loss of control has taught me: I'm going to get whacked eventually. Then again, these two seem to be handling their respective fates in style.

"El Jefe!" Howie points to Papa, on cue. My father is standing over an older woman who is focused on filling out a form, his hand reassuringly resting on her shoulder. He looks up when Howie calls and smiles at us.

"You even wear that outfit in the city?" Papa points to Howie's latest pair of drawstring pants—black with lush, white-pink hibiscus. You are a crazy motherfucker," he says under his breath as he greets us.

"And who are you, asshole? Pat Boone in the white buck shoes?" Papa, who is indeed wearing white bucks, seersucker pants, and a plaid shirt with a white collar and paisley bow tie, grins again and hugs Howie. I catch a glimpse of Joyce, still staring at Howie. Looking away, staring again.

"There's style and then there's chaos," Papa says. "This way," he puts a hand on my head and leads us toward the back. "Welcome to the next frontier in the war on poverty."

"Corner office, of course. He's El Jefe," Howie whispers to me, conspiratorially.

Howie catches the eye of everyone he passes, a black, white, and pink blur of kinetic energy. His friendliness is infectious—people can't help but smile in response—but the smiles are followed by a weak wave and a confused look: Does this guy have something to do with getting off welfare? Maybe he's *on* welfare?

Papa sweeps us into his office and reaches for a leather cigar box on the windowsill. "Cohiba?" Howie shakes his head and Papa shrugs, putting his nose to the long, brown stogie. He breathes deeply, pierces the tip with a gold-plated cigar punch, wets the end with his tongue, then his lips, and finally lights it with a scrimshaw Zippo.

"Cuban?" Howie asks.

"Dominican, alas."

"How about Hawaiian?" Howie pulls his own smoke box from his pocket—the Sucrets box—and reveals three huge joints.

"Ever heard of boundaries? This is an office, for Christ's sake," Papa says.

"*This* is an orifice," Howie replies, opening his mouth wide and mimicking Papa's cigar routine, licking the joint, biting off the tip and spitting it across the room.

"Put it away," Papa wags a finger, walks to the door to close it.

A young businesswoman walks by at just that moment, focused on a stack of papers in her hand. She slows for just a second, waves at Papa, takes in the fact that Howie and I are there, and keeps going.

"New staff member," Papa says cheerily. "I'll introduce you to her later. Smart, smart, smart. GREAT hire."

"Speaking of . . ." Howie says. "Are you hiring?"

Papa looks blankly at him. "Can you wear regular clothes and not get high in an office?"

"Did Franco Harris rush for one thousand yards last season?" Howie asks as if the answer is self-evident.

"No clue," Papa says earnestly. "But I've got a grant proposal in. If it comes through, we'll have an opening. You willing to stay on this coast for while?"

"You get me a job and you've got yourself a housemate, mate. Well, two housemates, in fact. Two for the price of one."

"Oh, there's a price," my father nods, puffing at his cigar.

He kicks us out shortly after we arrive, so we stroll the Combat Zone with its Boston Bunnies, Rap Booths, King of Pizza, nude photos. Howie leads me to The Book Mart, a small corner shop with blacked-out windows and a glass door stenciled with different typefaces: BOOKS AND MAGAZINES. MODERN AND TRADITIONAL. LARGE COLLECTION FRENCH SWEDISH CLASSICS.

Inside, a black guy in a royal blue southwestern-print shirt and large round aviator sunglasses blocks our way. "Hey man, you can't bring that kid in here."

"He's my son, it's cool. I give him permission."

"Pigs don't give him permission. Gotta go."

I glance around nervously: unfamiliar nude magazines are wrapped in plastic. *The Seeker* shows a man kissing a woman, her shirt fully unbuttoned.

"He's blind, man," Howie says. "He can't see anything anyway."

Then I see another cover—*Show-Off*—with a couple kissing on it, but the woman on this one has no shirt at all and the man is squeezing both of her breasts.

"Bull. Shit. Kid's eyes popping out of his head right now."

Twogether, *Skin Scene*, *Screw*, and *Dirty Old Man Coloring Book* with an illustration of a bald man on the cover that looks way too much like Gramps, a halo over his head and a sly smile spread under his extended nose.

"That's because he's *blind*," Howie whispers. "You know, usually he wears dark glasses so you can't see them. It's embarrassing. Don't talk about it, OK?"

"Out."

Howie asks two construction guys on a cigarette break from ripping up the sidewalk if they can keep an eye on me while he does a quick shop. They nod, pat the concrete sewer pipes they're sitting on, and invite me to join them.

"Your dad's got weird clothes," says one, shirt open, chest hairs dripping with sweat despite the cold of the Zone.

Howie emerges with a paper bag. "This kid give you any trouble?" he asks. "He's a tough one."

"Whatever, Sally." The sweaty one tosses his cigarette into the street and gets up.

"Well, thanks for the kindness, gentlemen. Off to new adventures. If you're ever in the San Francisco Bay Area . . ."

"Figures," says the other worker. Sweaty nods vaguely and picks up a shovel.

We meet Papa at "Naht" Station, and ride the packed sardine train home.

"We had a bit of drama here today," Mama says, handing my father a folded copy of the *Salem Evening News* as we walk in.

"These are the classifieds," Papa says, dropping his leather doctor's satchel, which doubles as a briefcase.

"Just read the announcements section, Peter," she says through clenched teeth.

"Right, OK, Historical Society meeting at Hamilton Hall, Thursday. Volunteer cleanup, Salem Common, Sunday. Blah blah blah. Gay Rights Alliance inaugural meeting, tonight, 31B . . . Chestnut St.?" He looks up at Mama.

"Uh huh."

"So, Frank's becoming an activist. Good for him."

"Yes," Mama says. "Good for him. I'm glad. But Glovey Butler isn't so glad that he's doing it *here*."

"Shit."

"She's the one who showed me."

"Shit."

"She says she doesn't care what he wants to do on his own private time, but she's worried about us. She thinks some local homophobes might do something, and now they have our address."

Papa strokes his mustache, considers, then loosens his bow tie and starts up the stairs.

"Where are you going?!" Mama shouts after him and my shoulders rise at the familiar shrill. Something beyond frustration there. More like panic. Like her brakes just stopped working and the car is jetting off the cliff at the Marblehead lighthouse. It doesn't happen often, but every once in a while my mother splinters, sharp and all at once. I guess everybody has their way of getting noticed.

"I don't think that's the issue. But we can certainly allay her fears. There's only one thing to do," Papa calls.

"And that is?" Her voice still frayed.

"Invite her to dinner."

"OK," Mama says uncertainly, but she drops out of DEF-CON 1.

"And Frank, too."

"Oh, God."

"It'll be fine! People can't sustain fear or bigotry when they've had a good meal together." Papa's voice fades into his bedroom on the second floor.

"And have Howie and Carly take the kids out?" Mama's head drops and she leans wearily against the banister.

"No! Everyone should be here," Papa yells back. "In fact, let's have everyone to Thanksgiving. That will give us a few weeks to figure all of this out."

"Oh God," Mama says again.

"We're not going to Grandma Wini's?" I sigh. "Come on. We don't want that old lady here. She'll ruin everything."

"I'm certain she has some other place to go," Mama says by way of comfort.

"I'll bet you a hundred bucks no one has the courage to invite her," Papa shouts. "And Howie! Let's play racquetball Sunday! You need a good ass kicking!"

Bewitched

Even my new school can't escape Salem's strict past. The Alternative School is housed in a big building on Hawthorne Street with FOR GOD AND COUNTRY and SAINT MARY'S SCHOOL carved in cement above the door. Its own scarlet letter to wear. Wild ivy coils the wrought-iron railing running along the speckled marble steps. An imposing statue of Hawthorne himself stands in the middle of the street, alive with texture in the folds of his coat, the bristles of his mustache, the great bunches of turquoise-bronze grapes scattered about the heels of his heavy boots. Funeral homes, burnt witches, dead writers—little room for the living, here.

I was promised a new kind of school, and I have dressed accordingly: Papa's tweed driving cap, turned backward, a green-and-yellow-on-white number eighty-eight jersey, and a pair of Mr. Green Jeans green jeans with a paisley patch Mama has sewn to the right knee. I feel like Howie: free, cool, and independent.

My teacher, Becky, who wants to be addressed by her first name only, greets me warmly with a handshake. She's wearing bell-bottoms, clogs, a white shirt, and a belt made of big tortoiseshell rings, all linked together. "We're so happy you're joining the class," she says, guiding me to sit with the group at a large round table. There are no desks in the classroom, and the students are doing art—a subject never even considered at Oliver. "I think you know Gretchen?" Becky asks, motioning to my neighbor sitting opposite from me. I shrug, noncommittal.

"You finally got out of Olivah?" Gretchen asks. I nod, scan the walls of the class, which are plastered with art, mostly by students, some prints by famous artists, or else collages of photographs of all the kids looking happy, wearing white-on-blue Alternative School T-shirts. I feel a wave of gratitude to my parents for springing me from Oliver: no grading on margins and crooked lines here.

"He lives around the corner from me," Gretchen tells the group as I settle. "But he's really from New York." The other kids at my table look up, acknowledge me vaguely as I settle in among them.

"I like your hat," says a tall boy to my right. "I'm Uli."

I smile and touch the tweed absentmindedly. The group is drawing on large pieces of colored construction paper, choosing from a massive basket of Cray-Pas. A blonde woman at the table, younger than Becky but definitely older than all of us, hands me a piece of tag board and slides the basket closer to my side of the table. She looks like Stevie Nicks on the album cover for *Rumours*—the same choppy, feathered hair, the same curve in her lips.

"You can try to do still life from one of these things in the center of the table," she says, pointing to a random assortment of objects that include an orange studded with cloves and a Polaroid Land Camera with a frayed leather strap. "Or you can just draw from your imagination."

"Can I go the bathroom before I start?" I ask her.

"I don't care," she says, not looking up from her own drawing.

Taken aback, I don't reply for a moment. Then: "But . . . Can I have permission to go?"

"Ask the teacher," she rolls her eyes.

"But aren't you . . . ?"

"What? A teacher? No!" The entire group starts laughing. "Why does everyone always ask me that?"

"Because yuh got big boobs," Gretchen tells her matter-of-factly.

"She's in our class," Uli leans in to me and whispers. "Come on. I'll show you where the outhouse is." *She's in our class.* I don't think I'd be more excited if I found out Farrah Fawcett was our teacher.

"You're lucky you got out of Oliver. That's like a concentration camp for kids. Here you don't have to ask for permission to use the bathroom," Uli says. His teeth are prodigious, almost horselike, and his mouth can't close all the way around them, but it adds a friendliness to his face that I take to immediately.

I nod as he leads me down a shining waxed hallway, most of the light coming from the tall windows at either end. Behind the bathroom's closed doors, Uli returns to the only subject that matters with a whisper: "Gretchen says Penny has such big boobs because her mom cast a spell on her." He answers my frown by telling me, "Her mom's a witch."

"No way."

"Yes, suh," his accent slacking on the *R*. "Laurie Cabot, the Good Witch of Salem. That's her mom."

"Yeah, right."

"Stick a needle in my eye. You never heard of her? She travels with the Red Sox and puts spells on their bats and gloves to help them win. Last year they had a ten-game losing streak so she went to Cleveland with them and broke the slump. Sox scored two runs *in the twelfth inning*. Longest game in, like, twenty years. So pissah."

"Have you met her?"

"A million times. She comes and does lessons at the school. Witch lessons."

"She teaches you how to cast a spell?" I ask, crowding into the urinal and unzipping my pants. But nothing comes out. Who can focus?

"No, she doesn't really teach us that. It's more like mind control and ESP and stuff."

"Can you read my mind?"

"Yeah. You need to pee."

I can't take my eyes off of Penny for the rest of the day.

"Hey. New kid," she says, holding a picture she has drawn. "What do you think? Everyone always tells me how good I am. You tell me the truth." I stare at the drawing but think only of her. Penny shakes the construction paper in my face, intuiting instantly the direction my mind has wandered. "Hello? What do you see?"

I look at the picture and it takes every bit of strength I possess not to say "It's good." It's great, reminiscent of *The Grey King*, a book I love. "A wolf with purple eyes. A ballerina, standing on an acorn. But she has wings, and something, like, wrapped around her arms. Like streamers? Or ribbons?"

"Leather," she answers plainly. "But I know what it's of. I want to know what it needs."

It's hard to answer the question. It's perfect. Her drawing is to the other students' drawings as her breasts are to all the other girls: on a completely different level. But Penny looks at me and her expression says *Please be different*. Whatever her need, I want to satisfy it. She's waiting for an answer. An irresistible tug in my chest pulls me to her. All I want is to make her smile.

"It's the skin," I say as confidently as possible. "She doesn't have real skin the way the wolf has real fur. The hair and wings look real but her body . . . It's just an outline."

Penny considers this for a moment, nods and smiles. "You're

right," she admits. "I had a sensation that you might be a member of the clan."

"My dad says I'm a member of the tribe."

"Tribe. Clan. Coven. Same thing. Want to come over after school?"

I touch the tweed of my cap and say: "Yup." I glance at Uli. He's mouthing the words: *That's . . . so . . . pissah.*

I tell Mama I'm not coming home when she rolls up in her battered Mercedes at pick-up time. She's annoyed, having driven across town to get me, but the fact that I've found a friend seems to mollify her. I hand her the address on a crumpled piece of paper.

"I'll pick you up at five. Mr. Nusselblatt is coming for your Hebrew lesson. You've already missed two."

"I could miss all of them."

"You promised you'd try."

"Papa says he doesn't even care if I get a bar mitzvah or not."

"I care. Your grandfather would have cared a lot. Will you try, just for me?" she asks.

I smile and wave, running off to find Penny.

We walk along Pickering Wharf, a faded briny little port where sailors unloading pepper and molasses have long since been replaced by fried dough stands and scrimshaw knickknack peddlers. The wind blows past the Misery Islands and surrounds us with the smell of the sea. We talk about movies, the new *King Kong*, how she loves Jeff Bridges ("He's a *god*") and I prefer Jessica Lange ("You just like when the monkey puts her under the waterfall and makes her all wet and see-through"), and which is better: *Close Encounters* or *Star Wars*.

It's the former.

We agree.

I stop in front of a Derby Street liquor store, whose unusual name is proclaimed in extravagant blue neon script. "The Bunghole? That's disgusting."

"That's what pirates call the part of the booze barrel where you stick a cork, dummy. I know this guy who works there—Timmy White—and he knows everybody thinks it's your asshole." I love the way Penny says asshole. I laugh freely. "The funny part is it used to be a funeral home."

I stop laughing. "This whole town is a funeral home."

"No shit. They used to make booze in the back, next to all the embalming fluid and the bodies, when it was illegal to drink, because the cops would never want to go back there."

"I should put some dead bodies outside my room. Then my sister would never come in again."

"Smart. Timmy says they still have all the funeral home stuff in the basement. I went down to see it once and he tried to kiss me on the stairs. I kicked him in the nuts."

I laugh again, but the thought grips my spine, unleashes such a flood of nervous adrenaline I actually consider turning around and running all the way home.

"You want a smoke?"

"I can't," I shrug. "Asthma."

"Sucks," she says, slapping a pack of Parliaments on the heel of her hand. "Mom says I can't smoke in the house so I have to do it before we get there."

"Your ma lets you smoke?"

Penny takes a long drag on the white cigarette and stares at the sky thoughtfully. "Does your mom tell you what you can't do?" *Now that you mention it*, I think, *it's been a while.*

All the streets off Derby are stifling and constricted, packed with narrow little harbor homes pressed close together, each adorned with a wooden emblem in the shape of a house declaring its year of construction in thick black calligraphy: 1844, 1845, 1862. Penny's house is around the corner from the Customs House and the House of the Seven Gables, local tourist spots that pale in comparison to the coming attraction.

A huge pile of stuffed animals dominates the twin bed in her room, so we sit uncomfortably close together, along the edge of a crocheted afghan, browsing copies of *Tiger Beat* and *Dynamite*. The room is cold but Penny sheds her turtleneck anyway. Her stomach makes a brief appearance before she tugs her tank top back down and shimmies, cross-legged, alongside me.

"Who do you like better? Shaun or Parker?" she asks. I stare blankly. I notice the Shaun Cassidy poster over her bed. "I like to look at him," she says, catching the direction of my gaze. "But if I were a boy I would want to be Leif Garrett." She holds up a copy of *Tiger Beat*. Cassidy and Garrett are pasted next to each other. They're both smiling and next to Leif is a block of text that says "Leif: The Right Way to Meet Him (Yes! There Is One)! See Page 49."

"You actually kind of look like him," I say, looking at the cover and then at Penny. "You have the same kind of hair."

"Mine's way curlier. Take off your hat, let me see yours." I follow her instruction, shaking my hair loose. I've been growing it as long as I can. "You know, if you put some grease in it, push it back, you'd look just like Spike."

"*Happy Days*' Spike?" That's not what I want to hear. I hate Spike. He's was the Fonz's cousin—kind of a mini-Fonz—who they replaced with Chachi a few seasons in.

"I love Spike," Penny tells me. "I don't know why they got rid of him so quick. Chachi's a loser. Try this on," she jumps up, pulls a black leather jacket from a tiny closet by the window and tosses it my way. "I'll be right back." She comes back a moment later with a plastic spray bottle and starts spritzing my hair with water before I can object. "Use this comb. Push it back. Put this cigarette behind your ear. Wear these mirror sunglasses. Yup, that's good. You look *just* like him. You could be in *Tiger Beat*, no problem."

I move to close the door to take in my reflection but it hits unexpected resistance. A gentle, almost childlike woman's voice calls from behind: "Why are we closing the door?"

"Jesus, Mom, he's just looking in the mirror."

"He? Oh. And who would this greaser be?" Laurie Cabot, the witch of Salem, sweeps past me to sit on the bed, her black robe covering nearly every inch of her body below her neck, black hair exploding out and upward like the silhouette of the tangled pear tree in our backyard. I shed the jacket and look at my feet. "Oh, don't undress on my account," she laughs.

"This is Louis. He just started in our class. He's from New York and he's probably the only cool kid at school."

The *only* one!

Her mother takes my face in her hands and scans my eyes as if she's dropped a diamond ring in my skull and is trying to find it at the bottom of my soul.

"Mom!"

"Oh. Yes. He's a good one," the witch says reassuringly. "Keep doing whatever it was you were doing." Two black cats emerge from under her robe and begin to tussle under Penny's bed. As Laurie Cabot turns, a black Lab pushes through the door, claws clicking against the splintered wooden floorboards. She sniffs between my legs, lapping my green jeans' crotch.

"Alpha, stop it!" Penny yells, watching me squirm. "You're being rude." And then to me: "You can pet her. She's a good dog. She just likes boys because we're all girls in this house. Me and my mom and my sister." Now the two cats emerge from under the bed, using my pant legs to claw their way up, and begin rubbing along either side of me.

"Wow, you're popular," Penny says. "They don't like most people."

"I just have a way with animals, I guess," I offer, but my shoulders rise anxiously as I feel the brush of animal fur on nearly every bit of my exposed skin. Atjeh is the wildest dog I've ever seen—a white-eyed devil dog—but she's also the only pet I haven't been allergic to. Ever. Not Grandma Wini's bitchy Siamese. Not the Weimaraner Papa had to return when I almost stopped breathing in the back of the car. ("Two hours back to return that beautiful animal," Papa recalls more often than I would like. "And I had to pull over in the Pentagon parking lot so she could barf. What a dog. Even her politics were spot on.")

Two more cats rush through the open door, leaping silently to the bed to sit beside me. Four cats, all black, all circling me, touching me, raising the skin on my arms and along the back of my neck. What is it about animals that makes them all want to play with the allergic kid? A fifth appears at the door but comes no further, choosing to stare me down instead, gold-flake eyes catching hold of my growing anxiety.

The room, so small and hot now, feels like a snow globe, the air raining a shower of dust bunnies and dander down around me, filling my mouth, nostrils, lungs. I look at Penny, who has slipped back into *Tiger Beat*.

I take a breath, prod two of the cats away, and try to stand. Alpha jumps at this, placing her front paws on my thighs and forcing me back to the bed. But I take a breath. Then another. The doorbell rings. I hear my mother introducing herself to Laurie Cabot. The two women chat happily about the Alternative School and the upcoming fundraiser as they navigate the hall to Penny's room.

"Oh, my God," Mama blurts.

"Any god in particular?" Laurie asks.

Mama's hand flies reflexively to her chest, asthma alert on high.

"Well, it's just that, all these cats. And that dog. Louis is so terribly, terribly allergic. He shouldn't have lasted five minutes in all of this." She shakes her head, puzzled.

The witch waves the thought away. "I wouldn't let anything like that happen in my house."

Mama and I both stare at her. There isn't even a whispered tickle or pinch in the lowest folds of my lung lobes or the most remote branches of my bronchial trees. Apparently some spell is at work here.

"That's . . . that's truly remarkable," Mama laughs nervously. "You . . . We normally . . . How long have you been here, Lou?"

"I don't know. An hour? A couple of hours."

"Amazing. Well, it's time to go. Amanda and David are in the car. I left it running, so let's hope no one's driven off with them!" Mom and I both laugh, for different reasons.

"See you at school, Spike," says Penny.

"Spike?" Mama and Laurie say together.

"Later, Mom. Ugh."

Mama wraps her arms around Laurie Cabot before we leave. "I don't know how to thank you." She looks like she's about to cry. "You don't know what this means, for him to be able to do this."

"So, we'll see him again, I hope?" Laurie asks.

"Oh, yes," Mama assures her. "You can have him any time. Yes."

Yes!

Nusselballs is waiting for me in the dining room when we get home, talking with Frank, who has let him in.

"I love them!" Frank reaches out to touch the dangling curls falling around the ears of my Hebrew teacher. "Fetching. That's what I'd call them, your little locks. Fetching!"

"Peyes," Mr. Nusselballs pulls away, turning plum. "A religious prohibition against shaving the corners of one's head."

"I love a man who understands commitment." Frank giggles like a girl gorilla. His furry shoulders, exposed by a tight white tank top, bounce up and down as he turns back toward his apartment. "Maybe I need a little coming-of-age ritual myself? Let me know if you do Italian."

I roll my eyes. "How does a head have corners anyway?" I ask. "It's round."

Nusselballs ignores me, opens a workbook, and leans in close to run through the Hebrew alphabet with me.

"I'm not going to go through with this," I assure Nusselballs midway through the lesson. "They want me to, sort of, but they don't care that much. And they're really busy. And if I don't care, they can't make me. They don't tell me what to do," I say firmly. "So it's really not going to happen."

"I can tell," he says, that perpetually venomous shtetl-belch of his breath filling all the available breathing space. There's nowhere to go. I slide my chair sideways, feel an asthma attack coming on.

"Hey, hombre, how was day one?" Howie pops in, shirt open, smile brilliant. Thank you, God.

I relay every detail of my encounter with my newfound crush.

"I give you an A for the day. Just remember, a woman's cherry is the most precious jewel in the known universe. Promise me you'll do a little Lou-Howie powwow before you go all the way."

"Which way?"

"Perfect," he says.

Nusselballs stands and gently closes his little Hebrew book. "This really should conclude our studies together. You need a different kind of teacher, I think."

In the Schvitz

Howie and Carly don't appear for Sunday bagels until close to noon. But when they do emerge, they are so beautiful: clothes flowing, all different colors. Silk. Linen. Velour. Fabrics none of us wear. And skin, showing out of all different places. It's cold in the house but Papa stokes the fireplace in the dining room and flaps and folds of fabric loosen and drape as the temperature rises.

"I love seeing you all around the table like this," Carly says warmly. "This is what family is all about." She leans forward to grab a bagel and I search her open collar for a line of cleavage. *I love seeing you like this, too.* But when she sits back I notice her eyes are red and swollen.

"You'll be our practice family, OK?" Howie says. "And the little ones are our practice kids."

"Take 'em away," Papa says, handing his friend a section of the paper. "And read the op-ed piece by Milton Friedman. Calls LBJ an interventionist. Wants a complete withdrawal from the war on poverty."

"Gimme that," Howie pulls the page from Papa's hands.

"Where were you last night?" Mama asks Howie, passing him a piece of Grandmother's Famous Cranberry Bread.

"I went into the city for a bit. *Mmmmm!* This is incredible, Princess."

Amanda, still clad in her nightgown and curled in her chair, looks wonderingly at Carly. "You have puffy eyes," she says timidly.

"Shhhhhh. . . ." Mama hushes her. "It's not polite."

"Do you need a hug, Carly?"

Carly nods, closing her eyes. Her tears come quickly, in a big stream down her cheeks. She's so raw it hurts. I look down at my bagel, a weird fist of shame pressing inexplicably inside me.

"Oh, honey, what happened?" Mama asks, standing to join Amanda and Carly, who have come around the table to wrap themselves in a standing hug by the fireplace.

"It's nothing," Carly sniffles. "Don't worry."

"It's my fault," Howie says. "I hurt Carly's feelings. We're working through it, but it's hard." He stands to join the hug.

"Can we not discuss it with the group?" Carly pleads.

"But it's *family*," Howie objects.

"No, Howie. Please." She looks as if she'll cry again.

"Cranberry bread?" Papa asks.

"What happened?" Amanda repeats.

"I wanted to spend some time with a new friend last night," Howie says, "and Carly is feeling a little jealous."

"I'm not *jealous*."

"Hurt."

"Ouch," Carly says softly. "That's all I want to say. Ouch."

"Where did you meet a new friend?" Amanda can't help asking. For the rest of us, it's a slow-motion car crash we can't prevent.

"Actually, at your dad's office," Howie says, like that makes this all a bit easier to swallow.

"Not Joyce?" Papa sighs.

"Re-Joyce!" Howie trills in a tone rife with admission, apology, and reverie. I recall the woman at the reception desk listening in on our conversation, blushing when Howie said her name. *Joy to meet you, Joyce.*

Carly leaves the room and Papa makes angry eyes at Howie. I've never seen him do that to an adult.

"Too much?" Howie asks.

"Might be," my father replies.

"I'll go talk to her."

"No," Mama says. "Let me."

"Well, I reserved the court for two o'clock," Papa says, clearing his dishes. "Still game?"

"Never more," Howie says, shaking off the mood that has soured the room.

"Good, because you could use a beating."

"Can I watch?" I ask.

"You never come to the Y," Papa notes, rightly.

"I know, but I want to see you play."

"I think he wants to see *you* play," Papa pats Howie on the back on his way to the kitchen.

"My game is ten times better when I have a cheering section," Howie assures me. "I prefer taller and blonder. But you'll do."

It's true, I don't care about racquetball. I bring a pile of comics but take breaks now and then to peer through the Plexiglas porthole when there's a heavy thump and Papa or Howie bounce off the wall. Howie shouts "FUCK!" every time he misses a shot. Papa says "Lucky, boychik," the few times he does.

After the second game they emerge, drenched and winded.

"Who's winning?"

"I came close that first game," Howie says to me, slick with sweat. "Fifteen-twelve. The second was tougher. Your old man's a killer. Killer instinct."

"Come on," Papa urges. "We only have the court for another twenty minutes."

They're out in seven. Howie's breath is labored and he's wheezing. Papa, on the other hand, is bouncing, ready for more. My father is hairy, weedy, and lithe. I think of him as strong, but with a toughness more mental than physical. His style is to cajole rather than menace. To outsmart rather than outmuscle. Howie is how many years his junior? Cut like a G.I. Joe doll! Ready for action! And now sliding to the floor in an exhausted pile.

"What was the score?" I ask, proud of Papa but totally disoriented by the scene.

"Fifteen–zip," Papa says, nonchalant in victory.

Hearing all that grunting on the other side of the wall, I pictured Howie clobbering him. "Zero?" I ask Howie, lying in a puddle of his own sweat on the dusty black linoleum.

"I'm fucked."

"You're all muscle, no lungs," Papa tells him. "You need to change your workout. Less iron, more running. Condition yourself for the long haul. Endurance! Come on, let's get a *schvitz*."

"Oh! It's so humiliatin'! I feel like a Samsonite after the Steelers give it a good wailing . . ."

"Yeah, only you didn't hold up as well as those pretty suitcases in the commercials," Papa digs just a bit more before climbing the stairs to the locker room.

I stuff my comics and clothes in Papa's locker and wrap a scratchy Y towel around my waist. They're already in the steam room, so I pry the heavy metal door open and the heat is so strong it makes me swallow and hold my breath.

"I should be hearing about that grant any day now. Get you on staff, earning your keep." Papa's there, somewhere deep in the steam. I try to call to them but when I open my mouth the air blasts my tongue. I turn to leave.

"Jefe, I'm honored."

"But you can't fuck my secretary."

I decide to stay, invisible in the scalding mist.

"Because . . . ?"

"Because? Do I really need to tell you because? You really think you're *that* different?"

"I'm a human being. You're a human being. You have the *niños*. Makes it more complicated, I know. But if we're being honest with each other, then it's not so complex. It's being human."

"Oh," Papa's voice cuts the heavy mist. "It's clearly not complicated for Carly."

"She's going to be a sex therapist. She understands."

"Understands that you're a selfish prick. That you can't keep it in your pants, even on your honeymoon. And you can't keep quiet about it, either."

Papa's words cut, and the anger in his voice twists my stomach into knots.

"That's the voice of your father, man. This is a different time. This is our generation. I can't hide anything from her. I love her."

"If you love her, you protect her. You don't cheat on her. And if you do, you don't *tell* her."

"Wow. Where do I start with that? Everything you just said is based on false assumptions. First: It's not cheating. We committed to each other, to be together, yes, but also to have an open marriage. We acknowledge that we're human beings with human desires, not to deny our natural instincts. That's why Carly is a part of any exploring I do—not in the bed, necessarily, but in the setup and arrangements. Second: We don't lie about it. I don't know how to be anything but honest, especially with Carly. I can't hold all that shit inside. I don't know how anyone could. One day of deception and I'm a mess. Two days, and I'm on a collision course for the cuckoo's nest. How can I do that to the woman I love?"

"You just *do*, you asshole," Papa says angrily. The verbal shrapnel makes me flinch. "You don't rope her into it. You carry your own water. Every time you get a hard-on for another woman you don't *tell your wife*. All that's going to do is hurt her. Carry your water. You don't talk about it unless it's going to affect the relationship, permanently. That's when you need to bring it up."

"Well, that's how they used to do it. And how did that go? Repressed masturbators and guys sneaking around on women they say they love. And then everyone ends up divorced or, worse, in separate beds. We do it differently. We tell each other the truth."

Papa snickers. "You know what?"

"What?"

"You're stupid."

I let loose a desperate pant in the heat of the steam. "Lou?" Papa calls. I don't answer, willing my invisibility powers into action. He pauses, sighs. "Did it ever occur to you that you could just be monogamous? Is that even on your groovy radar screen?"

"You know what monogamy is?" Howie asks in the fog. "Monogamy is racism."

"Ha!"

"I'm not joking. It's a moralistic, puritanical, fabricated judgment of our nature. *And* it's a violation of our human rights. We're trying to cure it."

Papa laughs for a long time. "You know how long I've been married?" he asks when he catches his breath.

"Ten years?"

"Fifteen."

"Beautiful."

Isn't it?

"You want to know what marriage looks like after fifteen years?"

The heat of the *schvitz* closes on me, but I want to hear more. I try to hold my breath against this scalding air.

"Never mind. I don't need to talk about it. You can judge for yourself."

"Maybe you should," Howie proposes, spinning my heart in my chest round the other way. I'm not sure I want to hear the answer.

"Maybe. But I carry my water. It's what we have to do."

"Do we?" Howie asks.

"Well, I do." Papa pauses. "Your revolution is a lot harder to support. Plus, it's a lot harder when I have your wife living with me. Takes a lot of the fun out of it when she shows up at the table looking like she's sitting shiva."

The steam is crushing me. I grab for the door and escape to the cool BO of the locker room. My arms and legs are bright red, my throat scorched. My chest constricts, asthma attack looming, even with no dogs in sight. Slipping on the tiled floor, I make for the stairs down to the pool, skip the mandatory shower, and jump in the deep end.

The water is a reverse shock, the exact opposite of the *schvitz*. My body convulses once, marrow solidifying, and then a second time when my superheated balls recoil at the new exposure as the towel falls away, surfacing in a nappy white swirl among the Sunday morning lady lap swimmers. A whistle shrills and echoes off the walls of the pool room. "ADULT SWIM!" the lifeguard shouts. *"Outofthepool!"*

The lady lappers have stopped and are bobbing around me like wet raccoons in goggles and rubber caps.

"Come on!" one of them screeches.

Slowly I let my body slip under the surface. Opening my eyes I see the metal ladder, a few feet away through the rippling ice blue. I try to swim the gap, insides still on fire, skin shivering. But my lungs give out a few feet shy and I surface again.

"I said *outofthepool*!"

I dog-paddle a few more feet, reach for the ladder and try to close my ears and my mind to the gasps and cries that follow my naked ass into the stairwell and up to the locker room, invisible no more.

Curls, Crowds, and Other Thanksgiving Arrivals

"I want you all to go into the basement. *Now*."

Mama's tone is unmistakable. An octave below eruption. We have worn out her welcome in the kitchen. Thanksgiving is bearing down and my father is nowhere to be found. We're well accustomed to the long workdays and overnight business trips, but this is a holiday. It's becoming harder to hold him still and get a bit of what I need. But what is that, anyway? Hugs? I'm too old now.

I grab David by his little hand and we hurry down to the basement, where all there is to do is listen to *Godspell*, Paul McCartney and Wings, and *Disco Duck* on the plastic portable turntable.

"Howie said he'd jump out the window if he heard that song again," I warn my sister as she flips the 45 from the A side, *Disco Duck* (part one), to the B, *Disco Duck* (part two). Damn you Rick Dees and your Cast of Idiots.

"Well, he's on the third floor. He can't hear," she says.

David rides a green plastic Inchworm around the basement until he tumbles into the cordwood piled near the back.

"I want Mama . . ." he sobs. *Sure*, I want to tell him, *we all want Mama*. He was a baby when we lived in Manhattan. Mama worked, but she was *home* when she was home back then. In this mess of a mansion, she's always here, but never settled. As little as we got of her back then, David gets less now. His solution is to always stay close to my parents, snuggled under dinner and coffee tables, sleeping at the bottom of the stairs just outside the dining room door—close enough that he is not quite alone, but not so close to the adult realm that he'll be picked up and put away for the night. His method seems to work.

"Come on, buddy. I'll take you for a ride." I kneel down and curve my back so he can climb on, the way Papa does. His little hands grab my collarbone, wet cheek against my neck. "Let's go to Fahntasy Island!"

"Hey, who's hiding down here? We have a big Thanksgiving dinner happening on Chestnut Street!" the real Papa says as he trots down the basement stairs.

"Peter?" Mama's voice, muffled by the long dark of the dumb-waiter shaft.

"One sec!"

"Papa!" Amanda runs to the base of the stairs to meet him. "David fell over and . . . What happened to your hair?"

"Do you like it? Raphael did it."

"Who's Raphael?" Amanda asks.

"It's curly." David points over my shoulder at the exploded Brillo pad on my father's head.

His hair has been transformed, from a familiar hippie helmet to a tight chocolate-brown poodle shag.

"It's like Arnold Horshack and Juan Epstein had a baby," I whisper, mortified.

"It's called a perm. Short for permanent. Raphael! Come down and meet the kids."

"Is it . . . permanent?" Amanda tests.

A tall man—dark skin, long curly hair—clomps down behind my father.

"Hay-lo," his accent is doubly foreign here in our basement. "I am so pleased to meet you."

"Raphael is my hairdresser. Though that doesn't do him justice. Artist is more like it. He suggested I do something different for a change."

"I hurt my foot," says David, kicking his right leg forward along my ribs.

"Ooh," Papa soothes. "Let me kiss it."

"My grandmother, she put—how you say?—pepper pods on my injuries and they go away," Raphael smiles hugely while saying this.

"We could try that!" Papa's so cheerful for someone who looks like he was just electrocuted. "But Raphael, I want *you* to try my hummus."

"Why'd you . . . ?" I nod at my father's hair as David slides off my back.

"Change of pace. Can't let things get boring." Papa picks my brother up, inspecting his little body for cuts and abrasions. Poodle hair notwithstanding, he is talented when it comes to tenderness. He just doesn't do it as much as I wish he would.

Amanda and I stay below, huddled by the dumbwaiter where Mama's voice is clearest. "Where have you been? You've been gone ALL afternoon? I did the stuffing, the turkey, the celery root, everything . . ." Pause. "What did you do to your hair?" Amanda looks at me, bug-eyed.

"You like?"

"His face? Perfect for this! I tell him so," Raphael says happily.

"Hello? Who are you?" Mama tries and fails to sound friendly.

"Raphael. I told you. He's from Havana, by way of Miami. Real success story, his business."

"Well . . ." Mama says slowly, "I'm so glad you stopped by. I've just got so much to do and, Peter, I could *really* use your help."

"I've invited Raphael for dinner. We've got space."

It's not unusual for Papa to spike the social punch bowl with unexpected dinner guests, but Thanksgiving seems a bridge too far. Our move to the North Shore marks the first time we aren't celebrating at Grandma Wini's house, where the guest list would typically be us, Grandma and Gramps, Aunt Leslie, Uncle Rick, and Cousin Greg, with the Freedmans making their annual pilgrimage up Rockaway Ave for pie and rocky roads at a predetermined time. That's it.

"Peter, you know I love spontaneity," she says, but it doesn't sound loving. "Any other night, this would be different. But we've got eighteen people coming, including Glovey, and the table's not even set."

"Right, I'm on that," Papa says, a snap in his voice. "But I promised Raphael his first taste of hummus. Let me just whip up a quick batch."

"Peter!"

"I'll set the table. You don't need to do anything else. Why don't you go upstairs and rest? Take a break and save your energy for tonight."

Mama erupts. "I DON'T WANT TO REST. I WANT TO COOK DINNER. AND I WANT YOUR HELP!"

"Mount Vesuvius," I whisper. Amanda giggles, then catches herself.

The front door slams and Uncle Rick calls from the foyer before the argument can intensify. "Pete? Phyl? We're early!"

Papa shouts back, "Welcome! Rick, Les, meet Raphael—he's

in the living room and he's the best hairdresser on the North Shore. Make him a drink and help yourselves!"

"Oh, is this the Cuban Cutter guy? How ya doin', amigo? I'm having rum, Pete. You want one?"

"I'm very well, thank you. You are Peter's . . . er . . . brother?"

"Great!" Papa shouts over the drone as his new Cuisinart whips garlic, lemon, chickpeas, and tahini. The sound is like fertilizer for the blooming cacophony. "Ice is in the bar. How'd Marblehead do, Rick?"

"I'm his brother-in-law," Rick says. Then louder, to Papa: "Swampscott killed 'em, twenty-five to six. Massacre. And it was wicked cold. We left early."

Unlike Papa, who can't stop moving, his sister Leslie and her husband Rick are "Marblehead forever," never having lived more than four miles from Grandma Wini and Grandpa Sam. Uncle Rick went into the Navy when he turned eighteen, got some tattoos, lived on a submarine, and learned electrical engineering. Now he works at the Sylvania plant in Salem, making lightbulbs. Leslie, for her part, is full of enthusiasm for everyone she meets: first to laugh, last to leave, rarely without a smoke.

Cousin Greg calls from the top of the basement stairs and we come up to meet him as Grandma and Gramps trundle in, along with my parents' friends, Steve and Enid Freedman and their kids Matty and Rebecca.

Steve is in the wine business. A "connoisseur," Papa says. He grew up on Rockaway Ave, two blocks down the tree-lined street from Papa. Like my father, he moved to New York to make it big. And like Papa, he's found his way back home. Steve is by far the tallest Jewish guy I've ever met.

Enid is my mother's best friend. She's the prettiest and kindest of all the moms, though lately she spends most of her visits whispering mysteriously in the corner with Mama.

All the guests are carrying bowls, Pyrex plates, square ceramic dishes covered with foil and plastic wrap. I swoon at the once-a-year scent of sweet potato and marshmallow. Special food, but *normal* food, made from Grandma's *Joy of Cooking*, not Papa's *Cuisine Gourmande*.

"It was a disaster, Pete," Steve shouts over the tumult.

"You're all fair-weather fans," Gramps huffs, hanging his coat on the iron tree in the front hall, then helping Grandma with hers.

"Hello, my loves!" Grandma Wini coos, pulling a wrinkled tissue from her sweater sleeve and dabbing at her runny nose.

"And you're the worst of all, Pete," Gramps says to my father, his son, who is sprinting through the dining room to greet them. "Who skips the biggest rivalry of the year? What happened to loyalty?"

Suddenly the bustle of everyone arriving, greeting, shedding coats, and stomping boots falls silent. They've caught sight of my father's new hair.

"Jesus, I guess loyalty put its finger in a light socket," Steve laughs.

"Peter?" Grandma Wini's face takes on a rare expression, disdain, stretched and distorted by a cringe of horror and the competing impulse to always, always smile.

Papa grins broadly, thrusts out his arms, and flutters his jazz hands. "Ta-da!"

"You're shittin' me," Uncle Rick coughs on his icy rum and soda, spilling a bit of Papa's as he hands it to him.

"What happened to your dad's hair?" Matty leans in to me and whispers.

"Meet the maestro, everybody. Raphael's a master with shears."

"And cuter than Warren Beatty." Frank appears in the doorway between the dining room and the front hall.

"Hel-lo! I'll take a shampoo, love." Aunt Leslie giggles, pushing through the crowd to hug Frank.

"Such a fag hag," Frank pecks her on the cheek. "And look at you, Peter. Aren't you just one . . . singular sensation!"

Papa waves it all away, impervious as always to jabs.

"Well, I think you can pull off anything," Enid says softly, kissing my father on the cheek.

"He looks like Richard Dreyfuss," Aunt Leslie offers, arm around Frank. She towers over his round, furry frame.

"He looks like Richard Pryor," Rick says.

"Gene Wilder with a mustache?" Steve offers.

"He is a beautiful man with brave hair," says Raphael, trying to end the debate.

"*Brave* is one word for it."

"Ricky!"

"What? I'm not the one who got a Bozo do."

"You're just jealous," Papa laughs, brushing the conversation off, kissing his mother, patting Gramps on the back, Steve on the cheek, and each kid on the tush. "Hold on. I just made some hummus. Let me grab it and then I want to play you something."

"Who makes hummus for Thanksgiving?" Gramps asks no one in particular.

"He was going to make Cornish game hen instead of turkey," Mama sighs, pushing hair out of her eyes with the back of her wrist. "But I told him you wouldn't eat it, Sam."

"Thank you, Sweetie," Gramps kisses Mama on the cheek.

"You sure Pete's not a fag?" Uncle Rick elbows Frank.

"Sweetie," Frank tugs coyly on Rick's Abe Lincoln beard, "you should have seen him in the fraternity. He's a man's man."

Leslie lets loose a cheery, phlegmy, ciggy-butt laugh.

Everyone circles Mama for hugs but she waves them off. "I'm a mess. We're a little behind and I need to change my clothes. Maybe everyone can go into the living room? The fire should be nice and warm." Then to Enid, who has lined up alongside her: "Everything OK? Want to come up with me?" Enid nods and the two slowly climb the stairs to the second floor, Mama a step ahead and pausing for Enid every few stairs as the rest of the guests move along as instructed.

"Got any new albums, Pete?" Rick shouts as he flips the thick metal toggle to the Marantz. The heart of Papa's massive stereo system, along with his prodigious record collection, takes up an entire wall in the pool room. There's a fire burning here, too, along with the one in the adjacent living room where most of the family is gathering.

"This is going to knock your socks off!" Papa calls, handing Raphael an overflowing bowl of hummus and Leslie a lyric sheet printed on the protective album sleeve of Meatloaf's *Bat Out of Hell*.

"Steve, is Enid OK?" Aunt Leslie scoops the hummus with a pita wedge. Steve's head bows, shakes almost imperceptibly.

"Hold on!" Papa instructs, dropping the stylus on the album and turning up the volume. "Hold . . . on . . ."

Everyone has to hold on a long time because "Paradise by the Dashboard Light" is an eight minute, twenty-eight second operetta—the epic story of a teenage boy trying to get into the pants of a teenage girl on a hot summer night in the front seat of a car. It wraps up with a mock play-by-play by Phil Rizzuto—all-star shortstop, voice of the Yankees, Yoo-Hoo, and The Money Store—as Meatloaf tries to round the bases. But before he scores, she wants commitment. He wants to sleep on it.

"Pete!" Aunt Leslie cries with delight when she grasps the conceit of the song. "This is *the nuts*!"

A half hour later a series of martinis and more rum has been poured and everyone's listening to the song for the fourth time, singing together:

> *Though it's cold and lonely in the deep dark night*
> *I can see paradise by the dashboard light!*

More guests arrive: Mama's Uncle Mo, eyes wide behind thick glasses, with Grandma Charlotte, Mo's sister-in-law and Mama's mother. "Is this Thanksgiving or a circus?" Uncle Mo, the retired butcher, rumbles.

"I made pie," Grandma Charlotte says in a tone that suggests it was all work and no joy. "And here's the Cool Whip. I bought extra."

"Cool Whip doesn't have any cream in it, you know?" Papa declares. It's a secret to no one that my father never gets along with my other grandmother. She kvetches more than she smiles. And if she loves us like Grandma Wini does, she hasn't figured out how to show it. Then again, until I met Howie I hadn't known anyone could shine as bright as Grandma Wini. The weak kiss and smile Papa offers his morose mother-in-law is unconvincing but he takes the big paper shopping bag from her. "No dairy in the Cool Whip," he repeats, looking into the bag as if there might be something else to redeem her. "But try the hummus. It's homemade."

Grandma Charlotte just glares, then splurts, "What the *hell* have you done with your hair?"

"Uh, Pedro . . . ?" Raphael materializes alongside Papa, head down, hand reaching out to my father's shoulder. Papa looks quizzically at him. "I . . . eh . . . the hummus. It was so good."

"I'm glad you liked it, Raphael."

"Yes," he chuckles, turning bright red. "Yes, it was so good. I think, perhaps, I ate it all."

"*All* of it?"

"Yes, I am so sorry," Raphael says, embarrassed. "You were right. It is . . ."

"So good, right? Jesus, Raphael. I made, like, three pounds. Did anyone *else* get any hummus?"

The knocker clacks before anyone can answer.

As dramatic as she is slow-moving, Glovey Butler has honored the invitation.

"Hello?" her creaky voice deadens the hubbub as she scuffs along into the foyer, followed by a young man with a red ponytail and the heavy slam of our front door.

Papa smiles again, another faint flourish of jazz hands. "You'll have to excuse me for a moment . . . Glovey! Welcome. I am *so* glad you could spend the holiday with us. And this must be your grandson. Johnny, is it?" The ponytail guy nods, shakes hands, and digs into his coat pocket for something.

"Hi Glovey," Mama says, fixing an outsized smile on her face, blinking uncontrollably. "Oh, Johnny, thank you . . . That's . . . Oh! That's really too much," to Johnny, who has found the bottle of whiskey he was evidently searching for in his coat and offered it to my mother.

"Welcome to our humble home." Papa is at his most deferential. "May I take your coat, Glovey?"

Her watery old eyes scan Papa's face. "Have we met?" Glovey asks.

The party falls dead silent. I catch an eyebrow-raising look pass between Rick and Frank, telegraphing the sentiment of the group: *Is the old lady batty?*

Papa is momentarily speechless. Then he holds out his arms appealingly and replies: "Peter. Peter Cove."

"You remember, Grammy," Johnny says softly. "Our neighbor."

"Well, of course, but you must be his brother. Peter has straight hair. Longish. Like a hippie who hasn't yet left the 1960s behind."

The circle holds its breath. It is a moment that even the youngest in the room understand. It may be Papa's domain, but the town belongs to Glovey, Empress of Chestnut. Being cantankerous doesn't affect her position. In fact, it only deepens the respect of those around her, and they grant her an ever wider berth: Glovey, the grand old whaling ship blithely navigating the social harbor of Salem, making all the smaller boats scramble sideways as she rumbles from port to port.

"Glovey," Papa ventures into the silent void, "You are a fucking hoot."

This is Papa: sovereign ruler of his court, eldest, flawless firstborn Jewish son, big brother, gracious host, racquetball champion. Mustachioed, newly permed, hero to the jobless, father to us all. Papa. He will not be put in his place.

Glovey looks my father straight in the eye, her lips crimped into a gray little anus of wrinkles above her pointy chin. "Well," she begins, dry tongue snapping at the roof of her mouth in reply, "that's what my father always used to say."

The collective sigh, dropping of shoulders, relieved chuckles, all retrieve the moment from frozen, awkward time to the chirpy familiarity of just another party on Chestnut Street.

"Now how about a drink?" Glovey asks, her tone switching to something far more benign. "It's chilly in here, Cove. You're not going to force me into a Jimmy Carter cardigan, are you?"

"I've got just the thing to warm you," Papa assures her, then to Grandma Wini: "And Mother, *you* need a martini. Raphael, do you know how to make one?"

"I'm an experienced mixologist!" Howie offers as he descends, as if on cue, from the third floor of the house. "I've been experimenting with fermenting tea and home brewing, but I've also been known to make a martini now and then. Quakin', not absurd, yes Wini?"

"The gang's all here," Uncle Rick says as the adults migrate to the bar.

Soup's On, Pants Off

The adults booze and the kids bolt: Matty and Rebecca Freedman, cousin Greg, and my siblings follow my charge to our parents' room upstairs. Uli breezes in, the one uninvited guest of the evening, and finds us all upstairs. "We finished our dinner a long time ago," he says by way of explanation. "Super boring." He's been here a few times since I started at Alternative, and it's a love fest between him and Papa so he knows he won't get turned away.

"Anyone know how to light their fingertips on fire?" I ask, grabbing a bottle of perfume from the gilded mirror lying flat atop my mother's dresser.

"I know how to make myself burp," Matty says, serving up a gamey tuna fish belch.

"Pissah," Uli says, balancing on his long arms in the doorway. And then he erupts with a belly volcano twenty times more sonorous than Matty's.

"Uli!" I call. "Come here, light my fingers." I pour a bit of perfume out on the mirror and dab each of the three middle fingers of my right hand in the slippery liquid. I hand him a book of matches and he strikes one, holding it before his face for a moment. Then adopting a Lugosi drawl says, "Vatch as I vill burn my friend to ashes! Bwah hah hah!" And with that he touches the match tip to my fingers, setting them ablaze in a translucent blue and yellow.

Rebecca screams and bolts out of the room. Greg and Matty stay, fixated.

"That's boss," Greg says, big buck teeth pulling at his lower lip, barely able to control his excitement. I think he is going to drool.

"He always does that," Amanda puts in, annoyed by the attention we're getting.

"Hey, what are you little people up to?" Carly takes Uli's place in the doorway, eyes watery and red, smile weak.

"Louis just lit his fingers on fire with my mother's perfume," Amanda says blandly.

"Oh, that's creative," Carly says. "Can I try?" As she approaches me the three other boys drop back a step or two, eyes on her purple silk evening dress, tie-dye splashed at the chest so the explosion of color turns sun yellow over her breasts. Carly takes the small square glass bottle and dabs the tips of every finger and the matching pads on her palm. She looks at me and nods. My hand trembles a bit as I hold a lit match before her doused fingers. "I'm not sure what happens if you have long fingernails," I say, pulling back at the last moment.

"It's OK," she answers softly, sniffling. "I'm an adult." As if I need to be reminded.

Moving closer to her, I feel Carly's breath stroke my hair, sparks erupt across my back.

My heart leaps with the liquid blue flame as Carly's fingers flutter and she laughs happily, eyes brightening at the vision. "I don't feel a thing," she says. "It's cool."

"Don't let it go too long," I warn.

"It feels good. You forget everything for a second." She licks her lips softly, letting the fire continue to lap at the space between us. I dash to the bathroom to get a towel.

"It only lasts for a little bit that, then it starts burning your skin. I don't want you to get hurt," I say, covering her hand with the towel.

"Too late for that, Sir Lancelot," she touches my head again, wraps an arm around me.

Papa added three leaves to the table but it still can't hold the entire group. He asks Uncle Rick to take Raphael to the basement and lug up the wooden worktable on which Mama has been cutting glass and framing pictures for neighbors and friends.

Mama's stress level has risen with the headcount, now grown to twenty with the unexpected additions of Raphael and Uli. We all take our seats and Uli sidles up happily next to Gramps, who pats him on the shoulder, and turns to Carly. "So how are you keeping yourself busy?" Gramps asks.

"I'm organizing a group here at the house—a safe space for women to gather and discuss their sexual lives," she says, her voice still soft, but resurgent.

"Sexual lives?" he draws back, faux scandalized.

"We all have them . . . Hopefully." Carly smiles at him. "Some are wonderful, some could use some adjustment, and some really need intervention and support. But they all need to be talked about."

"With strangers?"

"With other human beings. It's just human. I'm sure Wini would understand. Maybe she'd like to sign up."

Gramps chuckles uncomfortably and turns to Grandma Wini as if to say *You wouldn't, would you?* but Uncle Ricky has pranced into a political minefield by starting a debate with my father about welfare recipients—whether they truly want to work or are just living off the taxpayers.

"Of course they are!" Grandma Charlotte leaps in. "Society's leeches."

"Charlotte, honestly, you don't know what you're talking about," Papa says from the other end of the table. Grandma Charlotte glowers at Papa but says nothing. Although the regulars know this is standard thrust and parry for my father and my mother's mother, the newcomers are startled. As high as he has placed his own mother on a pedestal, Papa would take shit from Atjeh before he takes it from Grandma Charlotte. "Seriously," Papa goes on, the room simmering in wait. "You don't know *bupkes*. Spend one day in our office. One. Now I'd like to make a toast."

"I see there's a great deal of respect for one's elders in this household," Glovey says to Johnny loud enough so everyone can hear.

"Ah, forgive me," Papa bows his head. "You're right, Glovey. Charlotte, I apologize, that really wasn't appropriate at all. The fact is, you genuinely have no idea what you're talking about and it drives me bananas, but that gives me no right to speak to you with anything but respect. I hope you'll accept my apology."

Grandma Charlotte doesn't speak, and she is motionless save for the gentle sway of her towering gray-blue hair. She stares blankly at Mama while the rest of us stare at her. "*Did* he apologize?" she asks at last. "I didn't hear it."

"Anyway"—Papa raises a glass and clinks it with the side of a butter knife—"this is a very special occasion. We have all our loved ones together around the table again. Plus, we are fortunate enough to be able to welcome Glovey and her grandson, Johnny, to our home. Glovey," he raises his glass still higher in the old woman's direction, "you are the belle of our ball and we are honored by your presence." Glovey gestures gently in response, indicating that this is sufficient praise.

"What about Uli?" Amanda asks. "It's special that he's here."

"Well, yes it is," says Papa. "Uli, we are so glad you could make it." He pauses. "By the way, where's your real family?"

"Watching the Cowboys game."

"I got Cowboys by six," Uncle Ricky says.

"Well, we're glad you chose us. And the same goes for Raphael who, despite eating all my hummus, is my hero for the day. I feel ten years younger."

"Was that the point?" Ricky laughs heartily.

"I think Peter looks marvelous," Grandma Wini chimes, alive with her unique brand of maternal euphoria and her three-ounce martini.

"Anyway, if I can try once more?" Papa raises his glass. "It's a delight to have you all here. Not to mention our special houseguests, Howie and Carly."

"Amen!" Mama says.

"We love you," Carly says, her voice pure and full of love. None of the joking or irritation has affected her. And whatever had caused her heart to ache earlier, it seems for the moment to have melted away.

"I love you," I reply into the silence.

"Whoa, hombre!" Howie throws up his hands and I blush.

"I mean all of you. Duh? I love all of you," I sit up as straight as I can in the hardback chair.

"I love you all, too," Mama says, "And I'm just happy I have a son who feels comfortable enough to say it so simply."

"Hey," Amanda protests. "I love everybody, too, you know."

"We know," Mama whispers. "Shhhh . . ."

"Right." Papa regains the attention of the group. "It's a love fest. Anyway, as I was trying to say . . . What separates today from all other days is that we stop, take a moment to reflect on what we're grateful for, and do it in the company of those we care for. I, for one, am grateful for my family. For all of you. You add richness and texture to life. You keep the days from dragging on and the nights from ending too soon. We are better for knowing you all. L'chaim!"

"What did he say?" Glovey asks Johnny as the rest of the room repeats the salute.

"It's a Jewish thing," Rick yells to her. "I'm old hat at this now. The token goy. Ask me anything."

"I'd like to suggest that maybe we go around the room and each add one thing we're grateful for. Just a word or two. Phyl, do you want to start?" The guests, caught off guard, look uneasily at one another.

Uli's eyes widen admiringly every time my father opens his mouth. I realize I have stopped trying so hard to wrest Papa's attention from his many preoccupations—his friends, work, music, wardrobe, and *The New York Times*. I am more interested in trying to unlock the mysteries of the man from Berkeley. Yet now I feel a sudden pang of guilt. My communication with Papa these days is more the wordless kind, the reality between us more often done in significant glances than in conversation: angry eyes if I cross his line, approving wink and nod if I meet his standards.

Mama grins nervously, never one to make toasts or speeches. "I'm grateful that Howie and Carly are staying with us," she says softly, then passes the baton to Enid, sitting on her right.

"I'm grateful for the good health of my family," Enid offers as Mama quietly excuses herself and disappears into the kitchen.

"And good medicine," Steve adds, leaning his head against Enid's.

The kids go round: "Popsicles." "Burping on command!"

"No fire engines today." Cousin Greg, always terrified of sirens, looks genuinely grateful.

"No fire engines today!" Aunt Leslie seconds.

"My old shit spreader didn't need a new differential after all," Uncle Ricky informs us.

"I'm grateful for this invitation," Glovey Butler says, "though I do find you all a bit strange." The table laughs nervously at her paper-dry humor.

"Unity and love," Carly is looking right at Howie.

"Love and latitude," Howie replies.

"Papa's old hair," my sister says with more force than she may have intended.

"*Amanda*," Mama's scold floats along the fragrant warmth coming from the kitchen.

"It's fine. Fine. Keep going," Papa says. "David?"

"Bunny Yabba?" he says. Glovey Butler crinkles his brows.

"Moving on," Papa prods.

"My beautiful, glorious, to-die-for grandchildren," Grandma Wini scrunches her eyes shut, clearly experiencing some sort of secret rapture the rest of us can only imagine. "And Sammy. And my children. And their spouses. And all of you. Oh, it's too hard to narrow down."

"The buffet at Kowloon," Gramps says, betraying his deepest passions.

"Sammy, honestly," Grandma Wini shakes her head.

"Dad?" Papa asks. "Seriously?"

"What? It's the best all-you-can-eat on the North Shore. And the fried bananas? Come on!"

"Christopher Reeve," Frank clasps his hands to his chest.

"Who?" Three or four people ask simultaneously.

"Superman?" I ask.

Frank nods vigorously. "Good-bye Travolta, hello Sugar Tights."

The room erupts.

The table turns light and easy until Papa makes me read the poem I wrote last year. He had a local artist illustrate and frame it. I was smitten by that thoughtful attention but blush at this. "Off you go," he prods. "Wait until you hear this. Louis is turning into a real writer."

I return with the framed poem. Papa smiles, gives an encouraging nod. *You're making me proud. Now show everyone else how proud I can be.*

"When I'm Lonely," I begin softly.

"Louder!" Uncle Rick says.

"When I'm lonely I sit on my bunk bed and count my one hundred and forty baseball cards. I lay on the floor when I'm supposed to clean my room. I think of why I have no friends; I think of the same one hundred reasons, then I'm back to where I started from. I thumb through my dictionary or an astronomy book— the stars seem lonely too. I look for a toy I know I lost, or sit on my old tricycle. Sometimes I walk out of my room and let my mom scream at me . . ." I pause here.

"Go on," Papa says, eyes closed, listening with intent.

"I walk out of my room and let my mom scream at me about why I should be cleaning my room. Sometimes I'm lonely when I'm in school and want someone to help me with a story. I'm lonely when I'm the slowest boy in the class." I lay the poem on the table to indicate this is the end. It's over.

"My Louis!" Grandma Wini nearly shrieks. "That is simply mahvelous. Come here! Come here this instant!" she calls, not waiting, lifting from her chair and smothering me against her soft chest in front of the group. "*Oy gottenyu.* I'm going to die right here."

The others offer gentle applause. Amanda rolls her eyes. David says, "I'm lonely, too!" searching the room for a response.

Howie leans forward to me and points at my heart: "You have two superpowers in your corner, *niño*: that creative spark . . . and *that* grandmother. That's some serious unconditional love stuff right there. I've got a jealousy hard-on for that."

"I think that . . . that was so terribly sad," says Carly as the table quiets down. "It makes me want to cry."

Papa frowns. "Well, that's what makes it a good poem. It evokes some emotion."

Carly stares at me. "But I just think of you, up there, all alone, trying to keep yourself busy, but doing the same things over and over. Things that won't make the feeling go away." I glance at Grandma Wini who ponders this interpretation with a confused expression. "I think that may be the saddest poem I ever heard," Carly says, her eyes fixed on mine.

She's right. They're celebrating it, but no one really listened. Well, almost no one.

"It's the artistry that moves me," says Papa. "We all feel lonely now and then. But Louis says it so well."

"Where was *I*?" Uli asks. "I would've come over!"

Everybody laughs except me and Carly, our eyes still locked. I would feel bad over and over again just to have her attention like this. To be known as I am, rather than as I am wished to be.

Guests are beginning to stir. Mama, Enid, and Leslie go to the kitchen and return with steamy platters, gravy boats, bubbled-over dutch ovens and pink and green terrines—more than anyone could imagine would fit in our tiny kitchen or our stomachs.

The *chink* of silver on china fills the room, and the rustle of multiple conversations rises to fill the awkward spaces. Mama and Papa's dinner is alternately familiar and bizarre. Most of the adults compliment them, oohing and aahing over the variations, but the kids wait for the turkey and cranberry sauce, even if the latter is, they will discover, laced with unwelcome additions: candied ginger and almond slivers.

"This meal is far fucking out," Howie says through a huge mouthful.

"Mrs. Cove, your salad is divine," Glovey Butler croaks from her end of the table. "You must share the recipe with Johnny so he can make it for us sometime."

A warm blush fills Grandma Wini's face and she begins to list the ingredients—mandarin oranges, water chestnuts—but one of the other guests cuts her off. "So, our friends from California here must have some strong feelings about the defeat of Proposition 6, I assume?"

"What's Proposition 6?" Amanda asks, always magnetically drawn to the third rail.

Mama and Papa lock eyes. They both look at Glovey Butler, then back at one another. I sense that this is it: the conversation they never wanted to have with her.

"It was a terrible thing, love," Carly says to Amanda. "California voters were asked to ban gay and lesbian people from teaching in the public schools. They called it the Briggs Initiative and, thankfully, it failed."

"You know you're living in the Twilight Zone when Ronald Reagan comes to the defense of the gay movement," Steve adds.

"Mmmmm, let's not get ahead of ourselves," Howie answers. "He didn't *defend* gays. I'm sure he would have been very happy not to have them teaching in public schools. He just made sure that fucking Briggs didn't end up governor. Self-interest, all the way."

"California probably just avoided its own version of Kristallnacht," Frank says, uncharacteristically serious.

"A little extreme, don't you think? Comparing the plights of Jews and gays . . ." Grandma Charlotte says.

"Oy. And away we go . . ." Uncle Mo pulls out a green cigar to light between courses.

Mama shifts nervously in her seat. Papa keeps opening his mouth as if to speak but can't seem to get anything out. He's torn, wanting to join the conversation but also wanting to end it. His face turns deep red as he drinks more wine.

"I don't think so," Glovey Butler says, dropping her silver to her china plate with a definitive clang. "Just look at what happened in Dade County with Anita Bryant."

"Miss Oklahoma?" Gramps asks.

"Miss orange juice huckster turned zealot! She's a closet Nazi if ever I saw one." Again Glovey renders the group speechless. Even the kids, who have no idea what's being discussed, can feel the temperature of the room drop by ten degrees. Everyone stares at Glovey, who picks up her utensils once again and begins to carve into the turkey Mama has just placed before her. "You know," she creaks, "some of my best friends are homos."

"Yeah!" Howie cheers. Mama chokes on her wine. Papa grins happily, shoulders releasing as he leans back in his chair. He gives Glovey an almost imperceptible knowing wink and we realize, all at once, that the cranky old doyenne next door is just an act.

"I prefer 'queen,' myself," Frank replies. He sounds indignant, but when I turn to face him I see a wet smile quivering below his bristly 'stache.

The banter continues but I'm fixated on the look of silent love my mother is giving my father. He was right. This was the solution, and his tendency toward chaos has paid off. Glovey isn't a homophobe and Frank isn't her enemy. She wants the neighborhood to look one way, on the outside. But behind closed doors, everything is on the table.

Uncle Rick is laughing, waving a finger at Howie. "Hey, speaking of queen—I could use a pair of pants like *that*."

"Have mine," Howie motions to his lap.

"That's OK," Rick says. "You know what the guys at the Sylvania plant would say to me if I walked in wearing those geisha girl pajamas?"

"Let's find out!" Howie stands and, before anyone can say otherwise, pulls the white drawstring at his waist and lets the orange pants drop around his ankles.

"Oh, my God," Mama whispers, horrified.

"*Now* it's a party," Frank delights.

"A singular experience, Mr. Cove," Glovey says to Papa.

Amanda, Matty, Rebecca, and Greg squeal as Howie steps out of his pants and, conspicuously unhurried, walks around the table to present them to Uncle Rick.

"Thanks, you crazy freakin' loon," Uncle Rick shakes his head as Howie returns to his seat, naked from the waist down.

"You should all get used to seeing this anyway, people," Howie says, pointing south. "Because you're seeing the future."

"I've never seen anything like it," Glovey Butler replies.

"Put your pants on," Papa grumbles fiercely, eyeing Glovey and seeing how swiftly his victory has turned pyrrhic.

"Doesn't pay," Howie shakes his head. "But this does." He pulls something from under his seat—a magazine with big yellow letters at the top and a picture of a brown-haired woman with a man in the lower right corner, resting his head on her shoulder, nuzzling her neck, and smiling. Howie opens the magazine, grabs the top of the page, and releases it, accordion style, to reveal a single photograph of . . . him.

Propped on his right elbow, half-smoked cigarette between his lips, long hair blowing back from his head, chest tanned and shiny, just speckled with hair, stomach contracted into a knobby washboard, legs spread and held apart by his left arm, bare knee pointing toward the ceiling, thick veiny pink penis, haloed by a spray of light brown pubic hair, pointing past his hip bone to the floor, and a golden ashtray—the only other prop in the scene.

I look at Carly. Her eyes have dried, whitened. She's staring at Howie with that look of blissed-out love. I drop my head, inspect the soft little popover of my stomach. I look up again. And there he is, still naked. The room is silent.

"Meet *Playgirl*'s Man of the Month!" Howie does a game-show model kind of thing with his hand, keeping the centerfold in plain view. "I'm Mr. November. Glad to make your acquaintance."

Part II

Exposé

Man of the Month

Uli and I sneak up to my room with a copy of the magazine, one of a half dozen Howie distributed to the Thanksgiving guests while Papa circulated cigars and digestifs in the break between dinner and dessert.

"I don't really want to see naked guys," Uli says as I flip through the pages, trying to find Howie's section.

In one spread, there's a guy who looks just like Frank. He's got the bushy mustache, dark hair, and perpetual five-o'clock shadow. He's wearing a white hardhat, white tank top, blue and white striped boxers, and he's holding a huge chunk of watermelon that's been bitten into a few times. Someone removed the seeds. But he's much skinnier than Frank. And a second look at his boxers reveals that one side is riding higher up on his thigh than the other because there's a huge boner under there. This section is called "Brief Encounters—It's Underclothes That Make the Man."

On the opposite page there are four more guys in underwear: white briefs, Tarzan leopard briefs, red and white briefs, and a pair of green briefs with a big silver dildo pointing out of the waistband. Each guy has a title: White is The Art Director. Leopard is Tarzan. Red and white is The Accountant. And green, with the Steely Dan, is The Swinger. The Art Director is wearing green argyle socks. They don't match his underwear. On the next page are The Rock Star, The Swimmer, The Businessman, and The Producer. The final page is devoted entirely to The Jock. He's wearing one, and he fills it massively.

I stumble onto another spread on page eighty-one. It's innocent enough, nine profile shots labeled *A* through *I*. The guys all look different—a blonde, redhead, couple of mustaches. I can't help but notice that four of the nine have perms. Apparently Papa is on to something.

It's "*Playgirl's* Haven't I Seen You Someplace Before? Contest."

"Who are these men?" the text reads. "And why do they look so pleasantly familiar? Turn the page. You'll be glad you did."

We do, and we're not. There are nine numbered photos: eight dicks and one ass.

Your mission, should you decide to accept it, is to match dongs with mugs. If we're lucky, we'll win a lifetime subscription to *Playgirl*!

There's an entry blank below.

"Sick," Uli turns away. I keep flipping. There's an ad for a product called Caress. It doesn't really say what Caress is, but there's a photo of a woman holding a long rubber penis in her hands. Next to her black-and-white photo are the words "SOFT YET FIRM! Only $7.95."

I continue on to the "bumper crop of gorgeous men" in the Guys Next Door section. It leads off with an Illinois striptease from David Shuster, twenty-three, of Peoria, Illinois. "David is crazy about outdoor sports. Obviously."

Justin Wiener of Malibu, California, is walking down the beach naked. Gene Keefover from Glendale, Arizona, is "in the insurance biz." He has a mustache, and he's lying spread-eagle on an inflatable air mattress in the pool. Ryan Halley is in the shower. He's twenty-two, from Dracut, Massachusetts, and he'd make any pilgrim woman blush.

"Hey," says Uli. "My cousin lives in Dracut. I wonder if she knows him."

Greg Hamilton, who apparently was a centerfold in June 1976, doesn't seem to want to fade away so he sent in a snapshot of himself on his back deck. The head of his penis looks like a cherry bomb that someone taped to a sausage.

"Aauuuuuuggggghhhh!" Uli and I say in unison, pulling away from the page and laughing. "What happened to his dick? It's disgusting," Uli says and gags, returning to the picture like a pedestrian who almost stepped in the tangled entrails of roadkill.

How much time have I spent on this bunk, dissecting every nook and cranny of Barbi Benton? Monique St. Pierre? Debra Jo Fondren? All the *Playboys* I stole from Gramps's guest bathroom . . . The *Hustler* I pinched from Howie . . . Suddenly, I am forced to wonder, does Grandma Wini have a bunch of *Playgirls* under the sink in the bathroom upstairs? Does Mama?

"Does your mom read this?" I ask Uli.

"No!" he punches my shoulder. "Disgusting. But I bet Frank does."

"Ugh."

"Seriously. It's so gay."

"No. This is for women. That's the whole point."

"I'm gonna throw up."

"Hold on. It's in here somewhere," I promise.

"He's the *centerfold*." Uli frets, covering his eyes. "Just go to the middle!"

I do, and find Howie splayed naked before me, then flip back a few pages to the start of his section. There he is, left hand on hip, in a brown corduroy blazer and tight, umber corduroy pants cinched with a finger-thin, tan leather belt. A sweater pokes out from behind the wide lapels of his jacket, a busy pattern like something Grandma Charlotte might have crocheted into an afghan. The collar of Howie's khaki shirt, unbuttoned, is so wide it reaches his clavicle. He wears a brown knit tie, loose, squared at the ends and speckled with white dots. His cheek and lips are pinker than in real life. His hair, heavily styled, seems caught in a light autumn breeze. The mouth of a beer bottle can just be seen poking up between his thumb and forefinger. It's ringed with gold foil. Looking back at his left hand I notice his wedding ring has been removed. He's smiling, but not too much. His skin is tan. His chest hair is wispy, not too thick. The gray background makes him pop off the page in his many shades of brown.

He looks like a star.

By Howie's shoulder, in white and powder-blue letters that are nearly, but not quite, brushed by fluttering wisps of his hair, it says:

PLAYGIRL'S MAN OF THE MONTH—
HOWIE GORDON.
Actor, Artist, Lover.

"It almost doesn't look like him," Uli cocks his head this way, then that. "Is he wearing makeup?"

In every way, Howie stands apart from the Guys Next Door. They are caught in a moment in the shower or on the beach by a girlfriend or neighbor, but Howie looks as if he has stepped off a movie set, nowhere near his Berkeley cottage or 31 Chestnut. He is the idealized Howie, the Howie of Dreams. Plastic but real. Corduroy but silky smooth. I imagine running my fingers through his hair.

On the next spread Howie lays on his side, propped on his right elbow, Lowenbrau in hand, still completely dressed. There's a dog beside him, tail curled between its legs, skinny like a whippet, its coat yet another light shade of brown. Whose dog is that? I wonder. He doesn't own a dog. Why would they make him pose with one?

There's an interview with Howie in which he explains why November is the perfect month for him to appear in the magazine. "I've fallen passionately and madly in love with five women who were born the first week in November," he reports, and then explains how it has something to do with his "chart." Born May 5, 1948, double Taurus, Moon in Aries, six fire signs, two earth signs, and one air sign.

Who are the five women? What's double Taurus, Moon in Aries, with all those signs? What signs?

Howie's striptease takes place in three photo stages. It's slow, taking two shots just to get his shirt off, though his pants are already unbuttoned and folded back a bit so you can see the inside whites of his pockets and a hint of pubic hair. The third shows him grabbing his cords by the back waistband and pushing them down an inch or two. The stem of his penis is visible, but it's the articulated abs and squared chest muscles that catch my eye. His stomach is completely flat and there are carved lines at his hips that lead like riverbeds directly to his pelvis. This is why they wanted him. This is why women like him. This. And his crazy brain.

I touch my stomach reflexively, incapable of imagining my body hardening or sprouting, of any part of me strengthening or lengthening or thickening. I am just this. Soft and wheezy. For as long as I can remember.

On the next page Howie is really naked. There are three small photos at the top of the left-hand page. He's standing in the first, taking off his last sock. Even though he's bending over, and he's looking straight into the camera with an expression that says, *ready or not, here I come.* His penis is kind of shadowed somewhere between his hunch and his raised knee, but you can tell it's coming. In the second shot he's kneeling down on the ground, back to the camera, looking over his shoulder, right into your eyes. His ass is shiny, like he's wearing a lot of Coppertone oil. His elbow is on his raised knee.

"Is that the tip of his dick? Or is it one of his balls?" Uli's finger touches the page, just below the dongle in question.

"I have no idea. Don't touch it."

In the third frame he's standing straight up, hands on hips, elbows thrust backward, washboard sticking out, boner pointing toward another block of text.

The interview continues, and Howie follows up on this idea of falling madly and passionately in love. Does it come easily to him?

It depends. People know each other over long periods of time. Sometimes you meet people and you realize that your histories go back for centuries. When I met my last girlfriend we had the feeling we knew each other four thousand years ago. There is no word for that kind of feeling, but everybody knows when it's happening.

He loves life, and oh, yes, he wouldn't mind if someone in Hollywood sees this spread and makes him the next Starsky or Hutch.

"OK, if *that* happens then that would be pissah," Uli nods.

Below these three shots and the text is the big finale. Howie, spread eagle, all the brown and tan clothes on the floor beside him. His armpit hair looks like it's been sweating a little, bunched into thick strands, but there's no other sign of perspiration. He's just bronze. And a little pink. This time his penis is pushed back against his stomach and it looks like it's made of plastic.

Did they put makeup on it?

His pubic hair is pushed back too. Did they tell him to adjust himself or did someone get right in there and use a special comb? Or their bare hands?

Side by side, Uli and I continue to browse the spread. My fingers wander to my face. They smell like burnt perfume.

We're still analyzing when Howie appears at the door to my

room. "So? What's the verdict?" he asks, a new pair of drawstring pants covering the business again.

"It's cool," I manage, unable to find the right words.

"Really. You can say it's weird to look at pictures of my penis, you know?"

"I kind of see it all the time," I remind him. "But it's weird that everyone else can now."

"Touché."

"How many people were there when they took the pictures?" Uli asks.

"Photographer, makeup and hair girl, art director kind of person. And the centerfold editor."

"I would have been wicked embarrassed being naked in front of all those people," I say.

"Hazard of the profession. But I don't mind being naked in a group. You saw my wedding photos." He sits down beside us on the bed. "Hey, is this my *Hustler*?" I nod. "Just give it back when you're done. It's a new one. Stick with the back issues, Sticky, OK? But yes, I don't mind the public nudity. Though it's a little hard to keep it up when everyone's staring you down."

"That really is weird," Uli says.

"Yup," Howie concedes.

"So, how did you get so Lou Ferrigno for this?" Uli keeps going.

Howie smiles and flexes a bicep. "I was going more for Paul Newman, actually." He walks to Bunny Yabba's crate, leans over and sniffs. "When was the last time you cleaned this fucking thing? It smells disgusting."

"I don't really smell it anymore," I say.

"Trust me. It's bad. I'll help you clean it out tomorrow," he promises, sitting down beside me on the bunk and pointing at the centerfold in my lap. "This is thanks to El Jefe, in a way. Remember the way he kicked my ass in racquetball last time? That was just the latest in a string of humiliating indignities. He's almost ten years older than I am, but he is one tenacious motherfucker. And one of those times, a couple of years ago, he said 'This is middle age, boy. Use it or lose it.' And me, huffing and wheezing on the floor of the court? I realized he was right. El Jefe usually is, for what that's worth to you. Your old man *knows* shit.

"So I start working out with a sense of purpose, instead of just going to the gym to play a game. I start treating my body like a science experiment." He stands up and makes as if to pose in front of a mirror. "Oh! Pecs not big enough? Let's try to make them harder. You know what kind of a revelation that is for a former fat kid? I can carve my body into whatever shape I want to. Six-pack? Triceps? All possible. I started right away after that game. And breaking concrete with a sledgehammer for work didn't hurt. Next thing you know, I'm in a hot tub in Berkeley and a pretty lady across from me asks if I'd be willing to pose naked. Fuck yes! I'm beautiful now! But you saw the ugly truth: beauty can't slay the beast. Your dad still kicks my ass. He's a killer, that Papa of yours."

Uli, captain of the Papa fan club, nods vigorously. "But what about Carly?" Uli asks. "She seems super sad. Is she mad about the magazine?" I flash Uli the angry Papa eyes but the question is already out there.

"Yeah, well . . ." Howie starts. "I had a little fling with El Jefe's secretary. Remember the one at the desk?" he says to me and I nod, angry eyes morphing to saucers of surprise. "So I had to tell Carly that I wanted to. That it was going to happen. We made a promise to always tell each other whenever . . . whenever that kind of thing comes up. And she sets it up, you know? So there are never any surprises. I tell her who I want to be with and then she makes it happen, so that I'm not just out there sneaking around. Lies are what kill relationships."

"Seems like Carly wasn't that happy about it, though," Uli says. "I mean, if it's part of the agreement and everything."

"Point taken," Howie replies softly. "Sometimes love just hurts like a motherfucker."

Our Thanksgiving guests all have questions of their own:

"Do your parents know?"

"How much did they pay you?"

"What's the point?"

The questions are fast and relentless.

The magazine, it turned out, wanted a man with an erection. (Uncle Rick: "I couldn't do that if you put a gun to my head." Enid Freedman: "I thought that was . . . against the law. Being upright, I mean.")

"My dad wasn't too thrilled. He wasn't running down to tell the rabbi, you know? But my mother had a different take. She told my dad, 'Burt Reynolds did it! And look at his career!'"

Grandma Wini, never one to abide a gloomy moment, breaks in: "Well, this *grandmother* thinks it's very brave and very wonderful. I can't wait to show the ladies at mah jong. This is the perfect distraction from that dreadful game."

"Dayenu," Howie sighs, getting up to kiss her. "You are one of a kind, Grandma Wini."

"Hey, I don't care about the Pittsburgh perspective," Uncle Rick breaks in. "I just wanna know how they got you up! Let's get to the good part."

"OK, listen, before we get into the arousal part, can we have the kids go upstairs?" Enid beseeches.

"Lou," Papa calls. "Upstairs. Take all the kids. And your brother, too."

"I want to know that part, too, you know."

Uli nods feverishly beside me.

"Not on your life," Mama says, pointing to the stairs.

I stand reluctantly, appeal with my eyes to my father but he just shoots me an unambiguous expression of finality, then resumes his role as maestro of the table. "Steve! A little more wine? And Glovey, what can I get you? Cigar?"

As he doles out bitter servings of brandied apricots and crème fraîche, I have to reconsider Papa all over again. *"Your old man knows shit,"* Howie had said. The man I so admire, admiring the man who made me. Papa's not Lou Ferrigno. He's a skinny, short Jewish guy with a perm. Handsome, yes, but not a physical specimen. It's not physical prowess. It's tenacity. Discipline. Maybe even ferocity. He isn't in it to lose. He is going to win. At work. At play. As a father and a son and a brother-in-law. Even as the new Jew on Chestnut Street, living under the watchful eyes of Glovey Butler and the reproachful Salem royals, the backward townies and the sea captain wannabes.

Howie may be number one with a boner in a national nudie magazine, but Papa is El Jefe.

The Kicker

Yahweh must know what I've been thinking. Obsessing about Penny and Barbi Benton. Bailing on the bar mitzvah studies. Having fun.

So he decides it's time for me to get whacked.

I have seven days to adjust to the new reality that the man sleeping down the hallway from me isn't simply a free spirit, an unusual intrusion of cool—but a bona fide star. Only just enough time to imagine the kind of car he's going to drive when he becomes the next Starsky. And now . . .

"Time out, hombre. Gotta go home," Mr. November says when I find him stuffing his rainbow wardrobe into a duffel.

"What? Why?" Electric panic jolts me, top to bottom.

"My mom. She fell and broke her leg. Her ankle. I don't know. I'm not sure. But she can't walk." Steam wafts from the bathroom where Carly is showering. It's seven in the morning. I've never seen either of them up this early.

"How did she break it?" I ask.

"Strolling in the cemetery. Annual visit to see the relatives. Put a stone on a grave. Say 'I've come here.' I guess there was a pot-hole between Great-Uncle Mortie and Great-Auntie Flooz. There always was. And my mom is pretty heavy. Top-heavy, little bitty bones."

"What about your dad? Can't he take care of her?" I demand.

"My father couldn't cook a pot of pasta if you told him Jack Benny was coming for dinner. Plus my Uncle Izzy lives with them."

"So? Why can't he take care of them?"

"Because he's an extremely large fifty-year-old child," Carly says, walking out of the bathroom and kissing me on the cheek. Damp lilac-scented hair. Tea and honey and something else.

"What does that mean?" I say, intoxicated and angry at the same time.

"Uncle Izzy's retarded," Howie says. "He can't take care of shit. Carly and I need to go there and take care of *all* of them. It's going to interrupt our living with you for a while and that's a drag."

I start with solutions but quickly segue to pleas. "We need you here, you know."

"Hey, I like being with you, too. This is fun. And Pittsburgh ain't no picnic. It's going to be a production just to smoke a little dope. But listen, I want to leave you with something. Something to keep you company while we're gone." Howie hands me a small package wrapped in the Sunday *Globe* funnies. Inside is a black, hardbound sketchbook—a miniature version of the journals he keeps—its pages completely blank, except for the first, which bears the following dedication:

> *This book is joyfully given to Louis Cove from Howie and Carly and is dedicated to the million little voices in people's heads that like to have what they are saying be written down.*

An old writing teacher I once had told me that a person learns to write by writing. So, Lou, here's a whole book to write anything you want in it—even pictures.

The nicest thing about being a writer is that it doesn't stop you from being anything else you want to be. You could be a plumber and a writer, too.

So, here's your book, now,
hope you like it,
Howie + Carly

"You can use my colored pencils while I'm gone," he adds. "I'll leave a bunch in my room."

"So that means you're coming back?"

"Is Lenny Bruce's real name Leonard Schneider?"

"How should I know?" I almost cry.

"Hell yes." He hugs me, hard. I want to let go as soon as possible—of him and of this unfair feeling of loss. But I can't.

"Do you know how much I love you?" Carly asks, eyes searching mine. I shrug. "You can't possibly know. Now give me one of those hugs, too." And I do, holding on hard and wondering if the towel might just slip when I step away.

Later, outside, we are all crying as the powder-blue minibus disappears down Chestnut Street. Usually, when people go away, it's just one of us kids crying while the others comfort. Today, the family weeps as one, so there's no one left to tell us it's going to be OK.

"Now. Let's go get dressed," Mama says eventually, "it's still a school day."

I stop in Howie's room on the way, find the pencils, and retreat to my bunk bed to heed his counsel and write sad things. Bunny Yabba scratches anxiously from inside his crate but when I don't attend to him he settles down. Atjeh scrambles up the stairs and claw-skids her way along the hall to my room where she leaps up beside me, making my cheek sloppy.

"Quit it," I say, forcing her head down. "Lie down. Down."

She watches me as I stare at the white page, unable to conjure any words. Eventually I decide to draw instead: an eye, brown like mine, bloodshot, with a tear dripping from the corner. It's not very good, so I add a sword poking up through the bottom of the eye, color the teardrops red, and add a little spray of blood flying off and away from the pointy tip. Then I slide the journal under the mattress of the bottom bunk to the hiding space below and get ready for school.

"Do you think Laurie Cabot can read your mind?"

"Duh. She's a witch," Uli says as we cross the street on the way home. "Why? Are you afraid she'll read *your* dirty mind and make you stop hanging around with Penny?"

"I can't help it," I confess, a centerfold of Penny seared in my mind.

He laughs, punches my shoulder. "You better be careful. Or you get the curse!" He considers this for a minute. "That would be so freakin' basil, though. If you could read someone's mind?"

"Basil . . . ?"

"*So* basil."

"No, I mean, what does that mean? It would be . . . basil?"

"Oh. You know how some people say 'boss.' Like, 'it's wicked boss?' Which means it's really good. And some people say 'bitchin'.' Which is also good. But I wanted to make up my own word for something that is so totally boss and bitchin', so I called it basil."

"But, basil is a vegetable."

"It's an herb," Uli corrects.

I shrug, sniffing the last whiffs of Athens Bakery's bread still lingering in the unusually warm December air. Uli's different, which is why I like him. He's got weird ideas, all the energy I lack, and he's ready to try anything. But he's not Howie, and his not-Howieness is pronounced during the long Pittsburgh defection. In a lifetime of unwanted separations, I've learned to stuff the bad feelings away, but this one doesn't want to be stuffed.

We cross Broad Street, pass the houses at the tail end of Summer, and crawl through a hole in the wrought-iron fence and into the cemetery behind Oliver School. Having a creepy graveyard behind your school was just one of the many reasons I was glad to leave it behind. But it's a good place to hang out.

There are broken branches strewn everywhere among the headstones. IN MEMORY OF MRS. ELIZABETH. IN MEMORY OF STEPHEN COOK. IN MEMORY, MRS. MARY PUTNAM. HERE LIES MOLLY BRITTON, DAUGHTER OF EDWD. AND POLLY BRITTON. AT 15. WHILE YOUTH DOTH CHEER, DEATH MAY BE NEAR. And Pickering after Pickering after Pickering. Ruth. John. Eunice. Timothy. Mary. And then Mrs. Lucy Glover, wife of Capt. John H. Glover, who died October 22, 1830, aged forty-nine years. SHE LIVED RESPECTED AND DIED LAMENTED. Is this the mother of Glovey Butler? The grandmother? I try to do the math as we move. She's probably her great-great-grandmother I conclude. And she lived respected, just as Glovey does. But did she live feared?

I lay out an assortment of comic books, Wacky Packs, and Pixy Stix as we settle in a spot shielded by thick bushes and December-shriveled poison ivy. It's our regular spot, right by the Clifton crypt. I've used knives, elbows, anything to pry or pound open the doors to these crypts. I never really think about what we might encounter if we actually got in. Scapulas and clavicles, coccyx, femurs, and phalanges—the stench of rotten old Salem, composting behind those steel doors, built into the bright green knolls of this cemetery of which I don't even know the name.

On West End Avenue all that was under our feet was subway breath screeching and blowing through the teeth of the grates.

Better to be down there, rocketing through the tunnels of Manhattan to a new and exciting place, surrounded by *living* people . . . dancing, shuffling, hacking, ignoring, giggling, groping, sleeping, reading, yelling, rushing people. Every one of them alive. I don't even know where they put the dead people in New York.

But in Salem, the kids know where the dead are. We play alongside them, over their heads, mostly ignoring them but always knowing that they are there with us.

"Did you ever get into one of these?" I ask Uli, banging lightly on Clifton's final front door with my toe.

"Naw," Uli lays back and pulls a book of matches out of his pocket.

"I still want to see. I mean, I don't. But I do."

"Inside, you mean?"

"Yeah. Are they really still in there? Is it coffins or, like, bodies on little stone beds? Like a Dracula movie or something."

"We could check . . ." Uli offers, flicking a lighted match at his outstretched feet.

"Do you have more?" He hands me another book of matches, and we start flicking our little flaming projectiles toward Clifton's crypt.

"You ever hear DEVO?"

"What's a DEVO?"

"A band. *Are we not men?*" he starts singing in a robot voice. *"We are DEVO . . ."*

"No. Did you ever hear Eric Carmen?"

"What's he do?"

"That song, *All by myself . . . don't wanna be . . .*"

"Ugh! How can you like that? That's so bogus. SO bogus."

I shrug.

"You're a cool kid. You should listen to New Wave."

"I like rock."

"Well Eric Carmen is not rock. He's cock." He busts out laughing. "He's cock! Cock 'n' roll!"

"Hey! Trash mouth!" a loud voice shouts out.

We jerk up simultaneously and whip around. Two girls, one as small as the other is large, have appeared in front of us, arms crossed. They must be from another school because I don't recognize either of them. But Uli does.

"What's up, Charlene?" he asks the big one, sitting up in the dirt.

"You desecratin' somebody's grave?" she asks, sounding and towering like The Thing.

"No. Just lighting matches. It's not going to hurt anything." I look curiously at Uli, who seems far too conciliatory.

"It's a holy place, fahkwahd."

"Yeah," the little one repeats in her Minnie Mouse voice. "Holy. Fahkwahd." Her smile fans an unexpected spark of fury in me.

"Who's the trash mouth now?" I ask, scrambling to my feet to face down the little shit. "And you're a girl . . . I think," I say to The Thing looming over me, arms thick, and covered with an unnatural amount of hair and a skin eruption that isn't quite acne.

Uli grabs my pant leg. "He's just kidding," he says. "He's from New York."

"Bull*shit*. I've seen him. You should kick this cocksuckah's ass!" Minnie says, pointing at me.

"Charlene," Uli tries to intervene again. *What's his problem?*

"Shut up," Charlene says, low.

"Seriously," I chime in. "She's a stupid . . ." the word *girl* flies somewhere up over the Clifton crypt, along with the part of my tongue I just bit off. My body spins to follow my jaw, my feet fly out from under me, and I hit the dirt at the door of the tomb, breathless as whoever's left inside there.

"Charlene! Quit it!" Uli's up and yelling. Minnie grabs my feet and starts dragging me back away from the crypt so I'm an easier target for The Thing, whose arm is drawn back, fist balled, ready for strike two.

"Did you . . . Did you hit me?" I still can't believe it. My tongue, raw and wet, tastes like chicken soup.

"I'm gonna hit you again, you fahkin' fag."

She grabs my sweater as I scramble up and away. I feel it rip before I duck through the wrought-iron fence and start running like hell through the schoolyard, spitting blood.

"Kick his ass!" Minnie shrieks. My legs wobble under me and my head seems to be wobbling, too. Whether it's a concussion or simply bad judgment that led me up the service ramp at the back of the school, it doesn't matter. The heavy door is padlocked and chained and the drop over the side, though I'm prepared to take it, makes me pause just long enough for Minnie and The Thing to catch up and corner me.

And now the pummeling really begins.

"Kick him in the balls! Kick him in the balls!" Minnie cheers. I curl up, huddle against the attack, open my eyes and see the little one perched on the rusty railing, bouncing up and down and smiling that fucking smile again. There's no way I'm going to hurt The Thing—I can't get away from her thundering bombshells—but if I break away, even for a second, I am going to knock that puny freakin'—*Uggghhhh!*

She kicks just above my stomach, my back arches, exposing me to her big right meatfist, which doesn't hesitate. She crushes my balls with one pound.

"GetthefuckoffhimCharlene!" Uli issues a battle cry. From my resting place in the grit of the concrete platform I look up to see him riding The Thing, fists flailing, raining down on her as she spins. Minnie jumps away before The Thing smashes Uli against the railing, and uses the opportunity to try and kick me in my screaming nuts, but I grab Minnie's foot and she goes down lightly.

"Run, Lou! Run!" Uli's holding on, tearing hair, punching at her ears, bucking the bronco. I stagger down the ramp. "Run!" Uli yells again and I do. At the corner of Winthrop and Broad I look back over my shoulder to see him racing toward me. Minnie and The Thing howl at the edge of the cemetery, but stop. I start running again and don't stop until we're back at my house.

"Who the hell was *she*?" I ask, unable to breathe, wanting to cry.

"Charlene Smutch."

"How do you know that freak?" I ask, but Uli's looking away. "And that little runt. Is that her sister?" I puff on my inhaler and the mist stings the wounds in my mouth, but my lungs open at last.

"No, they're best friends. Same age, actually."

"No way."

"I know."

I survey my torn tongue in the rusty bathroom mirror of the third-floor guest room. Deli meat. And my balls. My balls. My balls.

"She's not so bad. She just comes from a bad home."

I turn to him, exasperated. I might cry, but I won't. "Are you kidding me? She's a psycho. She's a psycho mutant."

"She wasn't always like that. I've known her since second grade."

"How big was she back then? Did she have a beard?" I try to find my edge. Uli sniffs and looks away. His neck has deep red scratches on both sides from where The Thing tried to claw him. "Seriously. Look what she did to you. I can't believe . . . A girl . . ." The pain in my testicles shifts from hammering to humming and a deeper, more lasting kind of mortified agony emerges.

"We used to be friends. She didn't look like that. She was kinda pretty, in a way. I mean, she was pretty. More nice."

Anger replaces humiliation and it's empowering, even if I know in my core I am more powerless and wimpier than I ever realized.

"More nice? What the hell are you talking about? She's like The Rhino on gamma rays. Or The Blob. Or Kingpin . . ."

"Can we just not talk about it anymore?"

I take off my shirt and count the rising bruises in the mirror. "Hey, I don't want to talk about it at all. I don't want to talk about it ever. I just got beat up by a giant girl. You know, New York is dangerous, but we don't have *those* walking around. I look out for muggers and rapers and stuff. You can spot those ones. But why are you defending her?"

"I defended *you*!" Uli's voice cracks in a weird way. I turn back to him.

"I know," I deflate. "I just. What the fuck?"

"We kissed," Uli whispers.

"You kissed?" Silence. "You kissed that? *That?*"

"She was pretty. She changed later, but back then she was nice. She—"

"You kissed The Thing." I laugh helplessly. It hurts. Oh, it hurts.

"I'm glad you think it's funny." He stands up and starts to leave.

"Hey, stay. I'm sorry." He sits back down. "And thanks for helping me out. She was going to kill me."

"I know."

I don't know what hurts more: the image of Uli kissing The Thing or the memory of The Thing kicking my ass. How would it feel, to pummel the first girl you kissed? To ride her bronco, feel her Ben Grimm brawn against your chest and try to hold back those tree trunks from pounding on your new best friend?

"Wanna sleep over?" I ask. Uli nods, and that giddy grin surfaces again.

Uli's still beaming through my family's dinner conversation. It's embarrassing. I hurt in every part of my body, but he just smiles, bounces his knee nervously under the table next to me, hoots loudly whenever Papa says something, funny or not. Amanda keeps her eyes on Uli the whole time but he doesn't seem to notice her. He's focused on Papa's mustache, the bow tie he's loosened but not shed, and his perpetual, driving conversation.

"Let's talk music," Papa declares. "Uli, what's your taste?"

"I like Blondie."

"I like Blondie, too," Papa says. " 'Heart of Glass,' right?"

"Uh huh," Uli nods, smiling so his lips curl back until he's all gums. "I can't believe you know that. My dad wouldn't know that. That is so basil."

"What does basil have to do with anything?" Papa asks, staring out the window.

I giggle, then wince. Every place The Thing punched me feels like it's being punched all over again, from the inside out.

"What's wrong?" Mama asks.

"Nothing."

Papa zooms in now, scanning me intently. Why does he choose tonight of all nights to pay attention? "You have a stomachache?"

I nod, not wanting to say a word. If Howie were here, I could tell him. He knows all about getting whacked, and he wouldn't judge me for it. Or for who did it to me.

"You've been talking funny," Papa presses. "And you look swollen. What's happening to your face?"

Uli's smile evaporates. I stare at my plate.

"They got in a fight," Amanda says coyly before I can fabricate a response. "I heard them talking." She looks away from me, knowing well the penalty for spying.

"What fight?" Mama asks. "We don't fight."

"I hope you won, at least?" Papa says.

My mind is racing. I can't make anything up. Uli hammers his knuckles into my thigh under the table and it hurts like the purple in the core of my bruise—but not like the other hurt well-ing up fast again. That is the deeper pain of humiliation. And then I can't help it and I start to cry right there at the table, right into my stupid peas.

"We got beat up," I choke. "We got beat up . . ." I start again, looking at Papa's face. He looks back with concern, and anticipation. " By a girl."

Amanda cackles and I burn to murder her, but the confession is out and the oozing puss of exposed feelings eclipses my anger.

"We didn't start it!" Uli jumps in. "She wanted to kill us."

"I couldn't get away," I blubber. "She was so big, and she kept holding me down and punching me. I wish we never moved here. I hate it here. I hate it."

"OK, OK," Papa interrupts, holding up his hands. He's heard enough. "Look, this happens. You don't have to feel bad about it. I know what it feels like to get beat up. Everyone does. You can't beat *yourself* up after, understand? But you can do something different the next time." He leans toward me and puts a hand on my shoulder, leveling his gaze in a way that always precedes an important disclosure of fatherly knowledge. So rare, and so precious. If it takes getting smashed in the testicles to earn this, I may be willing to do it again. I look at Papa, nodding, waiting. Uli is wide-eyed.

"The next time, you need to defend yourself, you understand?" I nod again.

"Peter," Mama tries to intervene, a steady voice of logic and calculation, not emotion. But Papa holds up a hand.

"The next time," he says softly, looking me directly in the eyes, "you kick her in the cunt. And then you run."

"Peter!"

"What's a cunt?" David asks.

"Oh, God," Mama drops her head.

"You get it?" Papa beseeches us and we nod. "You *get it*?" He presses and I feel protected, like I've always wanted. Just when I think I don't need him anymore, he proves me wrong again. I need him so much.

"So, Uli," Papa continues over the din, "is the girl Blondie or is the band Blondie?"

New Traditions

The last day before Christmas break, after weeks of Penny insisting, I finally bring a copy of Howie's issue of *Playgirl* to school. We huddle in a gamy old stall in the boys' room and flip to the center.

Maybe this was a bad idea. Even clothed, I can see the soft folds of my stomach, the absence of chest or arm or pit hair. Only a few sprouts down below, but they don't constitute *pubes* exactly. They're more like sprinkles (in Salem, they call them Jimmies). Jimmies in my jammies, in other words, and not much else. Hard to imagine anyone wanting a centerfold of this. And here is Penny, spending far longer than I would like, lingering over the pictures of Howie in the buff.

"I didn't realize he was so . . . muscly," she says softly, slender fingers tracing his image, breath held. "You just told me he was a hippie. I was thinking of something different."

"Well, he . . . you know, he was working out a lot. It's because of my dad, actually."

"Uhhhh . . . I've seen your dad. Your dad's not built like *this*." More importantly, *I'm* not built like this. Next to Howie, I might as well be Nusselballs.

"No, but he inspired him," I say, playing the passion card. "He convinced him to work harder on his body because . . . Anyway, you know, they grease you up for the pictures, too, so it makes you look more muscly than you really are. If he was here right now he wouldn't look like this."

She nods, flipping back to the beginning of Howie's section.

I reach gently for the magazine. "We probably need to go back to class."

"He almost looks like Leif, don't you think? The way they did his hair? Can I keep this one?"

"Is there a girl in here?" a boy asks, from the urinals outside.

We stop talking. Penny grabs my hand and squeezes, smiling brilliantly. My skin burns hotter, and I shift closer to her on the wobbly toilet seat. She stands up and sits back down on my lap, eviscerating all the bad feelings that had begun to creep into the stall with us. She lifts my hand to her mouth, bites my index finger in mock anxiety. I lean in to her, trying to shift in such a way that our chests might touch. The witch shop incense smell draws me to the nape of her neck and I try to kiss the pulsing bit of her throat that moves as she swallows and pulls back, shaking her head slowly and smiling, pressing a finger to my lips.

"Hello?" the kid calls again. He's debating whether or not to pee. After a long pause he walks out without doing any business.

"Why not?" I ask. "I don't like anyone else but you."

"Gretchen?"

"Ugh. She's always following me around and showing up at my house without asking. And she talks like—"

"What about the girls from New York?" she asks, a little pout forming on her lips. "They're much better than I am."

"I don't live in New York anymore. And besides, I didn't like anyone there. I like you. I think we should be boyfriend and girl-friend." There. I said it.

"I don't know. You're kind of my best friend. I don't want to mess everything up."

"Just kiss me and see. Just try. Once." Her face broadens, open to possibility.

Penny leans forward, bringing her face as close as possible to mine, Bubblicious breath and sandalwood filling my nose. "You know what the thing is about boyfriends and girlfriends?" she asks, searching my face.

"No," I whisper.

"They don't last." And she pulls back, the spell broken. "But friends last forever. Everybody else could just disappear for all I care, as long as we can still be friends."

Ugh. The December chill seeps back into the narrow wooden cubicle that, only a moment ago, had been as hot as the sun. It is that special Salem chill, the one that rides the sea wind and smells of headstone lichen and wet black cat.

But she did say forever. I imagine myself in a loincloth, rifle in hand, and Penny clutching my chest as we ride a horse across the desert. Lady Liberty sinks in the distance, buried in the sand, but up ahead is a world all our own. Her rejection is a no with a maybe wrapped around it. I shake off the chill and try to keep the flicker alive. "We'll always be best friends," I promise. "Forever."

"Great," Penny brightens, stands up from my lap, rolls the mag-azine into a tube, and wedges it into her back pocket. "I'll give this back to you at the end of the day, OK?"

When the bell rings, she's nowhere to be found.

Bagels on Sunday and a Christmas tree for Hanukkah: this is the extent of traditions in the Cove household. Thankfully, the first of eight boring days happens to fall next Monday, Christmas Day, so we get to do presents then, like normal people. But the evening of The Thing turned out to be the start of an entirely new tradition: a secret Friday night ritual for Uli and me.

Mama and Papa make the holiday party rounds, filling the void left for them when Howie and Carly left for Pittsburgh. I miss them. They hardly call, and when they do it's brief, flecked with long-distance static and unfamiliar voices competing in the background. Meanwhile, my parents are making new friends in Salem: artists and judges, writers and priests. They host often, including a party they threw for the entire neighborhood and "anyone who can sled, ski, or snowshoe to our house" during a blizzard when the roads and schools were closed for days. We played all four sides of *Saturday Night Fever* over and over, all night long, while guests smoked cigars and joints and raised glasses of brown liquor on ice. There wasn't anyone who hadn't turned bleary-eyed and silly or just left by ten o'clock. And not many people left.

As disruptive as this parade of strangers can be, I take some comfort in living in the place that people think of when they want to shuck their calloused Salem shells. And Papa is happy to provide. The more, the merrier he is. Spike the punch bowl and dance.

When my parents do look elsewhere for their good times, they want to put me in charge to save money on sitters. I call Uli as soon as they leave, move the clock in the kitchen ahead to persuade Amanda and David to go to bed extra early, swipe a pinch of weed from the cigar box in my parents' closet, and let the ritual commence.

When we stuff the towel under my bedroom door and light the first bowl, I feel an unfamiliar sense of routine and belonging.

For this round, Uli arrives early with five new records. I pull five of my own. We agree on a playlist, check the *Salem Evening News* listings to see if the TV lineup has changed and who the guests are on *Donny & Marie* (George Burns, Chubby Checker, and Evel

Knievel) and on Johnny Carson (Johnny Mathis and Mel Brooks), divvy up the pile of porno mags Howie left behind and stack them on our respective bunks, and position our respective cum rags for later use. Then we hit Steve's Corner Store before dinner.

We load up on Ding Dongs, Big Wheels, Fruit Pies, Fritos, Cheetos, Doodads, and one giant box of forbidden cereal apiece. I go Apple Jacks. Uli always frets over the big choice: Count Chocula or Boo Berry? We get a half gallon of milk each and spend the rest of our money (raided from the trench coats and cluttered purses in the hall downstairs) on comics.

Steve busts us when we try to switch from browsing the twirly COMICS FOR ALL AGES wire rack to eyeing the adult titles behind the counter. He stops his habitual pencil drumming on the counter and yells at us before we're close enough to make out anything more than the titles. And Steve never yells. But this time he's waving a copy of the *Salem Evening News* wildly at us, open to a page with an article titled "Aid Sought in Smut War," and shaking his head.

"Cease and desist, junior jerk offs. This guy, Connelly? Acting city marshal?" Steve smacks the article with the back of his hand, " 'I'm doing an "out-and-out crackdown on smut," ' he says. Cops! Like that's the big problem we got in this town. Not robberies. Not gangs. Skin flicks and *Hustler*s. You know how much of my business is girlie mags?"

We shake our heads.

"Enough that I ain't gonna lose my license 'cause you horny wharf rats get me hung out to dry. This guy's a crusader. And nobody likes a crusader. Especially a Salem crusader."

"Like the caped crusader?" Uli and I say almost simultaneously.

"Like stick to the comic books and the munchies and find your titty mags somewhere else."

We settle for new issues of the *Defenders*, *Champions*, and *Ghost Rider* and head home.

Life has become predictable again without Howie and Carly to surprise us. The only magic now comes when Uli and I lock my door and light the match. It's too cold to smoke on the roof so we stoke the fireplace until the cover is blistering to the touch, then open the windows and put spark to bowl. Like Penny's cats, this miracle marijuana doesn't trigger my asthma. I'm free.

Time shifts with the weed, dragging and accelerating simultaneously, and before we know what's happened we've lost all restraint, laughing out of control, pouring milk directly into our cereal boxes, burying faces in pillows to stifle the ecstatic hysteria that flows from a wicked high with a wicked good friend.

We wrestle, land splat on the Fruit Pies, and unleash a Count Chocula milk tsunami across the solid green paint of the floor and debate endlessly about whether or not it's safe to leave the room.

"It's safe."

"Nuh uh."

"They're asleep."

"No they're not."

"I heard them."

"Fuck it."

"No."

"Yes."

"Wait. See?"

"OK. I'm going crazy in here! Aghhhh!"

Uli suddenly gets serious. "When's Howie coming back?" he asks, slumping to the floor in front of the fireplace. "Your house is totally more boss with him."

"I know. This sucks."

"No, it's already awesome. I mean, this is the only house I even want to sleep over at." He picks his nose, flicks the booger into the snapping blaze of logs, and chews his lower lip, squinting at the heat like there's something hiding from him there. "Seriously. Nobody else has parents like yours. They're cool and let you talk about stuff. And smoke pot."

"It's not as cool as you think. And they don't really let me smoke pot. They just don't . . . bring it up. There's a difference."

"You just don't know because *you* live here. Does my house seem cool to you?"

Those tiny rooms. The anxious mood. The soundless, stiff-postured, folded napkins, forks-on-the-right-side (left side?) meal-times. "No."

"Exactly." He slides to the floor, looks to the ceiling, and slowly shakes his head side to side. "And I hate it. I want to move out. I want to live someplace where people don't tell you what to do all the time."

"My mom keeps telling me I have to study Hebrew. To have a Bar Mitzvah." Uli frowns at the Jewish gibberish. "A thing you have to do when you turn thirteen. You have to read in Hebrew and everyone comes and then you become a man. Supposedly."

"You become a man? Right then?"

"That's what they say."

"Thirteen. See? That is so cool. I want to be Jewish so bad."

"Well, then there'd be two of us in this town," I say. "You sure you want to be the weirdo?"

"I am the weirdo."

"True. Well, talk to my dad. Maybe he'll adopt you."

"I'm going to."

"Right."

"I'm not shitting you." Uli tosses a HoHo my way. *"Rem, tongani!"*

Mangani. Tarzan's ape language. *Rem* means catch. *Tongani* is baboon.

I stand up and position myself in front of the door, arms akimbo. "This is my domain, and I protect all who come here, for I—"

"—am Tarzan, Lord of the Jungle!" we call in unison. The warbling brings Amanda knocking.

"GO AWAY!" we shout together, then laugh maniacally.

There are no words to describe what my mouth tastes like when I wake the next morning. Downstairs I find Uli, true to his word, deep in conversation with Papa about converting to Judaism.

"Not because I'm some big Jew," Papa clarifies. "But you should be free to explore any belief system you want. Not beholden to some mythology you can't get behind."

"So you have a Christmas tree because . . ."

"Because I like the way it makes my house smell."

"It's true," Uli says. "You don't notice the bunny poop as much."

"He's potty trained," Papa says in all seriousness. "But also because I don't want anyone to tell me what to do. What? I can't have a tree because I was born to a Jewish woman and a man with a circumcised penis? I'm not worshipping Jesus here. I'm putting up lights and garland and popcorn and cranberries. I'm not really a Jew or a Christian. I'm an American."

"I'm going to do it," Uli says.

"What?" I ask.

"Become Jewish."

"You're too old for a bar mitzvah," I say. "You just missed it."

"So I don't have to study Hebrew!"

"Upside to everything," Papa says. "By the way . . . did someone get into my stash yesterday?"

In the Running

I keep shoving ice cubes in my underwear while we play Monopoly, trying to stay awake until 1979 arrives. Mama and Papa are ringing it in somewhere else. Howie and Carly have us in mind—they call to send New Year's hugs, but the phone is a poor substitute for the real thing. "We wish we could be with you instead of homebound here. Back soon." Blah Blah.

"We'll do our own version when we're back, OK?" Howie says over the line from Pittsburgh. "Tonight's just another night, that's all it is."

"Can we have fireworks? They're shooting off fireworks in Times Square on TV."

"I'll bring the dynamite, pal."

Uli's parents make him go home at ten. Amanda falls asleep by ten thirty. Atjeh nods off at eleven. So it's just me and Dick Clark, who finally says, "OK, we're gettin' there!" He doesn't look cold at all, trench coat half buttoned, standing in front of a big vertical sign that says QUASIMODO. "Just a few more minutes and it will be 1979! People all over the world watch that giant, six-foot ball that stands atop One Times Square. It'll be a little hard to know exactly when it lands so you keep your eye on the digital clock."

The faint honk of cardboard horns rattles the tiny TV speaker as one year ends and another begins. Dick Clark kicks it over to Erik Estrada and Julie from *The Love Boat* in LA, where everything seems much more colorful. They introduce Barry Manilow, clad entirely in sparkly white, standing alone at a piano. He starts to play and it's so melancholy.

"Don't look so sad. It's not that bad. It's just another night. That's all it is."

I shut off the TV and take Atjeh upstairs.

By mid-February I've given up believing they are ever coming back. How long does a broken ankle take to heal? But there's a lot of shuffling and noise coming from upstairs when I come down for breakfast. I look around the table, count heads. Everyone's present except Papa, who went to the gym. My pulse quickens, and I feel like I've just surfaced from the water after holding my breath for a long time. Every fiber in my being twitches with excitement.

Howie Gordon—actor, artist, lover, friend—is at the bottom of the stairs now, decked out in a new velvet purple pair of drawstring pants, scratching his head with one hand, his butt with the other. I jump up and hug him before he can make it to the table.

"When did you get here? Are you staying for good? You grew a beard!" Amanda squeaks in quick succession.

Howie strokes his thick new facial hair, considers for a moment: "Last night. Who knows? And yes, I did," and he hugs my sister tight.

"Breakfast!" Mama's baked muffins and is bringing them to the table along with granola and yogurt. "Hello, Howie Gordon." She smiles broadly and walks around the table to give him a kiss on the cheek. "That was quite a night last night, wasn't it?"

"What did I miss?" I ask.

"Your Mama made the mightiest of midnight meals. The Hunan Princess prevails!" He grabs the newspaper Papa left behind, then calls to her: "Now, how can we serve you, your highness?"

Mama chuckles as she spreads our lunch around and drags David out from under the table. "Serve *me*? That's a new one."

"Well, until your husband gets his grant money and gives me a damn job I am going to work for you," Howie says, riffling through the Arts section of the *Globe*. "And we have to schedule some date nights, don't we, children of the princess? What's a prince of a princess, anyway? A princelette? Ha! Come, Princelette, what is your pleasure? I see *Thunderbolt and Lightfoot* is coming back around to the Salem Theater as part of a double feature with *Midnight Express*. Good time for the guys."

I step away from my place at the table and peer around Howie's shoulder at the mini movie ads scattered around the pages laid out in his lap.

"How about this one?" I point to a photo of a shirtless, long-haired, bearded man holding a woman with curly hair who seems equally (if more discreetly) naked.

"Huh. *A Star Is Born*?" His surprise catches me off guard, makes me question my choice. "I suppose there is a rock 'n' roll component there. But look at *him*," he says, pointing to a man balancing one foot on the handle of a gun so big it seems more like a cannon, the cigarette in his hand issuing smoke that rises above his head to frame his name—CLINT EASTWOOD. HE HAS EXACTLY SEVEN MINUTES TO GET RICH QUICK!

I nod, trying to get excited about the action instead of the romance. "Hey, I love Barbra Streisand," he says, changing tone. "So we'll go. But I *do* need a little help with something special." We all look at him, but he pauses to sip his coffee and build to the moment. "Today," he says dramatically, "is the day I begin my campaign."

"What campaign?" Mama asks.

"To win Man of the Year. To be . . . oh! Baby! Come on over here and join the family powwow." Carly appears at the door, a love mirage. I sigh reflexively with relief.

As she approaches the table I forget all about Clint Eastwood, Barbra Streisand, and my soggy cereal because her silk robe, which matches Howie's flowered pants, hangs open enough to reveal just how full and round her breasts are. The robe ends midway down her thigh so when she pulls out the chair next to me and sits down I can't help but stare.

"What are you talking about?" Mama says, finally sitting down and tuning in.

"I'm in the running, one of twelve, to be Man of the Year." Howie slaps a copy of *Playgirl* on the table—this one different from the November issue we've become so familiar with.

"Not again," Mama says.

"Picked this up in the airport on the way back. Right off the news rack. I didn't even know this was part of the deal! If you're one of the twelve men of 1978, twelve centerfolds, you're eligible to be Man of the Year for '79. Like Playmate of the Year. It's a contest. Write-in. And look how they advertised it . . ."

Of twelve contestants, only one is pictured in the contest announcement. Howie, boxed in at the bottom of page eighty-two, penis sticking straight out at these words:

VOTE FOR YOUR FAVORITE
CENTERFOLD OF THE YEAR

To cast your ballot for Man of the Year, just send a postcard to: Man of the Year, Playgirl, *Incorporated,*

3420 Ocean Park Blvd., Suite 3000, Santa Monica,
CA 90405. Results will be published in the May issue.

There's no denying that November '78 centerfold, Howie Gordon, *below and far right*, is irresistible. So what's new? The article says he was recently in Hong Kong filming a Brittania Jeans commercial set to air on Japanese TV.

"Too bad, you cry, that we can't see more of Howie in the States."

But then it offers comfort for *Playgirl* readers by announcing that Howie has a role in George Lucas' next film, *Purple Haze,* starring Ron Howard and Cindy Williams.

"When did you go to Hong Kong?"

Howie laughs. "Picture me. I'm in the airport in Kansas City and I read *that*! And there's me, and my Magnificent Seven incher, all famous. Sure, I *was* in a Brittania Jeans commercial, but it was shot in San Francisco for the Hong Kong *market*. They're spinning a little exotic PR fairy tale on my behalf, I guess."

"And the movie?"

"A sequel to *American Graffiti*."

I'm exasperated. Elated. In awe. "Who do you play???"

"Guy running."

"Who's Guy Running?"

"No, I mean, I play *a* guy. Running. They did this kind of comical reenactment of a '60s college campus protest run amok. And I'm in there, somewhere, running amok. Finding me would be like trying to pick out a buffalo in a stampeding herd. 'Look! See! There! The brown one!' "

"Oh."

"But it sure sounds good on paper. I'm not especially talented when it comes to self-promotion. But I'm learning."

The horizon suddenly expands before me: California, movie

cameras, flashbulbs, Hong Kong . . . a *King Kong* sequel! "Let me help!"

"Help? I need more than help. I need a partner. If I'm going to be Starsky, then you're going to have to be my Hutch."

Your Hutch. I picture us in the opening montage as the credits roll. We're racing in the cherry-red Ford Gran Torino with its white vector stripes, Starsky navigating the gritty city. He hop-slides the hood for a bust while I wrestle the wheelman. We take in a strip club. I'm distracted by the woman in the bikini, and he blows in my ear to remind me that we have a job to do. Friends and partners. The credits end with us in a half man-hug.

"Yes," I say. "Yes."

"Right on. And we've got a good head start with this bit of propaganda. Those *Playgirl* geniuses make me sound like the next fucking James Dean. Should win me a few votes . . ."

"That, and being the first guy with a boner," Carly chimes in.

"Hey, it was already a competitive advantage. And now they're using it to advertise the contest? I'd say I have a fighting chance!"

"Even if it looks extra small in that shot?" Carly chuckles beside me.

"Thank you, my love," Howie blows her a kiss. "I guess that's payback. You eating this, Princelette?" he asks as he grabs the uneaten muffin half still on my plate.

His Business

I use the dead time before the movies to dig into the *Playboy* archive I pilfered from Gramps. Unlike most days, this exploration is solely focused on strategy. I want to see what I can learn from the best in the business.

This obviously has to include Debra Jo Fondren, Miss November, 1977, and 1978 Playmate of the Year. She won a Datsun 280Z and was then featured on *Fantasy Island* and *Mork & Mindy*. But most impressive of all is her hair. Spilling well past her knees, Debra Jo is Eve if she just had a hair dryer in Eden. That's her trademark, and Howie's, while not exactly going past his knees, is his, too.

Who helped Debra Jo win her campaign?

Last year's winner, Patti McGuire, is wearing nothing but a Coppertone tan and see-through panties, standing next to a neon jukebox. Patti McGuire should be the Playmate of the Decade as far I'm concerned. I scan her winnings, see that she scored a Dodge Midnight Charger and got a part as Pussycat on . . . *Starsky and Hutch*!? A Midnight Charger is no Gran Torino, but it's in the ballpark.

The potential for greatness is sinking in.

Howie, as accommodating as he is indulgent, crafts a movie orgy for us. We see *A Star Is Born* first, though it is actually the second film in a matinee double feature with *Coming Home*. It is, as the poster suggests, a film about a woman with a perm and a guy with long hair and a beard. I wait patiently for nudity that never comes. In the end, I ignore the soap suds, devour the behind-the-scenes look at sex, drugs, and rock 'n' roll, and imagine Howie's ascent, conveniently overlooking the fact that this is actually intended to be a modern tragedy.

"That movie had to be written by a Jewish American princess," Howie says as we race out of the theater to grab cheesesteak subs before the next show. " 'John Norman Howard was once the best, but he was burning out. Until he met . . . Esther Hoffman.' Hee hee. Esther Hoffman! God love her."

We make it back just as *Thunderbolt and Lightfoot*, the first film in the evening's testosterone triple-play, is starting. The tagline is "Thunderbolt . . . the man with the reputation. Lightfoot . . . the kid who's about to make one!" Jeff Bridges plays the young side-kick to Eastwood's grizzled, legendary bank robber. This could easily be Howie once we win.

We end up staying for only half of *Midnight Express* because the beating scene in the Turkish prison is more than I can take. Howie and I walk home and he sends me off to bed. I wake with a movie hangover—my mind reeling from so many stories—but *A Star Is Born* stays with me the most. Carly and Streisand look nothing alike, but Barbra Streisand's character is all Carly. They're both confident, soothing presences tempering a fervid, burning star. Esther Hoffman endures her share of indignities and the pain in her eyes . . . I've seen that before. Carly's red eyes have become a common enough occurrence at the breakfast table that my family has named the condition *puffy eyes*. "Carly has puffy eyes again," Amanda will say, ever noteful. And Carly will nod and sniffle and say, "Yup. Just one of those mornings, little one."

Why Howie lets it happen so often, how he could fail to appreciate just what he has waiting for him at home, is a mystery to me.

My mother cries sometimes, but it's always over domestic frustrations: Papa slipped back to bed and left her alone to clean the kitchen, or surprised her with the news that he's not going to be home all day Saturday.

More than the conflicts or their frequency, though, it is the depth of passion and its naked expression that sets the couples apart. Howie may hurt Carly's feelings this way from time to time, but more often than not he is praising her as a goddess the universe revealed to him. The One True Love. "We're into some eternal love shit," he tells me.

When Papa uses the word *love* it's generally reserved for a new album or an exotic recipe he stumbled upon.

"Lou!" he shouts as I enter the dining room. "Goddammit this drip method is the ONLY way to brew coffee. Taste this. Taste it!" He pushes his tall ceramic mug toward me but I shake my head sleepily.

"You know I don't like coffee."

"You'll like this. No one could NOT like this. Try it. Drink it."

"I don't want to." I chew my muesli, the morning's cud. Atjeh rises unannounced from beneath the table, lands paws-first in my lap, scraping my thighs and toppling my cereal bowl.

"That dog is out of control," Mama says.

"You know, if you drank coffee and skipped breakfast you'd actually have far more energy," Papa says, inured to complaints about Atjeh wildness. I wipe my cereal and milk from the table back into the bowl. "That gruel's just going to weigh you down for the day. And it gives you gas."

"Peter," Mama rebukes him, as if she's never heard it before. The arguments don't change, they just go round and round.

"We don't need it!" he says again, tossing the paper on the table, not looking at her.

"*You* don't need it. Or you say you don't need it. But children need sustenance to grow."

"What?" He hasn't heard. "Well, I'm off. Stay busy today, OK? February vacation isn't just a time to do nothing. Try to be productive."

"Bye, Papa!" Amanda calls after him as he dashes out of the dining room.

"Pa?" I start as he grabs a long wool coat from the brass tree in the front hall and pulls on his gloves.

"Yup? In a hurry. What's up?"

"How come you never talk about the whole *Playgirl* thing? Do you like them? The pictures?"

He scratches thoughtfully at his perm. "I don't know if 'like' is the word. The photographer seems talented enough. And Howie looks good. He looks great. Aside from too much makeup. But I've seen him naked in the locker room. I don't need to see him like that in a magazine." He opens the door to the foyer and the hall immediately chills. "Gotta go now. Hug?"

I hug him but stay close. "Are you happy for him? Now that he's famous?"

"I'm not sure that's the kind of famous you really want to be. But it's his life. I don't judge. He's on his own adventure." He descends the front stairs, stops, and holds up his hands. The whipping snow almost carries him away. "I'll see you tonight, OK?"

"I'm going to help him win."

"Win what?" Papa sighs heavily.

"Man of the Year."

"That beauty contest? Jesus. He's a smart guy. He needs a job."

"When women win that beauty contest they end up on TV."

"That's women. This world loves a naked woman. Naked men, not so much."

His skepticism makes me flinch. "Well, are *you* ever going to hire him?"

"Hey, I'm not Santa Claus here. Every man for himself. But if the money comes in, then yes," he assures me. "Now good-bye!"

"Pa?" I gasp against the bite in my throat.

"Tonight!" he calls, walking backward and waving. I come down, follow onto the brick sidewalk, feet freezing in the snow.

"I just have one more question."

"Jesus, you're going to get sick." But he sees I'm not giving up, sighs once again, and grants a flustered, "What?"

"Did you know that Carly sets up . . . that she calls . . ."

He checks his watch, flips up his collar against the wind, and then kneels down to make eye contact with me. "Girls for Howie?" Papa offers. I nod. "Yes." I wait for more but there is none. "Is that it?" My legs are starting to shake, my pj's no match for the season. "I'm going to miss the train. Is there something more you want to ask me about it?"

"Does Mama?" Two words. I'm not sure what they mean or why I'm asking.

"Does Mama what? Set up affairs for me? Ha! Come on. You know by now there's a big difference between Howie and me, don't you?"

"I know."

"And between your mom and Carly."

"I know," I repeat, feeling foolish.

"Howie has his own way of doing things. He wants to show everybody his penis? He wants to play around with girls in the office? He wants to have his wife coordinate his extramarital affairs? His business. I don't work like that. I think that some things are meant to be kept private. You carry your own water, and you don't spill it all over everybody else."

"What water?" I shout against the gust.

Papa shivers and his curls dance to the whip of the wind. "To-night!" He yells, turning to walk. "Anything you want. We'll talk all night! OK? I promise!"

My head shakes so vigorously from the cold I don't need to nod consent.

What Salem Wants

Howie has painted a sign with a pink lady, naked, popping off a blue background, pointing the way inside, on the door to his guest room. She has a Jewish nose, one beauty mark under long lashes, and two acrylic nipples. Her breasts are petite but her hand is beefy.

I step in and take a quick inventory of all the things Howie and Carly have managed to assemble here since September. I don't see them shop very often but there's no way all of this stuff could have fit in the minibus. Every corner has something new: an easel and box of paints; three milk crates of magazines, plastic toy figurines, and Betamax cassettes; a stuffed Winnie the Pooh close to Amanda's size; a Kodamatic instant 35 mm and a video camera on a tripod; burlap bags filled with silky clothes; a gigantic water bong filled with tar and green murk; and, on the bedside table, a heavy, hardbound black book. Howie's journal.

I reach out to flip the cover with a finger, catch a glimpse of a brilliantly colored page, and hear footsteps coming up the stairs.

I can't leave without being seen so I go deeper, slip into their bathroom, pull down my pants, sit on the toilet, and pretend I've been here all along.

Howie's humming happily to himself on the other side of the door. There's a flick and a burbling sound like someone gargling before bed. Then his voice, muffled grunting like he's moving something heavy, *Mmphhhh. Mmmmppphhhhh. Caffffhhh. Unnkhhh. Ahhhhhhhhhh. Wooooooooosh.*

The bong.

The smell of pot creeps under the bathroom door. Howie coughs uncontrollably. Takes another hit when the spell subsides. Footsteps again, and the door opens.

"Oh! Hey, little man. Didn't know you were here. Everything cool?"

I nod, folding into my thighs. "You know, just because I've seen you naked doesn't really mean I want you to see me naked."

I stand, pull my pants up, flush the empty toilet.

"So today, we campaign for me. Are you in?"

I smile.

"Grab your paperboy bag. You're going to need it," Howie says, ripping off his shirt and bending back to the mirror, squeezing at his chin with strong fingers. He has different fingernails, shaped like perfect Preston Beach shells, so different from Papa's ridged, oily half-moons. The muscles in his back roll and flex under the skin. Not a single hair there.

I follow him back into the bedroom.

"Paperboy bag?" he repeats.

"Huh?" I'm staring at his nipples, lost in thought.

"You been smoking my stash?"

"No."

"Grab your *bag*, chief, and let's go."

.   .   .

No one's strolling Chestnut Street in the middle of the day, but I catch the lace curtains of the imposing old brick captains' houses drawing just a bit to one side as Howie and I walk by. The brittle leaves start to whisper over our heads with the wind as we stride along. Howie walks with my paperboy bag dangling from his shoulder, bulging with a dozen *Playgirls* and a pile of fliers made for the occasion. It's warmer than it was this morning, but still too cold to be walking.

"How come we're not driving?" I ask.

"Wow. Déjà vu. 'All truly great thoughts are conceived while walking.' Nietzsche."

"All truly great friends let their friends drive their minibuses. Me."

"All in good time, Mario Andretti. I know you've got a hard-on for my wheels. And that pretty Penny. Not sure I'd date a girl whose mom is a witch . . ."

"Yeah. But her mom likes me."

"She likes the Red Sox, too, but her spells haven't broken the Curse of the Bambino yet . . ."

"Her spell on her cats so I wouldn't get asthma worked."

"Why doesn't she just cure your asthma and leave the kitties alone?"

I never thought of that.

We cross Summer Street where Chestnut turns into Norman. Howie stops under the massive pink and orange Dunkin' Donuts sign. "Well, this is as good a place as any to start."

I stop him before he opens the door, feeling a sudden burst of anxiety. If it was awkward at our reasonably enlightened dinner table, how will complete strangers react? "What do we say?" I whisper. "When we go in, I mean?"

"I don't know. Vote for me? We'll figure it out. I haven't really given it that much thought, now that you mention it." Somehow,

I'm not surprised. Nor am I disappointed. Instead, I feel there's an opportunity here to learn, or get burnt, together. Starsky and Hutch style.

The doorbells jingle and the girl at the counter looks up.

"Howdy!" Howie calls, waving to her and the three people huddled at the far end of the counter. One of them, a man with slick hair parted down the middle and a black Allman Brothers T-shirt, stares at us silently.

"How ya doing?" Howie asks. The Allman Brother turns back to his companions—a gigantic woman in a blue golf shirt with pimpled pork-belly arms, and a teenage boy three or four years older than I am. His hair is jet-black; his dandruff chunks visible from across the room.

"Can I help you?" the counter girl asks, leaning forward over the glass to get a better look. She's oddly pretty yet not pretty. Her blonde hair hangs in curly waves, almost touches her shoulders, frames huge eyes—brown and blue at the same time. But her nose and her chin are hard, and her two front teeth stick out.

"Hey!" Howie says, like he's known her all along. "How *are* you?" He leans across the glass so the girl has to step back toward the sweet wall of donuts.

"Fine," she drawls.

"You are. You are. So, I'm Howie Gordon. This is my personal attaché, Alexander von Snugglepuss."

She laughs.

"Your ashtray?"

"Ha! You're swell. *Attaché*. That would usually mean a personal assistant to an ambassador, pertaining to a military campaign, perhaps. But in this case, it pertains to my personal campaign to become *Playgirl* Man of the Year. Know the publication?" Howie pulls a copy out of the bag with a flourish.

"Oh, Jesus," the Allman Brother says, wiping his mouth with the back of his hand. "Circus is in town."

Pretty Unpretty blushes. Howie just stares, waiting. "You're kidding," she says, finally.

"Nope. I'm November right now, but I want the year."

The girl looks toward the trio at the counter again, maybe for help. The Allman Brother shakes his head. Pork Belly may have swallowed something bitter.

"So . . . Do you want any donuts?"

"Éclair for my attaché. I'll take a black coffee. But would you mind . . ." he pauses, reaching back into my paperboy bag for a flier, "posting one of these in the window of your fair establishment?" He hands her an eight-and-a-half–by–eleven-inch sheet of white paper with a xeroxed image of his smiling face from page fifty-nine of his Playgirl spread, strategically cropped at the waist. Above the photo he's sketched a hand dropping a checked ballot into a box that says "Man of the Year" on its side. "CAN I COUNT ON YOUR VOTE?" is stenciled in colored-pencil letters at the top of the page, and at the bottom there's something else, typed. Howie pulls out a second, differently colored copy and starts to read in a loud voice that immediately drives me backward toward the door.

"Hi! My name is Howie Gordon. I'm from Berkeley, California, living in Salem for a bit, and am currently appearing in the November 1978 issue of *Playgirl* magazine as a centerfold. Whether you read the magazine or not, your vote could make a big difference in my life. I know this isn't everybody's cup of tea, but it could be my ticket to bigger and better things. So please vote. Thank you for your support!"

Pretty Unpretty doesn't say anything. Allman Brother sighs. Dandruff Chunks is glowing red.

"By the way," Howie adds, smiling, "I like your freckles," and he lays three more fliers on the counter.

.   .   .

Our campaign's success rate does not improve. Down the street from Dunkin' Donuts we hit the Irish bar (no go), a stationery store (no go), and then a place called Off Your Head Smoke Shoppe.

"My dad says I'm not allowed."

"Why?" Howie asks, halfway in.

"Dunno. He just buys his cigars there and tells me to stay outside."

"Cigars, huh?" He looks down the street like he's looking for a bus that's late. "OK, this time you stay outside. I don't believe in this kind of hierarchical, separation of church and state shit, but he is El Jefe and we don't want to question his wisdom unless he's here to defend it." He kneels down, looks me in the eye. "That doesn't mean we don't question authority, understand?" Then he pats me on the cheek and slips into Off Your Head.

The plate glass window is taken up entirely by two posters, one above the other. The top is of a roughly drawn bald man in a yellow dress-length tunic with a long white beard and a finger pointing to the sky. MR. NATURAL. Above him is a comic book bubble with the words "QUEST into the UNKNOWN!" Below that there's another image, striped white and yellow with big script lettering in red and black, familiar because Papa has the album in his collection: *Big Bambu—Sobrinos de Cheech y Chong*.

I stare absentmindedly at the displays when suddenly the *Big Bambu* poster comes peeling away from the glass on one side, replaced with Howie's smiling face.

At Steve's Corner Store, the eponymous Steve pulls nervously at the loose fabric of his Hawaiian shirt, cleverly peppered with bold-color drum kits.

"You can't post your fliers here," he says, tapping a staccato beat on the counter with his pointer fingers after he hands the sample back to Howie. "What's up, kid? Stay to the clean side of the store, right? Where's your other buddy? The nose picker?" I shrug, head for the comics for all ages rack.

Howie, unfazed, admires Steve's arrangement of behind-the-counter products and pulls a beaded Asian change purse from his pocket to get a few packets of Pop Rocks and Wacky Packs for me and a pack of Camel unfiltereds for him.

"You a Chet Baker man?" Howie asks, tucking away his purse.

"Max Roach," Steve keeps tapping, chewing gum, warming.

"Right. Drummer," he points at the print shirt.

"Right," Steve smiles.

All the walking and talking is making me tired. I find an unsold copy of the final *Doc Savage* Marvel published last year, pull it off the rack, and sit on the dusty floor with my back against the cooler.

"You want that?" Howie says to me, pulling his purse out again. "We'll take that, and a Yoo-hoo for him, too. Seems a little low energy for a kid, don't you think? Yoo-hoo's the trick. And I'll take a *Oui*, *Hustler*, and a *High Society* . . . wait, I have that one. Just the *Oui* and *Hustler* then."

Eventually Steve agrees to keep the fliers behind the counter and put one in every bag that has a nudie magazine. "And they all want a bag," Steve assures us.

"I've got my own," Howie smiles, holding up my paperboy bag. "But thanks for the support. Remember: Your vote counts!"

"I'll do the bag stuffin' thing cuz yer a fahkin' laugh riot, but I ain't sendin' my name in to a gay guy magazine, no matter how many packs a' butts ya buy."

"Fair enough. Though you can always use a pseudonym. You know, like Stephanie instead of Steve?"

"Don't press ya luck. The cops are breathin' down all our necks about the dirty rag biz, so watch yourself."

"Right. You're a mensch. Thanks, Steve."

Steve gives a reluctant nod and grins.

It's our second win, but our luck turns as we zigzag across town, circulating through the business-heavy section of Essex Street. Most stores are too established or too conservative to consider posting a flier of a naked guy. It's a big *NO* from the manager at the men's clothing store, the lady at the counter at Pewter Pot, the ticket booth girl at the Witch Museum, the impossible-to-understand cobbler, the iron-armed baker at Athens, even Mr. Getchell, my wrinkled paper route boss at the *North Shore Sunday*.

"I like you, kid," he says to me as if Howie isn't here. "Don't get mixed up with this kind of thing. It can only lead to drugs. And jail."

"Hey, this is news," Howie waves the flier cheerily.

"You end up in the pokey, don't come cryin' to me," Mr. Getchell's eyes stay fixed on mine.

"Come on, there's a story here." Howie leans over the counter. "You're a newsman. Think of the headlines."

"Tell your hippie friend I'm in distribution, not editorial. They tell the stories. I just sell the stories. They're a mixed bunch in the newsroom, but at least they wear real pants."

We have better luck handing fliers to strangers on the street. Well, at least with the women on the street. Some run away or just look horrified, but most read it, do a double take when they see the photo is actually Howie, giggle, fold it into their purses, and do a triple take as they walk away.

The bars and restaurants speckled around Pickering Wharf have more of a sense of humor about our cause. Most let us post, but only in the bathrooms, alongside the Bruins and Celtics scores.

Howie bursts out laughing as we approach the Bunghole.

"I gotta think this is a joke," he says, staring at the swooping neon letters.

"The Bunghole? That's what pirates call the part of the booze barrel where you stick a cork."

"Oh. Well, *excuse me.* Now get in the frame Doctor Etymology," he says, raising his camera to his face and motioning for me to stand in the doorway. "Lou, about to enter the Bunghole," he narrates. "Ready to sniff out clues to the secret of the universe, buried deep within its hidden folds and twisted passageways."

"Can I help you guys?" A man asks, his face hidden behind a stack of beer cases.

"Let me help *you* out, pal," says Howie, pulling a case away to reveal a man whose mustache and bourbon-hued aviator glasses are so comically oversized they look like they come from a Serpico Halloween costume.

"Hey there," Howie says as I pull the door open and we all walk in. "Ever heard of *Playgirl* magazine?"

"Yup. We sell it behind the counter if you want a copy. Just give me a sec."

"No, that's OK. I don't need it—I actually have about a hundred and fifty copies."

The man drops the cases with a thud at the end of the aisle and walks back to join us at the front of the store, the smile fading from his face. "Well, I ain't buying. And I'm not sure I like the idea of you and him together," he adds, tone shifting darkly as he stares at me.

"It's not like that," Howie corrects him. "This is Alexander von Snugglepuss, my attaché. He's helping me with my campaign to be *Playgirl* Man of the Year. Still have November's centerfold hanging around?"

"You're shitting me," Serpico says.

"I shit you not, Mr. Bung." The man frowns. "I mean Mr. Hole." The expression remains, rigid. "Hole . . . lotta love, that's what I got for you. Really, check it out." Howie hands him a copy of the November issue. "That's the boring stuff up front," Howie nudges him along. "I'm dead center."

"I know, I know," Serpico chafes. "Whoa! Shit, man, that *is* you." His face twists, impressed yet appalled, and he shuts the magazine. "So? Great. Everybody gets a peek at your kielbasa. What's the point?"

"The point, my good man, is this." Howie pulls a few fliers from the bag with a flourish. "Would you consider hanging one of these . . ."

"Ix-nay on the oster-pay, chief. There's a guy in town trying to stop all the stores from selling nudie mags altogether. I put up your poster, I'm just asking to get shut down." Serpico hands the *Playgirl* back and crosses his arms definitively.

"Who's this mysterious guy trying to stamp out free speech?"

"Acting city marshal," Serpico says.

"Acting?"

I tug at Howie: it's time to go. We've been turned down enough for one day.

"Hey. Good luck to you," Serpico yells as we move to the door. "And buy some pants."

Out on the street, Howie lights a cigarette and looks thoughtfully at the rippling in the wharf, ice cold and bereft of ships. His face turns downward, taking on a pall I've never seen before.

"I like your pants," I assure him.

He grunts then chuckles and puts an arm around me. "It's not the wardrobe that's holding us up, hombre. It's the story. We need to make it less freak show, more hero's journey, you know what I mean? More *Rocky*, less *Man Who Fell to Earth*."

"But Rocky doesn't win in the end," I remind him.

"He wins your heart. And that's what we need to do. Rocky's not that smart, and he's not that lucky. But then he gets this break and he just *kills* himself to make the most of it." Howie tosses the cigarette in the gutter and starts walking up Derby Street. "Salem doesn't want Bowie. Salem wants Balboa."

The Rocky Campaign

Who's that teenager in the shower? Plastic curtain threaded under his arm, covering the right half of his chest and the wet white of his blubbery belly, a man boob hanging free. *Hard Day's Night* hair. Big smile. How could this tubby kid grow up to be Howie?

I flip to the next photo. Same kid. Younger. Hair parted to the side and greasy. He's wearing a jacket and tie and he has virtually no neck. Even fatter than in the shower.

"*That's* Rocky," Howie says. "That's the Italian Stallion. The Jewish Jaguar. He doesn't look the part, but he's the kid next door, so you want to root for him."

"I'm with you," Papa nods. He's come home early from work, a rarity, and we're gathered around the pool table playing a quick round of eight ball.

"Of course you're with me," Howie sniffs. "You were a fat kid, too. We need the rest of the country with me. How do you go from having the biggest boobs in the seventh grade to being a male centerfold on every news rack in America? Hard work! Millions of sit-ups! That's what I've been doing. But if you look at my photos in the magazine you only get one part of the story: just another good-looking guy with no tan line and a flat stomach. Someone you can't be. But then you see these," he flaps the eight by tens, one in each hand, "and your whole view changes. Suddenly you can get behind this horse. Because that's the whole American Dream thing. Rags. Riches. Fat. Thin. Same thing."

"Still with you," Papa nods. "Two in the corner." Sunk.

"Terrific. One down, twenty million to go. Thanks, Chubby."

"Hey, don't alienate your base, pal. First rule of politics." Papa lights his dormant cigar and smoothes his mustache as he hunts his next conquest on the felt.

"Point taken," Howie concedes. "Now here's how you can really help me, because this whole self-promotion thing is not me. I may have been born Jewish, but I didn't get the memo on how to succeed in business without really trying."

"Step one," Papa says, "is *try*."

"I'm all ears."

"Ten in the side." *Bang*. "Step two, get those photos out there. You hit on just the right thing—a narrative. Fat boy makes good. Universal appeal. Now sell it. Have you shared these photos with *Playgirl* yet?"

"Nope." Howie looks pensively at the glossies, his old self staring back at him.

"Don't they have a PR office? Let them do some of the legwork."

"They're not going to do *bupkes*. Can't pick favorites. Besides, they don't get what I'm up to here. This takes the idea of men's sexuality beyond John Wayne. Past the unattainable falsehood . . ."

"Don't get ahead of yourself."

Howie jumps up, spreads his arms: "Look at me! I'm five foot eight, one hundred fifty pounds. Not what your average steak-and-potato-eating American thinks of as a man's man. Dustin Hoffman with muscles, that's me. The fact that I could be Man of the Year could mean a lot, to a lot of guys. And women. I can't compete at that 'put up your dukes' bar brawl level. I'm not a *that*. I'm a *this*. It's a different way of being sexy."

Papa huffs. "Too lofty. Listen, it's about the competition and how you distinguish yourself from *them*, not from John Wayne. Right now, the *Playgirl* folks need a guy they can put in front of the press. A guy who makes them look good. They've got a new publisher facing an uphill climb, right? A million-plus subscribers a few years ago, down thirty percent this year."

"How the hell do you even know that?" Howie laughs.

"I read." He points at the six ball, the far corner, and buries it. "But ask yourself: Why are the readers bolting?" He doesn't wait for an answer. "Simple. People think it's just a cover for a gay magazine. No one really believes that women are buying it. And if the women won't buy, the advertisers won't buy. The whole business goes splat. But if the women really like you, which they seem to if my secretary is any indication, then maybe you can change *Playgirl*'s story from homoerotic to Homo superior. You were a blob. Now you're not. A guy like me can get behind that kind of thing, but so can my mother. *That's* your competitive edge."

Howie sparks a roach, takes a hit, stares out the window, then stares back at my father for a long, silent moment. "This?" Howie says to me, but he's pointing at Pa, "this is one strategic motherfucker right here. Your dad. They don't call him El Jefe for nothing."

"You're the only one who calls him El Jefe," I say.

"Fat kid made good," Papa sinks the eight and ends the game before either of us get a chance to draw a cue. He crosses his arms, satisfied, and Howie grabs us both up in a bear hug.

"A-fucking-men!" he shouts. "Let's do this."

"You two can do this," Papa says, breaking the huddle. "I've got to go make a living."

The next day our new campaign strategy begins in earnest. Fat Howie versus Thin Howie. He lets me write the new tag line above the photos: "Would you vote for this boy?"

Below my headline Howie pleads his case in his wiry pencil scrawl.

> *I've been given a ONE IN A MILLION chance! But I can't claim the title without your help. It's the 15th round, I'm on the ropes but fighting back. I'm no gym rat—I'm just like you. I needed to put a roof over my head so I broke concrete with a sledgehammer sixty hours a week for $5 an hour. It made me strong and it made me skinny and finally SOMEONE noticed!*
>
> *If you were ever the chubby kid, or you felt like one inside, you know what this would mean to me and to all the other fat kids out there. If you think I'm worthy of the title of* Playgirl *Man of the Year, PLEASE VOTE!*
> *Your Pal and Salem Transplant,*
> *Howie Gordon*

"Better be careful they don't find out that the 'someone' who noticed you was in a hot tub with you," Papa says, reviewing the new poster.

"What's wrong with that?"

"Sounds too lazy. Goes against the sledgehammer story. Nice touch with that, by the way."

"Half true."

"Oh, my God, that is the cutest thing!" Mama joins us at the table, grabbing the new flier in her hand and smiling. "You were such a soft little plum."

"Ripe for the picking, Hunan Princess."

"How come you never call Mama the Hunan Princess?" Amanda slips into Papa's lap.

"It never really occurred to me," Papa says slowly. "It's more Howie and Carly's nickname for her than mine."

"What *is* your nickname for her?" Amanda reaches absent-mindedly to his cheek to stroke the weekend stubble.

"I don't know. Phyl, I guess."

"Even though he knows I hate Phyl." Mama sighs.

"It's just easy. Like an abbreviation. Try this smoked salmon. Had it shipped in from the promised land. Zabar's." Papa holds out the sliver of oily fish he's carved himself.

I shake my head and slide back away from him. It smells like low tide at Devereux Beach.

"You need a nickname for Mama," Amanda stays on point. "You should call her the Hunan Princess, too."

"The last thing we need is royalty in this country. And there's a lot of negative association with Jewish American princesses, Poopie. It's a meritocracy and it should stay that way."

"I don't like you calling me Poopie for a nickname, either. I told you a million times."

Howie says, "I know you've been married a lot longer than I have, Jefe, but I'm not so sure that political theory should be applied to the boudoir." He takes a slug of coffee.

"I agree with Howie," Mama says.

"Of course you do," Papa shrugs dismissively. "And Poopie is a term of endearment, my love," he says to Amanda.

"A little more reverence couldn't hurt, you know?" Mama poses this as a question, looking lovingly at Papa, urging him to change his tune, which has become sharp and off-key.

"Great news!" Carly sweeps into the dining room, a wave of india ink hair streaming behind her. "I just sold out my first group!"

"That's wonderful," Mama says, hugging Carly lightly.

"My wife! My life! I am a fountain of pride, shining with the awesome alrightness of being with this beautiful human being." Howie takes Mama's place, lifting Carly off her toes.

Papa delicately separates a thin film of salmon from the orange-pink slab, and glazes it with a spritz of lemon juice before popping it into his mouth. "Well, we just hit the Salem erotica trifecta," he laughs. "Frank's organizing an army of gay activists in the back. Howie's running the city flag up his pole, and now Carly's going to be hosting little-lady tea-and-crumpet sex sessions in our living room. They're bound to resuscitate that anonymous Chestnut Street gossip rag just to cover the goings-on at number 31."

"About time," Howie slaps Papa on the back. "It was a little dull around here before we arrived."

Our campaign relaunch seems to be working. When we canvass the town this time, shop owners and store managers laugh more, scowl less. Many still refuse to post, but at least they smile. And more than a few take a flier as a souvenir.

"Come on," the Dunkin' Donuts girl says, her jaw dropping. "That's not really you."

Howie nods, flashing a pitiful, pouting face.

"Well, I still can't put it up here, but if you give me a bunch I can put them in the girls' bathrooms at the high school."

I look at Howie, electrified.

"That," he says, "would be the equivalent of a triple lutz in my book."

"That's ice skating," Pretty Unpretty scowls sweetly. "I do gymnastics."

"Triple backflip?"

"Better," she says approvingly, reaching out and grabbing a small stack of fliers.

Howie buys a half dozen éclairs—a thank-you and a reward—and we step out into a brightening Salem morning.

"Well, my young campaign manager, the battle is on. Time for reinforcements." Howie takes a deep draught of the winter sea breeze, nostrils widening. He pauses dramatically, then marches to the pay phone in the Dunkin' Donuts parking lot. "What's Grandma Wini's number?"

Brisket, Herring, and
Pinched Cheeks

Howie asks if I want to drive the bus as we approach the Salem-Marblehead border on Lafayette Street. I try to contain my excitement, my favorite action fantasies playing in my head as he pulls me out of my seat.

It looks good, NASA One!

"Your legs are a little short, so sit in my lap," he says at the stoplight. I shimmy over the tall stem of the gearshift to settle against him in the driver's seat. The wheel is huge. I take it in my hands, ten and two, and turn to and fro happily.

We have separation.

"Keep it straight," Howie charges. "This isn't a toy. Can you reach the gas pedal?"

"Which is it?" I ask, feeling around with the cracked rubber toe of my sneaker.

"On the right. The light's changing! Do you feel it? Press down. Not too hard. Harder. I'll shift. Move a little. I need my left foot for the clutch."

OK, Victor. Landing rocket arm switch is on.

We lurch through the green light, bucking along Lafayette Street at a modest clip.

"What's this picture of?" I ask, looking down at the steering wheel emblem between my hands: a castle with a dog atop it, water flowing beneath.

"Eyes on the road, hombre," Howie bumps against me from behind, setting me to attention in my seat. "Driving's a big responsibility. Takes concentration. Focus."

We cruise gently along after that, making the uncrowded lights and following a tight course. Howie gives instructions now and then, but for the most part he lets me navigate the winding road.

Here comes the throttle. Circuit breakers in.

I like the feel of the hard plastic steering wheel in my hands, arms spread wide to hold it all. It could be a submarine or an eighteen-wheeler in a convoy. It's everything I ever wanted to drive, all wrapped up in a funky white and blue tin package. I look back over my shoulder to see that the curtains are pulled open, the road whizzing by on every side, receding from behind. The foldout camper table rattles faintly between the yellow seats.

"Eyes!" Howie says again, bouncing me in his lap. "Right on Maple. And ease up on the gas when you do."

I turn the wheel, but not hard enough. Howie has to reach forward and grab it to compensate before we hop the curb into the scrub on the right shoulder.

"Where's my weed?" he asks as we settle back into a straight cruise.

"The light at the bottom of the hill is turning red," I say as we pick up speed.

"Tap the brake," Howie calls, body twisted, rummaging behind the seat.

"Which one's the brake?" I ask, knowing it must be near my

foot. There's a red knob by the gearbox diagram, rimmed in rugged gray rubber and white, all-caps: EMERGENCY.

Pitch is out! I can't hold altitude!

"The brake. The brake. In the middle. Come on," he turns back, scans ahead, and screams: "Hit the fucking brake!"

The bottom of the hill shoots up at us so fast I can't imagine stopping in time. We fly past Glover elementary school, hurtling toward the red light. Cars putter in either direction ahead, where Humphrey and Tedesco converge at the bottom of Maple. I imagine the minibus smashing through them.

Correction, Alpha Hold is off . . . Threat selector is emergency!

Howie wedges his hands under my butt and shoves me off his lap back into the passenger seat.

"We're not going to make it!" he shouts as we fly under the red light, into a swarm of veering, honking cars. Howie jerks right and squeals onto Humphrey.

Flight Con! I can't hold it! She's breaking up, she's break—

Neither of us speaks until Howie turns left on Rockaway and pulls over. "Put on your seatbelt," he whispers, looking at his trembling palms.

We can rebuild him. We have the technology.

"But Grandma Wini's house is two blocks down."

"Put . . . on . . . your fucking seatbelt," he says again, even more softly, if that's possible.

I buckle up and stare at him but he won't look at me.

Better than he was before . . .

"Sorry," I offer.

"Not your fault."

"Can I try driving again?"

"Not with me you can't," he says as he throws the minibus into first, gently negotiating the rest of the block and pulling to a stop in front of my grandmother's house.

.   .   .

"You don't need my help!" Grandma Wini dismisses the idea with a shake of her blonde beehive, pulls a bowl of grapes from the refrigerator, and adds it to the mix crowding her round, white Formica kitchen table. We graze from a casserole dish of shag carpet brisket, carrots and prunes, a crystal container of walnuts, a platter of rocky roads, a jug of ginger ale, and the remains of the banana bread Gramps left after his late-night fridge raid.

"I need your help eating all of this . . ." Howie tells Grandma Wini, standing to grab her little body and hug her in a gentle restraint before she can fetch yet more nosh. "And I need your endorsement. I'm like Jimmy Carter going to the editorial board of *The New York Times*."

"Oh, so I'm the Gray Lady now? Is that it?" Grandma Wini wriggles free from his embrace and heads reflexively back to the refrigerator.

"Come on now," Howie coos. "You're the platinum princess as far as I'm concerned. And your stamp of approval means everything. Can't you see that? It will give the mothers of America license to join the fight. They're afraid of letting their hair down, but you can change all that."

"How about some chicken?" She says, staying the course while unwrapping a blanket of crinkled foil from a blue glass plate to reveal a pile of ashen, gelatinous leftover meat and bones.

"Have you seen this *pupik*?" Howie lifts his shirt, flashing my grandmother his flat, still-tan belly.

"Oh, it's *marvelous*," Grandma Wini says. "You know how I feel about you, Howie."

"Then have mercy and give it a rest . . . and help me make it famous." He takes a knee, braids his fingers imploringly. I can't help but laugh at Howie, in prayerful worship at the foot of

Grandma Wini, who is holding yet another plate, this one filled with pickles and herring.

"Howie! Get up, silly! This is ridiculous. Really. You'll do just fine without me."

"OK, I didn't want to resort to this . . ." Howie says ominously. "Lou, go on. Show her."

I try hopelessly to slide the food out of the way and make room. Reaching into my newspaper bag, I feel for the slick glossies, draw them out carefully, and lay them side by side on the table.

"Grandma Wini," Howie says softly. "Please. Just look at these before you make your final decision."

Back turned, still rummaging for something else to offer from the bottomless belly of her fridge, Grandma Wini calls over her shoulder: "I've seen the pictures, darling. And it's wonderful for you. But I don't need to see your altogether all over again. Once was enough."

"That's not what this is. One look. It's all I ask."

She emerges from the fridge with a green Jell-O mold, pregnant with canned mandarin orange slices. Sighing, she finally lowers herself onto the white vinyl cushion of the kitchen chair beside me. It exhales a familiar, satisfied whisper as she sinks into its softness.

"Oh, fine, let me see what you've got up your . . . Oh, the *punim*! That face. That plump little boychik! Howie? This is you?"

"Mmm-hmm." He nods, sporting just a half pout. No need to overplay it.

"Well, you look just like Peter did when he was that age. A soft *kneydlekh*! A little ball of deliciousness. I had no idea."

"He worked hard to get into shape," I chime in, finally. "He didn't always look like this." I point to Howie, still amazed and believing every word. "We have to help him win, Grandma. He deserves it."

"I look at these," she whispers dreamily, "and all I can think about is what your *polkes* must have felt like. Chubby bundles of . . . ooohhhh . . . I bet you were the most scrumptious little baby alive." She turns to Howie, caresses his cheek, pinches lightly at the end.

"I'm still the same inside," Howie says softly. "I just look different now. But if I win this, it could change everything. It could make me into a star. Modeling. TV. Movies. Anything will be possible."

"Well," Grandma Wini shrugs, "I don't see how I could possibly help you with this. What difference does a little old lady from Marblehead make, anyway?"

"Lou? How much difference does Grandma Wini make?"

"All the difference in the world," I answer instantly. Truthfully.

She looks thoughtfully from me to Howie and back again, a shy smile emerging in spite of herself. "Who could resist two beautiful boys?" she asks, grinning. "Tell me what I have to do."

The Crowd Melts in a Thousand "OY!"s

Grandma Wini's a reader, not a card player. But she likes her ladies so she begrudgingly attends the weekly gathering. Everyone's dressed up and the room is a riot of horizontal stripes, wide collar blouses, high-waisted polyester pants, and bleached bouffants.

When we enter, Howie and I are assaulted with offers of powdery mints, supermarket cakes, and big glasses of milk. We're directed to our seats at the end of the room while the ladies assemble on an orange velour couch and scattered rope chairs. The chatting and gossiping commences, each seeming to feign surprise, shock, or delight. But the moment Howie instructs me to fire up the projector and flash the black-and-white fat boy photos, everything changes. Pearl, Belle, Shirley, and Zella melt spontaneously into a collective grandmother's ooze, helpless against the lure of a plump little boy and his innocent smile. "It's frickin' Pavlovian," Howie observes in a whisper.

The idea of helping a California hippie with no tan line and a bulging shlong is a nonstarter for the little old ladies of Marble-head. They're not so rigid as to reject him out of hand, they simply can't wrap their heads around how, in the social circles they run in, they can justify even speaking about his campaign. But the picture of that dressed-up little fat boy, tie tight to his neckless chin, hair parted painstakingly so? It's too much for them to bear. They can't *not* help him.

"I don't believe it," the ladies say. "That can't be you!"

And Howie tells his story. Not about getting his picture taken in a fancy studio with Jacqueline Smith's photographer and dog, or having the women on set help him pop a boner. No, the one about a fat little boy who makes good: a story they can all relate to. One they had wished for their own children but didn't come true.

Howie points to the black-and-white school photo of himself. "They didn't call kids like me 'fat' back then. They called us 'husky.' Wonderful euphemism. I'm thirteen here."

And the crowd melts in a thousand "Oy!"s.

"Wini! Where did you find him?"

"He just fell into our lives. Isn't he delicious?"

"Around the age of seventeen, after a poor showing on the college boards and not much success at . . . boyfriend-girlfriend activities . . ." *Titter titter.* ". . . it was time to do something serious about it. It's not easy to connect with girls when you're carrying around all that blubber and you have the largest cup size in the seventh grade. I had to change."

"He's so funny! But it's not funny, it's sad. Just imagine. My Earl was like that. Amy Finkelstein broke his little heart."

"So I stayed home from school for two months during my junior year. I lifted weights and ate nothing but lettuce and meat and studied for college boards. And in two months' time I dropped from heavyweight to welterweight."

"See? A little discipline."

"What? You want Eugene dropping out of school just to lose weight?"

"I went back to school confident, in charge. I took the college boards again and raised my scores a hundred points. I got elected class president."

"I'm pulling Eugene out tomorrow. What's a couple of months?"

"And having this body was like having a new toy."

"And what a toy."

"Ethel!"

"The first half my life I was Quasimodo. I wanted the next half to be Clark Gable. And let me be clear, ladies: I want to be healthy and handsome, yes, but I don't take it too far. When the frog turns prince, he still knows he's the exact same person inside. That's when you realize how silly it is, what people reward you for. This?" He points to a photo of his washboard. "It's so superficial," he says softly, dropping his gaze and pausing for effect.

"And values! He has his heart in the right place. After all that getting naked. It's a mekhaye. A mekhaye."

"But it sure feels good when the ladies want to take a second look!"

The ladies erupt in laughter and questions. "Howie! Howie! What kind of diet are you on? Wait! Let me get a pen."

He smiles, circulating among his new fans. "It's not a diet you just jump on. You want to get it off and keep it off. So you need to *live* a diet. I eat one meal a day."

"That's not healthy. Look at him. He looks famished."

"Oh, shush. He's a doll."

"And since these days I make a living off my body I keep that one meal real lean. I eat a lot, but I eat foods that don't make me fat. Vegetables and meats. Brussels sprouts and chicken. No skin." My back to the audience, I make a barfing face at him but he ignores me, his gaze moving skyward, appealing to the heavens. "Oh, but I do look forward to a time when I can let my natural pig emerge and just turn into Orson Welles."

"That'll be the day!"

My presence at these events provokes a predictable reaction. The well-meaning ladies look aghast when I join Howie at the center of the circle to discuss our campaign for *Playgirl* Man of the Year. They try to shuttle me away, into their arms, covering my ears or eyes with their warm, wrinkly hands, holding me tight against their soft chests. It's like being taken into the bosom of a thousand Grandma Winis. And while none of them could ever come close to the love super nova she showers onto me, I allow myself to fall fully into the fine galaxy of their affection.

"He's a big boy," Howie assures the ladies of Marblehead. "And I promise that all the adult images are for your eyes only, and only for those who wish to see them. This is a G-rated presentation and my campaign manager is privy only to those photographs and materials that fall under that strict rating."

"Isn't that lying?" I whisper.

"Selective omission."

"Lying?"

"Prestidigitation."

"Lying."

"Don't be a buzzkill." Then, to his audience: "Who here has a grandson with a *punim* you can't help but squeeze?"

Out of the Closet

Howie and I have not just hit on a path to victory, but the jackpot for being smothered in love gravy. It's a bonanza of affection that satisfies so many needs. But the warm glow of any success proves challenging to sustain in the midst of a Salem winter. The bricks freeze, the streets empty, and the natives get restless.

And so does Amanda. Feeling left out of the adventure Howie and I are on, she voices her dissatisfaction and Howie promptly offers to take her on a date. He wears a sports jacket similar, but frumpier, to the corduroy job he wore in the Mr. November spread, and dons a pink tie, to the amazement of all. "A bit of dining at the York Steak House for the lady?" he asks in his best Clouseau, pinning a corsage to her red gingham dress. "Followed by a little *Revenge of the Pink Panther*?"

"Mama!" Amanda squeals. "A corsage! A corsage!"

My sister's joy can't be contained.

·   ·   ·

The next morning Carly tells us an odd story of how she and Howie put Amanda to bed after the movie and then Amanda sleepwalked into their room in the middle of the night. They called to her but she ignored them and proceeded to step into a big bag behind the bathroom door filled with toilet paper rolls.

"It looked like she was in a sack race," Howie chuckles.

"It looked like she wanted to pack up and live with us," Carly gives her own impression. "Poor little pooh seemed so lonely."

Atjeh and I retreat to my room after breakfast, reading comics and *Hustler*s on the bunk. The door swings open without a knock and Gretchen appears, shaking a Howie flier at me from down below.

"My sistah found this in the guhls' room at the high school yestahday," says Gretchen, her voice like foil on fillings.

"What are you doing in *my* room?" I groan. Atjeh, who I'd pulled up the slatted ladder to laze alongside me, raises her eyebrows sleepily at the sound of Gretchen's voice. She makes a jealous *Her again?* teeth gnash, smacks her lips, and drops back to sleep.

Gretchen climbs the ladder, jamming herself between me and my dog. I let Howie's *Hustler* slip down the back side of the bunk between the bed and the wall, safely out of sight.

"How come you didn't ask me to bring it ovah there? You know my sistah goes to the high school."

"I don't know. It was some girl from Dunkin' Donuts. I didn't do it." I feel defensive, and annoyed.

"Who? Mahcy? Was it Mahcy Dubriel?"

"I don't know her name. She does gymnastics."

"*That's* Mahcy. She's a wicked bitch. I can't believe yuh gave these to huh!"

What is it about me? I'm like a magnet for the weirdos—mutant girls, outcasts, bullies.

"She seems nice to me." Nicer than you, I want to say. It's a miracle Howie likes me at all, now that I think about it. The one person in this town I genuinely want to be around who feels the same way.

"Whatevah," Gretchen repeats, then starts to explore my room. She leans over the edge of the crate to look at Bunny Yabba. "There's no rabbit in here. Just his dookies."

OK, two people. Grandma Wini never equivocates—the unambiguous maharani of love.

"Good-bye . . ." I nudge from the top bunk, staring at the ceiling.

"What's in this closet?"

I pop up. A shriek of adrenaline stabs me in the throat. She fingers the latch. "Stay outta there!" I shout as the door flings open.

"Oh my gahd. There's a frickin' million paypahs in here. Didn'tcha delivah these? What the hell?" She laughs, kneels down to rifle through the little landslide that's spreading across the shiny green paint of the floorboards. "And *Hustlah*s? Lookit all these dirty mags!"

I flip over the side of the bunk, scraping my stomach on the wooden lip as I slide down. Atjeh leaps after me, spinning on her paws before banging into Bunny Yabba's crate. I try to slam the door to the closet shut but it's blocked by the surge of yellowing *North Shore Sunday*s. Papa can't know. Atjeh starts digging at the pile as if a wharf rat just disappeared down a hole in the floor. She shreds dozens of papers as she burrows, destroying the collector's edition scratch 'n' sniff issue of *Hustler*—"WARNING: to be smelled in the privacy of your home"—before I can tackle her. Not anymore.

Gretchen starts laughing again, that Salem townie laugh that betrays an accent, even though there are no *r*'s or *aw*'s to soften it. That chortling version of *fahkin' A* versus *fucking A, yuh muthah* versus *your mother*. Atjeh must smell my shame over the scratch 'n' sniff because she turns from the tattered ribbons of newspaper and hops to her hind legs, black nostrils flaring, white eyes reddening with fury, and slams her front paws right into Gretchen's little boobs, pointed teeth clacking shut with a spray of tongue lather, a hairsbreadth from Gretchen's stunned face. The girl falls backward, wailing: "Get yuh dahg offa me! She's gunna kill me! She's gunna kill me!"

I grab Atjeh by the collar and fling her aside, watch her spin across the floor.

I turn back to Gretchen but she's out of the room and down the hall, shrieking at the top of her lungs: "That dahg tried to kill me! I'm tellin' my fahthah! I'm tellin' my fahthah!"

I trail her down the stairs, through the second-floor hall, and around the bannister to the second set of stairs, which empty at the door to the living room. Carly is leading her first women's group, and Mama is sitting on the stairs just outside, within earshot but not participating, reading *The Murder of Roger Ackroyd*.

"Shush!" Mama hisses. "What the hell is going on? Gretchen? What are you . . . What's wrong honey?"

"His stupid dahg . . ." Her normally alabaster cheeks are splotched red. She can't catch her breath. "My face . . . bit . . . my sweatah . . ."

"That's *it*," Mama says, menacingly. "That dog is out of here this weekend."

"What? No! It's not her fault. She didn't bite her . . . she was . . . defending me. She thought Gretchen was going to . . ."

"Was going to what? Gretchen? Little Gretchen? What was Gretchen going to do to you?" She points at the frantic girl who is pulling on her down vest and heading for the foyer. "Don't be ridiculous."

"He nevah delivahd his paypahs," Gretchen shouts, standing

before the open front door and pointing at me. "Look in his clahset. Theahs a million paypahs in theah. And pahno magazines! I'm tellin' my fahthah that. And he can get yah fieahd from the *Naht Shah Sunday* and get tha dahg catcha' to come and put that stupid mutt ta sleep. That's what he's gunna do!" She screams this last part at the top of her lungs. Her voice cracks in a way that makes me laugh out loud. Mama whips around and glares at me. Gretchen, hair flying in all directions with the wind, screams again, even louder, as impossible as that seems: "I FAHKIN' HATE YOU, YOU LOOZAH!!!" And with that, turns and runs down the front steps without closing the door behind her.

"Jesus Christ," Mama says, palms out toward me, begging for an explanation. "Are there papers in your room? Papers you never delivered?"

"A few," I lie to the defunct iron heating grate at my feet.

"I want you to go upstairs," Mama says softly, moving to close the door against the wind, "and get Atjeh and get those papers and go bring them to the houses that are still waiting for them."

"Mom! They're old. And it's Thursday! Come on!"

"Deliver every last one of them, and then take that dog and tie her up in the backyard."

"I'll keep her in my room. I'll bring her food up . . ."

"In. The. Back. Yard." She grabs me by the ear and drags me to the stairs.

"I've never had an orgasm . . ." A woman's voice trails from the living room. "I mean, not with Bruce."

"Go!" Mama whisper-yells.

"I come all the time, but only when I'm watching the soaps." A chorus of women's laughter erupts from just beyond the doorway.

"Ugh!" Mama pushes me to the stairs. "And don't come back until they're all where they belong."

"So what is it about the soaps that allows you to let go?" Carly's tender voice rises from below and slows my climb. She's been attracting more women to these groups which, until now, have been held at semipublic locations. It's no wonder—her gentle, embracing style carries over seamlessly to the work. "And how can you bring that spirit into your bedroom so you—and your husband—can both enjoy it?"

"Can we bring Dr. Chuck Tyler in with us? That would be a good start!" The suggestion is rewarded with huge, raucously dangerous lady laughter.

Back in my room, Atjeh watches with that unconditional dog love face as I pull all the papers from my closet. I put about thirty or forty in my paperboy bag and set it by the door. The rest I bunch into seven stacks, each about two feet high, bind them with kite string and, one by one, hoist them out the window onto the thin blanket of snow covering the flat roof. I'll deal with them later.

I take Atjeh outside, tie her to the Seckel tree with the long rope, and leave her whimpering between the frost heaves and roots. It's too windy and cold to ride the Apollo so I set off on foot, heading up Winthrop Street. I turn on Endicott and stop, staring at a slick and steaming manhole cover. Wherever I start dropping these things, it's going to be arbitrary. And whatever papers I deliver might be a week old, or they might be six months old. Whatever sequence there might have been—and there wasn't much of one—it's been completely disrupted by the avalanche Gretchen started, then scrambled into an Atjeh omelette. I twirl slowly in place, looking for a spot to dump them, but there's nothing—just houses and yards and open streets. No garbage cans. No Dumpsters. I wish I could just open the manhole and stuff the whole load under the street.

I resume my trudge, turn on Summer, again on Prescott, and make a quick loop back to Winthrop. Halfway down there's a large wooden box on the sidewalk, hinged and latched with a rusty, open padlock. I scan the neighborhood for spies and, seeing none, unhook the lock with an angry metal scrape. A shiver, uncontrollable, shakes me beneath the stiff wool of my peacoat.

The box is full of salt, oversized gray and black crystals stored for snow emergencies, piled so high there's virtually no room for the newspapers. But having started this thing I can't seem to stop, even if the mission is utterly futile. Every drop of blood in my body surges with a message to my brain: ABORT. But my muscles are acting on their own, desperate to be rid of the secrets that have been piling up. I can't come home with them again, but I can't leave them on my neighbors' doorsteps, either. They'll know. They'll report me. I'll lose my job and everyone will say *He never delivered! He stole our stupid* Naht Shah Sundays*!* They'll brand me with a scarlet *T* for thief.

I force the musty papers into what small spaces are left inside, smooshing them, folding, crumpling, and rolling them into the salt box. A fine spray of sea air and February rain twists around me and showers the belly of the box as I lean into it, softening the newsprint and turning the secrets from my closet into a formless batter of guilt. Sharp moles of dirt and salt freckle the mass. It's melting. Melting. And then . . .

"Get the hell outta that frickin' salt box, ya dumb kid!" The lady, still in her sweat-stained nightgown at noon, is apoplectic, squawking from a rickety porch above me.

I freeze, face cast down into the dark mess of the box.

"Get outta theah, I said! It ain't yah trash can, dumbass. Out!"

I refill my bag with the sludge and skulk through the back side of our neighborhood where I am less likely to be seen. The people who live in the house behind ours are renovating their garage. A Dumpster sits on the curb, filled with fragments of wood and plaster. I sigh at the nasty irony—it was here all along—and dump the salty bolus of bad memories into its belly.

I return to find Atjeh croaking against her collar, unable to escape the confines of that pitiless rope. The last of her claws have been scraped raw in a circular trench she's dug racing round and round the pear tree. She barks sharply, trapped in the turned and frozen dirt of her backyard prison. A squall hits: thousands of loose pages of remaining *North Shore Sunday*s I had left on the flat roof two stories above, their reports of weeks long past, cascade and whip around me in a vicious circle, the sorry smell of my closet lost at last to the gray skies of Salem.

"Not delivering the papers . . . not getting good grades . . . not doing the Hebrew study . . ."

"You said you don't care if I get a bar mitzvah," I latch onto this sole chink in my father's angry armor.

"I don't. That's off the table. But I care that you work. Hard."

"But—"

"And I don't mean the 'campaign.' No more play time."

I suck in my breath, "You're not—"

"Oh, yes, I am. Discussion over. Get to work. From now on, you focus on grades raised and papers delivered. Votes come last."

I Can Be the Tomorrow You

When *The Man Who Fell to Earth* finally airs on TV, I watch with an uncanny feeling of recognition. "You're really a freak," Mary-Lou tells an alien Bowie. "I don't mean that unkindly. I like freaks." It sounds promising, but in the end the alien's family dies on his home planet. He's left behind in a world he doesn't belong to. I know the feeling, Mr. Bowie. It may be the most depressing film I've ever seen. More importantly, it's a message from the universe. The question is, is it the universe that will break me or is the universe yet to be conquered?

The answer comes as the *Man Who Fell* credits fade, in the form of a commercial for a new movie. It's *Hooper,* starring a bubble-blowing Burt Reynolds as an aging stuntman and Jan-Michael Vincent as his youthful, rugged protégé Ski. "Hooper's in a dangerous business, but his reward is excitement, adventure, and a fortune . . . If he lives to collect it!"

"Burt Reynolds did it!" Howie's mom had said. "And look at his career!"

Hooper and Ski race chariots, flip cars, and explode fuel trucks. They're on movie sets, in helicopters, popping dirt bike wheelies, and outrunning falling buildings. There may be danger, but there's no sign of alienation. No one's ever had so much fun in a bar fight as Burt and Jan. Excitement and adventure, a fortune to collect— and most importantly, friendship and loyalty that transcends all the risks.

In an alien land where everyone wants me to be something I am not, Howie and I can be something out of this world. If Papa only understood. School? The *North Shore Sunday*? These will break me. If he wants a son who follows in his footsteps, who chooses conquest over being conquered, then he should know: nothing will come between me and this campaign.

I spend the next few weeks keeping a low profile, giving every appearance of being the hardworking student but mostly using my time in the library to slip copies of the promotional flier into the New Arrivals titles and all the magazines for girls, and my time at school to lobby the undecideds and the uninitiated.

I try my hand at the bathroom postings, as Pretty Unpretty had done at the high school, but they get pulled down by day's end and I am called into the front office to explain, since everyone seems to know that I live with a centerfold. While their MO is to pass no judgment—true to the spirit of the Alternative School— they can't help but deem the behavior "inappropriate for school."

Martha, one of the substitute teachers, is more understanding when I return to class. "Give me the rest," she smiles conspiratorially. "I think my sister and her girlfriends at Salem State might be able to help."

"I can arrange an in-person signing if you think they'd be interested," I offer.

"Let's start simple."

"Do they have a speaker series? We could do a slide show."

"Math," Martha puts the fliers in her backpack. "Let's do some math."

The conversation gives me an idea. Howie has drawn a clear policy line: sixth grade isn't a place to campaign, but when I tell him that Laurie Cabot is scheduled to teach us something witchy today, he eagerly accepts an invitation to visit.

His lunchtime appearance on the playground is a breath of fresh air. Red and white silk baseball jacket, hair golden and greasy, Howie is the imaginary me I want them all to see when they look my way. Uli, Penny, and Gretchen circle us while the others edge closer.

"Is that the guy from *Playboy*?" Scotty, not the brightest crayon in the box, asks.

"*Play*girl."

Howie sits beside me and unwraps a tuna sandwich, twin to mine. "Just joining you guys for a little lunch and witchcraft," he says. "Best school ever!"

I surge with pride. "How come you're in magazines?" Scotty, the resident class knucklehead, asks. "Are you a movie star?"

Penny and Uli crack up. Howie clears his throat, puts down the sandwich. "Well," he begins, "I'm an actor and an artist . . ."

"And a lovah!" Gretchen blurts.

Howie actually turns red—a first. "I'm all those things," he admits. "And most recently I posed for a magazine . . . called *Playgirl* . . . a magazine that has pictures of men without clothes on."

Surrounded by twenty-three twelve-year-olds he is suddenly reserved, thinking far more carefully about his answers.

"Ugh! Why?" Katrin, who somehow missed the news, stares openmouthed, tails and faces of the sardines her father had packed in her lunch all mushed in a slurry on her tongue.

"Listen," Howie continues, "the human body is beautiful. The female and the male body. Who here has gone to the big art museum in Boston?" A flurry of hands. "And did you see any Greek statues?" Nods. "And were they naked?" Giggles. "Same thing. But in the museums they call it art and in the magazines people call it . . . something else."

"Porno?" says Scotty.

"My dad gets *Playboy*," Uli pipes up.

"My Grandpa Al does, too," says another girl.

"*My* father doesn't. My father would never. It's disgusting," says Katrin. What a little prude.

"The Greeks believed the human body is a work of art," I say, echoing Howie. "Getting all uptight about nudity is so"—I search for the word, find it—"puritanical! Salem was filled with Puritans and look what happened. They ended up burning innocent people at the stake."

"Wow," Howie says. "You've really been paying attention, hombre. I better be careful what I say."

"Do you get fan mail?" Scotty asks.

"A lot. Most of the people who write to me are girl-in-dormitory types who say things like 'I love you Howie Wowie.' " We all laugh. "There were some letters from men, too. I don't play that way, but I certainly appreciate being appreciated."

I look around, predicting who will get it and who won't. Katrin's all sardines again.

Penny raises her hand. "How'd you get so Man of Steel?"

"A lot of fucking work," Howie laughs, shaking his head then catching himself. "I mean, sorry . . . I mean, a lot of hard work. When I was your age I was the fattest kid in my class."

"No, suh," Gretchen shoots back.

"Yes, sir," Howie repeats. "Biggest tits in the eighth grade."

My classmates howl. Katrin puts her face in her hands, turning from the group.

"I looked a lot like this guy, here." Howie points at Scotty, who gasps at being singled out. "It's OK," Howie offers gently. "I look at you and I see me. So you can look at me and see you. You're the yesterday me. And if you want, I can be the tomorrow you. Not that you have to be. But it's possible. You can be whatever you want to be. I'm the experiment that proves the theory."

"Well, I wouldn't want to wear pajamas around town every day," Scotty splutters.

"They're drawstring pants!" Gretchen, Uli, Penny, and I all say together. Gretchen sticks her tongue out at me when we make eye contact. I grimace back, still furious about her betrayal at my house. And then she just smiles and blinks, innocently, like we're in love.

"*I* saw the pictures," Penny reveals to a round of gasps. "Louis gave me my own copy." Her confession exposes our closeness. We are meant to be. She goes on: "And you've got those six-pack abs. A kid like Scotty's never going to look like that," she says, apologetically.

"Hey!" Scotty cries, miserable.

"Sorry, but you're wrong," Howie says, rising to stand by Scotty, hand on his shoulder. "This little shlub has every chance that I did. It may not look it now, but it didn't look that way for me, either." Heat ripples in waves around Scotty's tomato face. "Before," Howie points at Scotty. "After." He points back at himself. "Before. After. I'll take you on if you want, little guy. You can be Grasshopper Number Two to my Master Po." I hope the offer is nothing more than flattery.

"No, thanks," Scotty pulls away.

"Invitation stands," Howie says happily. Penny can't take her eyes off him, and I realize she's not seeing the imaginary me. She's only seeing him.

"I hope you'll all vote for me in the Man of the Year contest. Will you? Can I count on your vote?"

The group cheers its support, as we head back to the school.

"You're the best. Lou has the fliers with all the info. Now where's the witch?"

"Present and accounted for," Laurie Cabot says, standing in the doorway, flanked by Penny's older sister Jody. Both are dressed entirely in black: Laurie in her black robes, Jody in black jeans, a button-down black shirt, and a matching pentacle necklace.

Howie joins the group and stares at Jody, who sniffs lightly, eyeing Howie's pants with knowing amusement.

"Let's get started," Laurie says.

"Is it true you're helping an oil company search for oil in Iowa, Laurie?" Becky asks. "I saw it in the *Washington Post*!"

Laurie sighs. "Ah, yes, well, they said they'd give me two hundred thousand dollars if I'm successful. It shouldn't be too hard. It's just a question of energy, connecting with it, revealing it. But I'm afraid the stakes are high this time. You know, the house we live in is for sale and if we can't buy it ourselves we might have to move altogether."

"Move out of Salem?" Katrin asks hopefully.

"I'm afraid so. Unless the community can find a way to help us raise the 43,000 dollars we still need to buy the house. It's the oil company or the citizens of Salem. Otherwise, we're off to who knows where. It would be a terrible loss for all concerned, I think. Don't you?"

Everyone nods.

"Ever been to Berkeley?" Howie asks Jody, who shakes her head silently, eyes locking with his.

"Oh, Jesus," Penny whispers. "She always does this."

"Does what?" I ask.

"Makes eyes at guys that I . . . that I know."

"Oh," I look at her quizzically, see her beautiful face darkening.

"I'd like to make a request," Howie says to Laurie. "Do you take requests?"

She looks curiously at him and he flinches away from Jody as if he touched an electrified cow fence. "Say more," Laurie offers.

"Well, I've been entered into a contest. It's a beauty contest, kind of . . ." The whole class bursts out laughing. "Well, it is."

"Ah, you're the *Playgirl* Man of the Month?"

"Mr. November," Howie bows.

"I sense your intentions are good in this pursuit?" Laurie asks, her words careful.

"The purest," he promises.

"Then I can assure you every success," Laurie Cabot vows, "as long as they *remain* so." Her eyes widen and fix on his, as if to ensure that the message she is sending has indeed been received.

"Understood. Loud and clear. Pure as the driven snow, that's me." Howie searches the room, spots the big clock above the door. "So, I'm going to have to miss the class guys. Big campaign meeting back at Mr. November HQ." My face scrunches, perplexed. "Thanks for having me. And Lou, I'll see you back home, OK?" I shake my head but he nods definitively and gives me the bug-eyed, getting-whacked expression I've come to know well. "Bye guys. Bye!"

Laurie exhales peacefully. Jody glowers at her mother, Penny glowers at her sister, and I just look at Uli who rolls his eyes and mouths, "Freak show."

Laurie's lesson is held on the stage in the auditorium and it takes up the rest of the afternoon.

"We have to begin with what I call the Crystal Countdown to go alpha," she explains, hands smoothing the air in front of her like she's wiping away the wrinkles of a tablecloth. I look at Uli suspiciously but he just shrugs. Ladies from the school office look on, whispering to one another from shadows at the back of the hall.

All the kids follow her instructions, practicing a magical version of meditation. Then, trying to "stay in alpha," we surround a table in the middle of the stage, lay our fingertips gently along its edge, and try to make it levitate with our collective energy. I feel it rise, and I'm not alone. We all question one another furiously afterward, trying to determine who, if anyone, did anything more than rest their fingers on the heavy wooden surface. Everyone denies playing a larger role, though Scotty is convinced that Penny conspired with certain kids in advance to lift from underneath.

"He's a skidmark," I assure her. "Don't listen to him. We all know it happened."

"It's not him I'm worried about," she mumbles, distant. *Then who? Me? Howie? Wait. Jody? Because Jody makes eyes at guys that . . .*

"Want to hang out?" I urge. "We haven't hung out in a long time. I swiped some pot from my dad. Uli made a pipe out of a potato . . ."

Penny shakes her head. "I gotta do homework, Cheech and Chong."

"Hey! Come on. I was just . . ."

"I know what you were doing."

"If you don't like it . . ."

"A girl doesn't like a boy to worry about what a girl doesn't like."

I stare, dumbfounded.

"A girl wants a boy to want to be a man, not a boy." I try to quickly parse her word puzzle, wanting very much to be a man right now. "But even if he wants to be a boy she doesn't want him to worry about the fact that she doesn't like it because that's even more boyish. You know?"

"Oh yeah, no, I know. I'm not worried about if you like it." Wait, that sounds totally wrong. "I mean, I want you to like it. Me. What I want." This is going badly. Hindenburg bad. "And I *want* to be a man," I say, my voice rising like a girl's. "I do." She frowns, shaking her head. I try one more option: "I want to be what you want me to be."

"You should want to be yourself, Spike."

"But that's what I'm trying to be," I reach tentatively for her.

"I know." She sighs, stepping back. "That's the problem."

Say Uncle

"What's the word, Thunderbird?" Howie asks when Uli and I get home. He and Mama are at it again, scraping paint bark from a rotting sill.

"Nothing," I shrug.

"Well, that was quite a visit today. I mean, that witch is the real deal, huh?"

"Peter says she's not," Mama says, "but I've seen it for myself. She can definitely do some kind of magic."

"You can't help but feel it," Howie marvels. "Why would he doubt her?"

"Well, he hasn't ever met her, for one. But mainly he just thinks she's a huckster. You know, she did manage to trick the governor into declaring her the official Witch of Salem."

Uli looks perplexed. "She did?"

Mama nods, leaves, and returns with a newspaper clipping that bears a surprise headline:

GOV. DUKAKIS UNWITTINGLY GIVES
"WITCH" HER WISH

She points to the way *witch* is set off by quotes and begins to read: "For six long years, Laurie Cabot has been struggling, doggedly, to get herself proclaimed 'the official witch of Salem.' This week, Ms. Cabot apparently worked her magic on Governor Dukakis, and he unwittingly did for Ms. Cabot what Salem mayors and councils have refused repeatedly. With the stroke of a pen, or more likely a signature stamp, Dukakis sanctioned Ms. Cabot's claim to being Salem's official 'witch.'"

"I don't get it," I say. "Why was it unwitting?"

"Well, some politician asked the governor to give Laurie what's known as a Paul Revere citation in recognition of her good work with sick children."

"But she *does* that . . ." For Penny's sake, I don't like the direction this is taking.

"She does. And it's wonderful. But the citation said 'Laurie Cabot, Official Witch of Salem' and technically, she isn't. Or wasn't. Oy. He must sign a hundred of them every week. But no one is really the *official* Witch of Salem. It's a made-up title."

"But with the Duke's John Hancock, it became official," Howie gets it before I do.

"Why does it matter? I mean, who cares? She's definitely a witch."

"I don't doubt it," Mama says. "I saw what she did for you. But the city council thinks she tricked Governor Dukakis so she could make money from the 'appointment.' And they think it's their decision and no one else's."

"'Council Says Phooey to Witch,'" Howie takes the article and reads aloud. "I don't think I've ever seen the word 'phooey' in a newspaper headline before. Very Salem." He passes it to Uli, who picks up reading.

" 'The city council wasted no time Thursday night repudiating Gov. Dukakis's faux pas in naming Laurie Cabot as Salem's official witch. Ward 5 Councillor Jean-Guy Martiseau recommended that the city council 'go on record as not acknowledging any person or spirit as the witch of Salem.' "

"Oh, I love this," Howie grins, moving along to another chipped and rotting sill.

"It gets better," Uli continues. " 'I don't think the governor should have anything to do with this. I just hope the witch doesn't put a whammy on me.' Ha! That's pissah." He hands the article back to Mama, who hands me another clipping.

RECOGNITION DESERVED

To the editor: I saw the article about my mother, Laurie Cabot. The way it was written was meant to make my mother look bad. But it also made Gov. Dukakis and Elaine Noble look bad.

If the Governor did things unwittingly he would not be Governor of any state today. I respect Michael Dukakis for his recognition of my mother's work and his right to declare her "Official Witch of Salem."

PENNY CABOT

Age 12

Salem

I read it twice and my heart balloons, renewed with feeling for her.

Why didn't she tell me?

"That's good spin," Howie says. "Sounds like she has a press secretary doing some ghostwriting for her. Turning it back on the paper and the council and making them the ones calling the guv's integrity into question."

"She's protecting her mom," I interrupt. "And I'm sure she wrote it herself. Why don't you stop making fun of her? You're being a big . . . dick."

"Whoa!" Howie bellows, not believing my anger.

"Lou . . ." Mama says as I bolt from the room.

I've thrown a gauntlet, and I don't know how to retrieve it but I know I'm not going to apologize.

"Hey, gringo," Howie taps softly on my open door. "Can I talk to you for a sec?"

I nod and he joins me on my bunk. "I was in no way trying to shit on your girlfriend. You know that, right? Friends don't do that, and we're best friends. So I'm sorry. OK? I'm sorry. I should know better. I *was* being a big, fat dick."

"Even though you don't even have a big dick," I crack.

"I have the smallest fucking dick in show business, buddy. That's why they made me get it up for the pictures. If I stayed soft you'd hardly see it." I laugh with him. "Hey!" He slips a magazine out from under the pillow. "You still have my *Hustler*. And now it's all sticky! Ewwwwwww!" He throws it at me and I scream and we roll on the bed together in a pile, his strong arms pinning and squeezing me just hard enough.

And then just hard enough becomes too much. I try to flip onto my side, to get an elbow underneath me for leverage, but Howie's mass seems to increase in direct proportion to my resistance. I fight with my legs and hips but I'm pinned. My forearms are free to flail but with Howie's hands locked on my biceps there was no way to reach him. I harden with a poison mix of anger and fear. The smell of Brussels sprouts fills my nose from somewhere ugly inside.

"Get off!" I scream. Atjeh barks warily from the bunk below.

"Say uncle," he laughs, adopting the goo-goo voice that adults use with babies.

"No! Just get off!" I buck and try to roll over.

"Uncle!" he repeats, singsong.

"You're not my dad!" I shout, surprising myself.

"No, *uncle*!" Atjeh yaps again, scrabbles around the room, trying to get a look at what's happening.

"Ugggghhhhh!" I flex one last, futile time against him, then scream "GETTHEFUCKOFFMEYOUFUCKINGASSHOLE!"

Howie springs up, realization dissolving his dumb handsome smile. "Hey. Hey hey." He reaches for me but I'm off the bunk and on the floor, face down in the beanbag chair by the dormant fireplace, Atjeh alternately licking my face and snapping up at Howie, who hangs his legs over the edge of the bunk, shaking his head. "Hey. I was playing. I'm sorry. It was just a game. I guess I'm . . . I'm just doing a shitty job of being the adult." I don't reply. "What's going on? This vibe is off. I can see that."

I roll over on the beanbag, my face so hot I could melt him just by staring. His expression betrays a hurt I haven't seen before and I can tell he isn't prepared for conflict. I reel in a tide of love/hate I've known with only one other person on this planet: Papa.

What hits me, suddenly, is the impermanence of the situation. For all the excitement, the campaign will only delay the inevitable: Howie and Carly will move on, and the Coves will go back to regular family life. Which is what, exactly? We've hardly given ourselves enough time in a single city to bother finding out. I should never get attached, to any place or anyone. It always ends. Badly.

I don't want to do the campaign anymore, I admit to myself the moment before I say it aloud to Howie. And as I do I start to cry.

"Fine. Done. Campaign over. We're out of the politics business." I look at Howie, his expression unreadable through the film of tears. "Does that help? Is that better?"

"But you . . . You have to win. I want you to be Man of the Year. I want you to win. I just can't be . . ."

He sits next to me and I can smell him. I smell Carly, wood

smoke, pot smoke, cigarette smoke, everything that makes up Howie all wrapped up in a fragrance as familiar and comforting as that of my own bed.

"Hey, it's almost April. The June issue comes out in May. So if they haven't stopped counting votes, they're going to any day now."

"But every vote counts."

"True. True. But let me let you in on a little secret. This whole campaign thing? It's not going to make a difference one way or the other. You know that, right?" I stare at him, unsure of what he's saying. "Salem? Marblehead? If we were in LA, maybe. New York. But here? It's just for fun. Just a way for us to pass the time."

"But you said you wanted to win." It can't be for me.

"I do, little Jefe. I'm trying! Oy, am I trying! But at the end of the day they're going to pick who they're going to pick. The thing is rigged. You know it is. They probably don't even count the votes. It's like your dad said, they just want someone who will make them look good, who they can send out on a press junket. Maybe I'm that guy. Maybe I'm not. But there's nothing you or I can do about it."

I know it's true. But I believe it's not. If it came down to the wire. If Mr. April was closing in . . . We could have made all the difference. I stare blankly at Atjeh's snout, settled protectively over my lap. "What about being your campaign manager?"

"You were," Howie says imploringly. "You *are*. But if it's causing you grief? That was never the point. It was a fun game while it lasted."

That last part scores the nerves, settles in the marrow.

A game. We're not Starsky and Hutch. We're Alice and Bobby Brady.

"I just want to be alone for a while," I say.

The Nuclear Sleepover

The April 1979 cover of *Time* is a full-bleed photo of two big, purple towers and red alarm lights blinking in the twilight. I had never seen one of these structures before last week. But there isn't a person alive who doesn't know what they are now: cooling towers for a nuclear power plant. They are in a place called Three Mile Island and they are not cool. The headline is two words long:

NUCLEAR NIGHTMARE

The adults stop talking about it when I come into the room but it's impossible to miss the new vocabulary: fallout, core breach, radiation poisoning. I read the newspaper every day, trying and failing to convince myself that apocalyptic disasters only happen in the movies. A few weeks ago it was *The China Syndrome*. Now it's Three Mile Island. And if *The China Syndrome* is real, then what else can be?

President Carter and Rosalynn fly to the site to prove it's safe, but there aren't many people there to greet Air Force One because they've all fled their homes. Headlines in *The New York Times* proclaim "Milk Safe" and "Area Now Safe for Pregnant Women" but do little to calm the panic.

Howie has taken the "accident" in Pennsylvania more seriously than anyone else, retiring to bed for the past two days. My disappointment in him softens as his own frailty and fear come into stark relief. "We're getting whacked. Again," he says from under the covers when I try, unsuccessfully, to draw him out.

There's lots of pot smoking in the house but none of the giggles. The fissures in our nuclear family—the one that includes Howie and Carly—are illuminated and 31 Chestnut is now lonelier and more solemn than it's ever been. But it can't just be because a stuck valve in a power plant in Pennsylvania spewed coolant and torched the heart out of reactor number two. Howie is offline. Answers from Mama and Papa as to how to survive in a world with a nuclear meltdown are few, and I suspect the adults in my life don't have any. I retreat to my Secure Position but there's little here beyond the shrieking bite of the March wind. I'm losing all my hiding places.

Well, almost all.

Penny calls. Her husky voice is oddly high. She's scared. "Sleep over tonight?"

It's Friday so I don't even ask. I just go and call Mama later: announcing, not requesting.

Penny, clad in loose waffle long underwear and black T-shirt, pulls me into her room as soon as I arrive, brings out a thick, furry blanket, and invites me under, side by side, knees bumping. Occasional shivers rumble up my spine.

"Spike," she whispers. I look into her eyes, wet and desperate, and nod. "I don't think, if something happened. Like the radiation meltdown thing. I don't think my mom . . ."

"She'll always protect you. She knows how."

"Not this."

And it's true. It's Three Mile Island, not pet dander. And she's the most beautiful girl I have ever seen.

"I always wished that, one day, my powers would come out. Superpowers. When they were needed most. Just . . . *flame on!*" I say.

"That's a comic book, not real life," Penny says.

"I know. But things happen. Look at you. Look at your mom."

"It's different."

"Why?" I shift closer to her. She sits up.

"Let's change the subject."

I turn onto my back, rest my head on her thigh, and stare up at Leif Garrett, visible in the moonlight.

"What if I had the power to . . . I don't know . . . something like Johnny Storm."

"I don't think being a flying flame is going to help you if a nuclear power plant blows up."

"OK. Sue Storm, then. She can create force fields, like protective bubbles."

"Great. Then you can be like the boy in the plastic bubble. You have a John Travolta thing, kind of. A Jewish John Travolta—"

"No, not that kind of bubble—"

"Like a shorter, not hairy John Travolta."

"A force field bubble. They're impenetrable. And they make it so she can fly, so it's better than Johnny."

"I really need you to stop," she says, lifting her knees to her chest and pushing me off.

"OK." I drop it and we sit in silence for a long time.

"I'm sorry," she says finally. "Let's just go to sleep."

We curl together under the warm blanket. *I'm actually spooning a girl*, I think. Penny's hair smells like the woods, making my penis swell, and I have to pull back a bit so she doesn't feel it.

"Come back," she says.

I try to get as close as I can, folding at the waist so just that one part of me doesn't touch. But it's sticking out so I have to pull my hand back to tuck it under the waistband of my underwear. I pretend I'm just scratching.

Penny flips over to face me again. "Where are you going?" she whispers.

"Nowhere," I promise.

She puts her face right up to mine and kisses me. The touch of her lips overrides the emergency cooling system of my internal reactor and my face floods with radioactive isotopes. She pulls back, smiles softly. Fusion.

"I thought you said—"

"Shhhh."

"—they don't last." I remind her, unable to stop. I need to hear her say they do. It will.

"Don't."

I lean in to kiss her again but she shakes her head, smiling. It's over. "Once is enough. Now go to sleep."

I know that nothing will ever be enough, but this is so much more than I could have hoped for. I tuck my raging plutonium fuel rod away again, press my chest against her back, wrap my arms around her stomach and feel the bottom of her breasts graze my forearm every time she exhales.

Nothing but a thin layer of waffled cotton between us. Then the door opens and Laurie comes in, robes catching the twilight.

"Is someone in here with you?"

"It's Lou," Penny says without sitting up. I hold my breath.

"Oh, good," Laurie says. "I'm glad you're not alone. Louis, it's nice that you came over tonight. This is such a terrible time and friends need friends."

"Uh huh," I say from under the blanket.

"So just take care of each other," she says finally, closing the door. "And sleep on the floor, Louis. OK?"

"Uh huh."

"You two are so good to one another," she says from the crack she's left open in the door. "Maybe you'll get married one day. Wouldn't that be something?"

Penny's face is hidden in the pillows so I can't see her reaction. Mine could light up the room.

Laurie leaves the next morning to join the Red Sox in Florida for spring training and help them break the Curse of the Bambino. I stay over a second night and we kiss once more. Just once. I don't dare touch Penny in any way that could screw the pooch and she doesn't invite it.

I get home Sunday night, blood racing. Amanda grabs me the moment I walk through the door—she wants to show me the loft Mama built in her bedroom. "And she let me pick out new wallpaper! It's bright green with yellow flowers and we painted the loft bright yellow to match!"

I indulge her briefly on the way to my room. It's a sight, for sure. Mama's skills are undeniable.

Behind closed doors I flop onto my bed, close my eyes, and think of waffled long underwear and black cats.

Penny's Been Thinking, Gretchen's Been Drinking

Spring pops in Salem. Our campaign scuttled, the Man of the Year voting period ends with little fanfare and the nuclear fallout does have a half-life. Penny says I can't come over while her mom's away. President Carter gets attacked by a swamp rabbit while fishing in Georgia and Howie slowly returns to his old self. We make up like brothers, a couple of hugs and soft punches. The money for the job Papa keeps promising for Howie never comes. And with the work of lobbying voters in the most important election in modern American history behind us, we devote our evenings and weekends to house renovations and trips to the movies. All we can do is wait.

Papa and I sit in the backyard under a new sun that is warm enough for T-shirts. I can almost imagine being in this yard forever, in this place I never wanted to be. Even the bickering and whining of my little brother and sister take on a warmth and comfort that I have never felt before. Family, for all its mayhem, is warm, and it holds me.

The sudden lack of drama on Chestnut Street is as unsettling as it is comforting. For months, each day has been an unexpected adventure. Now, in the quiet aftermath, things feel more orderly. I can't help but feel the other shoe is about to drop.

Down the street, Glovey Butler approaches, her face determined. "I'd argue that *this* is more like what a centerfold should be," she says, marching into our yard with a yellow-framed *National Geographic*. The cover flutters in the breeze, a deep blue photo of a submerged scuba diver reaching up to pat the underside of a dolphin.

Papa takes the magazine in one hand, offering cheese, crackers, and nuts and a seat under the tortured branches of the bare Seckel tree. Glovey, dressed in black, opens a black umbrella to shield her white hair and whiter skin. I sit quietly reading *Doc Savage Magazine #3: Frenzy in a Frozen Hell!*

"Hey, take a look at this, Lou," Papa shifts. "Bird's-eye view. You're sitting right . . . about . . . here!"

I toss my comic on the chair between me and Glovey and lean over Papa's shoulder to get a closer look. "Wicked! It's our street."

And it is: A full-bleed of Chestnut Street covering pages 578 and 579 of the April issue. A thin strip of white space at the bottom carries this caption:

Tea from China and pepper from Sumatra helped build houses in Salem in the early 1800s. The town ranked among the nation's leading ports when it sent its sailing ships racing to the Far East for exotic goods. Chestnut Street, above, exhibits many of the handsome Federal-period homes built by sea captains and merchants.

Our house is right there at the center of the spread, six chimneys, my bedroom window, the patchwork slate of the roof, dark where shingles chipped off under my scrambling feet. The bay window of Frank's living room is half hidden behind the trees, which are full, just beginning to turn. The photo was snapped in autumn, from a helicopter. I search the windows for a sign of my face, staring out to see what was making that sound overhead.

"They did Chestnut Street and Marblehead Harbor," Papa says proudly, "the two most beautiful spots on the North Shore. They really got it right, those *Geographic* folks."

"So they did," Glovey agrees. "Apart from the grifters there at the end."

Papa ruffles the matte pages forward to a slightly smaller photo of Laurie Cabot, flanked by Penny and Jody, the three of them surrounded by Laurie's magic circle—thirteen or fourteen more witches, all in black. Aside from the three Cabots, I don't recognize the others. They might have worked at Laurie's magic shop downtown or been at the house on a past visit, but my attentions are always on Penny. Laurie has her hands on the shoulders of a young girl, but Laurie is barely smiling, and neither is the girl. Penny and Jody are also stiff-faced. Most of the other witches are smiling. There is one guy, the tallest, who stands beside Jody, his face nearly covered by his long frizzy hair, who looks especially angry, ready to jump off the page and go all warlock on the unsuspecting reader.

What are the chances that I'd live with a male centerfold, in a house that appears in a centerfold of a national magazine, in which the girl-witch love of my life shows up in the pictorial as well?

I'm thinking: *low*.

"They say witches find a more tolerant reception here in Salem than they did in 1692," Papa reads. "Louis, you're certainly a case in point," he adds, chuckling.

"Perhaps in some quarters." Glovey sighs.

"But look at this. Did you see the blue lightning bolt across the bottom of the page?" Papa holds the spread up and it's true: there is an odd, cobalt fracture that runs left to right, at the witches' knee level, from one side of the photo to the other.

"Is that radiation from Three Mile Island?" I ask.

"No!" Papa seems taken aback by the question. Then he pats my back reassuringly. "But it's unexplained."

"Hocus pocus," Glovey waves a wrinkled claw.

"Really, Glovey? When have you ever seen a photograph in the *Geographic* that was anything but flawless?"

"Read the sidebar," she says. "The people at Eastman Kodak say it's static electricity."

"Glovey, I hate to take issue with you, but I've had thousands of rolls of film developed in my time and I can't remember ever seeing anything like this, not just on a roll, but even on a single frame. And they say 'the same phenomenon occurs on every single shot, across multiple rolls' of the coven. I've been a skeptic all along, but this is pretty convincing."

"Cove," Glovey fixes on him. "I count on you to be a voice of reason in this otherwise unreasonable city. Please don't fail me now."

"They quote Laurie as saying the electricity present in the room forms the perimeter of their magic circle," Papa says. "Hard to argue with the evidence."

"I really can't abide this."

I surge with pride at my father's defense of Penny and her mother. He may revere Glovey, but that won't keep him from speaking his mind. And in his mind, as in mine, the magic is real.

We go inside when it gets cold, eat dinner, and I settle down to watch *Fantasy Island*—an episode about two kids who send their divorcing parents to the island hoping they'll fall back in love. Howie plops down beside me a few minutes in.

"I'll take *Fantasy Island* over Three Mile Island any day," I muse.

"A-fucking-men."

The phone rings. I don't answer it—I never answer it—but

Mama calls from downstairs a minute later and tells me it's Penny on the line. I jump up and into the hall to talk to her.

"Hey!" I launch into a stupid spiel about seeing her photo in *National Geographic*. "So wicked." But she doesn't want to talk about it. She wants me to know that she's been thinking. Thinking really hard. About me and our friendship. About what happened in her bed and the kissing and the whole superpower thing. About how she loves me so much, but not the way she thinks I think she does. And she meant what she said, back in the bathroom stall. "Remember when I said boyfriends and girlfriends never last?" she asks. I nod but can't answer out loud. "I thought a lot about that. About how good a friend you are. And I decided we're not going to kiss like that again. We can't. OK?" I shake my head, still unable to make words come out. "OK? Everybody else could just disappear for all I care, as long as we can still be friends. OK?"

I have nothing to say, so I just let the call end awkwardly, my throat tightening with grief. Because it's *not* OK. Maybe boyfriends and girlfriends don't last, but the panic and loss eating my brain will never stop. The gash in my heart won't heal. What is meant to be will never be. That's not how stories are supposed to end.

"How do I get her back?" I whisper to Howie when I return, fighting the urge to cry.

"Women just want one thing, gringo. They want to be heard. Listen to what she's saying. Be true to yourself, but make her feel heard."

"What if I don't like what I hear?"

"Then you just check in to Fantasy Island for a bit and hope for the best." Howie puts an arm around me and we go back to watching the show. A few minutes pass and the phone rings again. I'm up and answering before the second ring can finish.

"Hi," I say, heart hammering, hoping she's had a change of heart.

"I need you to come ovah heah." Gretchen. Ugh.

"Where?" I ask, shoulders sagging, eyes searching the ceiling for help.

"To the Fletchah's." Is she crying? "I'm babysitting. But I stepped on a nail. I'm bleedin' wicked bad."

"Call 911."

"I can't you butt fuckah! I'll get in trouble. Get ovah heah. NOW!"

I walk down Chestnut to Botts Court, where the Fletchers live, taking my time as I go.

Gretchen opens the door standing on one foot. Blood has soaked the sole of her striped sock and is dribbling small puddles on the floorboards.

"That's bad," I say, letting her put her arm around my shoulder as I lead her to the living room couch. It smells like cloves in here.

"No shit, shuhlock," she tries for edge but only gets to fear. I find a dishtowel in the kitchen and put it under her heel, then pull the sock gently from her foot.

"That's so gross," I say, staring at the violent wound, open wide enough that the gelatinous white meat deep within her arch is visible. "I think I'm going to barf."

"Shut up! Get me a Band-Aid, yuh puss bucket."

"You're going to need more than a Band-Aid," I reply, heading for the bathroom.

"Don't wake up the kids!" she shushes me. "It took me two ow-ahs to get them to sleep."

I come back with a roll of gauze, a near-empty bottle of Bactine, and some aluminum butterfly fasteners. Gretchen squeals when I douse the hole in her foot with what's left of the Bactine and grabs my shoulder, digging in with her stubby excuses for fingernails. "That huhts like a mutha fuckah," she moans softly.

I tell her about the electricity in all the photos of the witches while I wrap.

"Guess how much I caih?" Gretchen pulls away, finishing the bandage job herself.

"I'm just saying . . ."

"Whatevah. Do ya see the bottle of schnapps on the table theah? Bring it ovah." I do as she instructs and watch her chug three or four swallows before she takes another breath. "Now fill it with watah up to heah and come back ovah to the couch."

"Sure, your highness," I bow mockingly.

When I come back she sits up and has me put a pillow under her foot. Then she pulls off her sweater, revealing a thin tank-top blouse that I can see her bra through. "I need ta make out," she says. "Come ovah heah." She leans forward enough that I can smell the mint bite of schnapps, see the white curve of her breasts, which are bigger than I remember. "Come on!" she urges, pulling me toward her by my shirt and opening her mouth wide. I didn't brush after dinner and my tongue tastes like cottage cheese and noodles. But Gretchen doesn't seem to mind. Her tongue swirls around mine, licking it clean and searching around in the farthest corners of my mouth, clearing the dull taste and leaving a bracing alcohol-and-mint sweetness that makes me think of TV ads for fresh, clean feelings.

It's everything I want, just with the wrong person.

I press into her, trying to imagine Penny beneath me, but it's Gretchen, in all her fury. I reach beneath her blouse and she arches instead of contracting. I push her bra cup up and over, taking her full and naked breast in my hand, growing braver, squeezing in rhythm with her sharp, husky breath beside my ear. Gretchen jams her hips against mine and I feel a power surging that is new. Fearlessly, I push my hand down into Gretchen's pants. Instead of buckling up and bolting out, as I worry she might, Gretchen sucks in her silky belly and lets my hand pass, over the front of her panties to the soft drop and into a mysterious slipperiness.

We don't have enough time to button or compose because the front door opens right into the living room. The Fletchers are home early, staring straight at us. At Gretchen's bloody foot dangling. At my hand, emerging from her pants, unsure where to go.

I leave Gretchen to be berated by her employers in glaringly unheroic fashion, but even as I turn to watch the front door slam behind me I see the expression on her face, and it is one of affection, not anger.

As much as I am in Penny's thrall, Gretchen has unexpectedly carved herself a space in my heart, and just in the nick of time. She's the unforeseen radioactive catalyst in my own *Marvel Tale*, Issue #13, April 1979. Her mom may not be a witch and she may smell like cigarettes and talk like the late-night drunks at Dunkin' Donuts, but she believes.

I know what she feels like, and I want to feel it again.

What You Cling To

Bunny Yabba is paws-up. Pink eyes gone white. Finished.

Papa yells at me for twenty minutes straight. *Irresponsible. Lazy. Stupid.* I stop listening after a while and start thinking logistics for making a waterless bong I saw in *A Child's Garden of Grass* called a "steamboat."

Mama cries more than I expect. I'm not sure if that's about Yabba or me or something else—my heart's gone flat. The losses are piling up and I'm shutting down.

When I drop by Howie's room he's filling a bag with magazines and clothes. "Time to hit the road, Cochise."

"What? Where?"

"Home."

"Why? Again? Is it your mom? Her ankle?" I think *this can't be happening* but of course this is happening. It always does. "Can't we just wait until the votes come in? You're going to win. I know it."

"And that pays . . . a complete wardrobe. But no cash. Brother gotta work."

"But it will mean lots of work—"

"In LA," he says, and I know it's true. He puts his hands softly on my cheeks. "It's just . . . time."

"It's not time," I shake my head, "Not yet."

"The Buddha says you only lose what you cling to," he says. Another one of those sayings that say nothing to me.

"Well, I lose everything." Not just the houses. Everything. "Every friend. Every house. And now you. I didn't want to move to this stupid city. But then you came. You came. And for once, I was happy. We all were." This much is true.

"If you think of things that way you'll always be unhappy," he says softly, sitting beside me on the bed. "The Buddha says 'a spoon of salt in a glass of water makes the water undrinkable. A spoon of salt in a lake is almost unnoticed.'"

"I don't care what the fucking Buddha says. Or Lenny Bruce. Or Bob Dylan."

"OK. What *I'm* saying is that if you think of your life as a little glass then the hard moments, like this one, seem to fill every bit of the space you've got and they taste like shit. But if you think of your whole life as a big and magical lake, a wide-open adventure, then a few teardrops are just seasoning. They don't spoil the whole thing."

"*You're* spoiling it."

He gets up, softness leaving him. "We gotta go home. This isn't real life anymore."

"You mean it's starting to feel like real life. For the first time." Papa appears, right on cue.

Howie laughs. "Maybe *your* life, Jefe."

"Right. My life. Welcome to it. It's about time, you know?" He points to Howie's beads and the paintings and papier-mâché sculptures and the plastic toy characters all fucking each other in different positions on the mantle and the windowsill and the bedside table. "This den of iniquity is a fantasy. You can't live like this forever."

"Can't hurt to try," Howie argues.

"Really?" Papa snaps back. "Really can't hurt? Try raising a family while you're high all day. Making *bupkes*. Cheating on your wife. Try doing it that way."

"It's better than being gone ten hours a day and taking martini lunches. What's the difference?"

"Everything I do, I do to make sure my family is safe and sound. Everything you do, you do to make sure your dick is stroked. By *Playgirl*. By my secretary."

Howie goes back to stuffing his bag. Not looking at us. Mad but not mad. Processing it all. Uncomfortable with the way this is going. This isn't the Howie and Carly vibe.

"Hey, maybe if you got that mythical grant and hired me then you wouldn't be saying any of this," Howie blurts suddenly. "I can't support my family if you're not paying me. So I've been taking care of *your* family for you. I thought that was our deal."

"Sure. I appreciate everything you've done. But that's not a real job. And it's not my job to get *you* a job. Carry your own water."

"Thanks for the pep talk, Dad," Howie snips in a tone so unlike him. "When did you start believing you're The Man?"

Papa flashes red when Howie says this. Those wide Papa eyes, telling you that you just crossed a line. "I believe in reality," he says in a whisper. "You lost touch with that a long time ago."

"So many realities, Jefe. You just have to know how to dance between them."

"Look," Papa appeals suddenly, his color drained, an unconvincing smile fixing his face. "You're my brother. I don't want you to go. But I can see you've made up your mind—"

"No he hasn't," I push in, finally, feeling like this may be Papa's fault. And if it isn't, he's not doing enough to help stop it.

"He has," Papa snaps. "He's an adult. I'm sorry the grant never came through." Then to Howie, in a political shift that is as jarring as it is mollifying: "Louis is right. The two of you? Being here.

It's been one of the best experiences our family has had in a very long time. There's no way we're going to end it on this note. So tonight's a bon voyage party . . . Right after the bunny memorial. What a day."

Howie sighs heavily but he's smiling.

"I need you to give me a hand with this," he says, handing me a duffel when Papa is gone. I help, but I know he doesn't really need me.

"She was a little rabbit whose presence was rarely seen but always felt, here in this great house on Chestnut Street," Papa says, officiating over the funeral that precedes the bon voyage. We bury Bunny Yabba at dusk under the pear tree in the backyard. Atjeh paws the fresh earth and I kick her away as we take turns remembering our fallen family member.

"I can't believe this is happening all at once," Amanda shakes with new tears.

"April showers," Carly whispers, wrapping her arms around me and my sister. "But it's almost May. It's the cycle, love. Everything ends. Bunnies die, flowers fall, friends take different paths. But the flowers always come back. And it's all right here with us," she says, rubbing her warm palms on our cracked hearts. "We carry each other. Wherever we go. Do you feel it?"

"I feel it," Amanda whimpers.

"I feel it," Howie says convincingly, joining us low to the ground.

"I feel it," Mama says, and she's crying again.

"I feel it," I confess.

"We feel it," Papa adds, bouncing David in his arms. "And we feel hungry! Let's eat."

We say good-bye for the last time before bed. When we wake up, just like that, our friends are gone.

Part III

The
Center
Folds

The Anticlimax Doesn't Last Long

One week drags. Two. Penny averts her eyes in class, demateri-alizes when school is over. Gretchen deliberately fills the void, re-sponding to any opening I provide. We try hanging out after school at the pool at Salem State. She rides my back in the water, nearly chokes me with her ferocity, grinds against my tailbone, and lets me reach behind and push aside her red one-piece. The excite-ment is bracing but when I get home my mind drifts. I never imagined fingering a girl would feel like a consolation prize, but there it is.

Truthfully, everything is a consolation prize. The naked won-ders are gone. The extravagant scents, evaporated. But what I can't understand, or even admit, is that the unity Howie and Carly brought to our family is gone, too. I thought their spirit had rubbed off on all of us. How could it slip away so easily?

I spend my nights waiting for a ring. What I wouldn't do for a phone call, a telegram, a set of dashes and dots. There's no way to know what's happening out there in America. How many votes have come in. Who's in the lead. Whether the boner is truly the competitive advantage it seems or the turgid nail in the campaign coffin. They don't handicap this kind of race in the papers or on the *CBS Evening News*. It's a blackout.

Until today.

"Hey, *niño*." That voice, staticky and far away, pops the brittle bubble of feeling I've been holding inside. I hard-swallow a sob. "We won!" he shouts. "We won! Fuckin' A, motherfucker! Pat yourself on the back, son."

"I knew you would," I tell him. Grief plus distance plus victory equals numb.

"*We* would," he says.

But this is far from the triumphant scene I imagined of us sitting on the front steps, surprised by a Publisher's Clearing House type with an oversized check. We'd be dancing in the street, TV reporters jamming microphones in our faces. Uli and Papa and the converted Chestnut Street snobs lifting us on their shoulders and singing "We Are the Champions" at the tops of our lungs.

"So listen, they're sending me on a press junket as soon as I get back. Gonna see the world, score the new wardrobe, meet with the Hollywood elites, wine, dine, feel all fine."

"Wicked," I answer, aware there can be no real party without Howie here.

"And it looks like the tour's going to bring me back to Boston in July or August. So we'll get to celebrate together then, OK?"

My heart leaps a little. Settles. Too little, too late.

"Oh, and you're not going to believe this. We're in a truck stop in Nebraska and they're playing 'Disco Duck' on the jukebox. Somebody paid to put that on. I gotta go before my head explodes. But listen, you're the man. You're my *main* man. And you should feel all kinds of proud right now. Do you feel it?"

"I feel it. I do," I tell him, softening. "But mostly I'm proud of you. You worked so hard for this . . . I just wish you'd come back."

"Soon. Soon."

"Congratulations," I say. "I love you."

"We love you, too!"

Carly calls "We LOVE you!" over "Disco Duck" and they click off.

I stand in the front hall looking at the phone, the wallpaper peeling behind it. I pull at the frayed strip, stick the tip of my finger into the horsehair plaster, and dig a hole. The house has fallen quiet.

Playgirl received four million votes during the four-month voting period for Man of the Year. I have no idea how many came from the North Shore of Boston, but that doesn't diminish the thrill of pride when my signed issue arrives in the mail.

From a business standpoint, though, the June issue is a bit of a disappointment. Howie's not on the cover like Monique St. Pierre is for *Playboy*. It's just some guy and some woman, fully clothed and not particularly sexy. There's an interview with Joe Namath, an article about "What Men *Really* Do on Business Trips," and a blue and yellow banner in the bottom right corner that says: "Special Sixth Anniversary Issue: Our Man of the Year Contest Winner." It doesn't even have his name!

The Inside *Playgirl* letter from the publisher, Ira Ritter, introduces Dianne Grosskopf as the new executive editor but doesn't mention the contest.

Howie shows up first at the top of a painter's ladder opposite Jimmy Hakim, Mr. October 1975, and twelve other former centerfolds, as part of the sixth-anniversary centerfold reunion. Hakim is doing a Tony Manero: bright red polyester shirt with oversized collar spreading out over the shoulders of his black leather jacket. Howie's in a powder-blue three-piece, jacket slung over his shoulder and a look on his face that says *Hey, wait a minute* like something funny's going on. Because something funny *is* going on. Why, for one, is he sharing the ladder with Jimmy Hakim? I think he's one step higher, so his head is a millimeter or two closer to the top of the page than Hakim's. Higher than anyone else, as you'd expect for the Man of the Year. But it's by a hair.

The next page has an outtake from his original photo shoot. I haven't seen it before. It's a full nude, lying on his side, biting an apple, come-hither eyes. His circumcised penis, held loosely in his left hand, still has that plasticky makeup look to it. If you look closely you can see the tan line where his wedding ring should be. Maybe that's why they didn't use this shot the first time? But why now? And why not a whole new shoot? It's not even an exclusive spread because he's sharing this one with Rock Pamplin, Man of the Year 1976 and Man of the First Five Years. It says Rock just cowrote a song with Brian Wilson of the Beach Boys called "It's Like Heaven" that Shaun Cassidy will sing on his next album. But after the Brittania Jeans Hong Kong baloney I don't trust anything I read in *Playgirl*.

"I do know one thing," writes copy editor Dale Weintraub, who chauffeured Howie to a local LA morning show hosted by some guy named Regis Philbin, second name even stupider than the first: "Spending a day with this adorable creature convinced me that our readers made an excellent choice!"

And that's it.

"Bit of an anticlimax," Papa says, tossing the magazine on the bar and racking up the billiard balls for a game.

He's right, but I'm in no mood to concede. "He still won," I say, scratching on the break.

"Some victories matter more than others."

I drop the cue and it clacks loudly on the floor.

"Hey! That costs money!"

"Why don't you ever support him?" I ask hotly.

"Support him?"

"Yes."

"Did you not notice him living in our house and eating our food for almost twelve months?"

"And helping. And taking care of me and Amanda and David . . ."

"And that."

"*You* weren't." I gulp at the words, too late to pull them back, knowing it's unfair to compare his presence in the house to someone without a job.

He doesn't speak, just glares. Papa eyes. Then: "Where'd you get those sneakers?"

"Bradlees."

"Who paid for them? And that pile of comics in your room? Or this house?"

"That's not what I mean."

"That's what taking care of your family looks like," he says. "Not like smoking pot on the roof or driving a VW bus before you're even thirteen or going on a speaking tour of the ladies from the yacht clubs and canasta cliques. That's playing, not parenting."

"Maybe you should try playing sometime," I say.

"What the hell do you think I'm doing right now?!" he shouts.

The anticlimax doesn't last long. Within a week we learn that Howie and Carly will be on *Donahue*. Mama lets us stay home from school, eat popcorn, and watch in the TV room. We never get out of our pj's.

Phil holds up a copy of Howie's spread to his audience. "Can we talk about it for a second? Just for a second?" he asks plaintively. "Women have been posing nude in magazines for a long time, so it's about time that women have the same opportunity to look at men."

A bucktooth blonde lady in a white collared shirt and black vest raises her hand and Phil rushes to her with the microphone. "I agree, it's been too long. Men sit around all the time looking at women. It's our turn." She smiles proudly, having taken a stance, but the audience isn't going along.

"But I've heard from some," Phil says, scratching at his silver helmet, "that women are not as . . . how can I say this? . . . *positively* affected by that as men are."

"Well, they've never given us nice ones to look at before!" the bucktooth woman grins into the mic. This time she gets a laugh.

"Oh! Well, it's alright then. How many think it's alright?" Phil turns to the crowd. I've never watched this show before but I know it's huge and I'm amazed by it. One man in a room full of women, leading a conversation about the issues of the day. He claps along, kind of egging them on, but makes a face when not everybody joins in. He squints, holds the mic to his chest like something's hurting in his rib cage, and plays devil's advocate when needed. "It's, ahhh, just a little bit vulgar . . ." he says, allowing the prudish holdouts to vote their conscience. Phil approaches one of them gingerly and asks softly, "Will you talk to me? Help me out? Stand up for just a second. It's easy, really. If I can do it, you can do it . . ."

I've gotten so used to Howie and *Playgirl* and men posing nude I hadn't quite internalized just how radical this whole notion is for Middle America.

Sort of.

Phil lets us know that the magazine's annual readership has broken the twenty million mark, pushing it to number six of the most profitable newsstand magazines for women and sixteenth most profitable of all magazines for the decade. *They're all reading it.*

He takes the hand of an old lady objector and helps her to stand up.

"I think the children get into these magazines too much these days," she says.

"And you think it's worse for a man to pose nude than for a woman?"

"Oh, I think so. There's more there!" The crowd laughs wildly and so does the old lady. She rides the wave, then adds, "We're from the old school. We just don't go for a lot of the new things."

"I understand," Phil assures her. "You're going to be able to stay for the show, though?"

"Oh, sure!"

Phil holds up the fat boy photo first. "Cute, huh?" The audience agrees. "Well, here he is today." He holds up a *Playgirl* calendar with Howie on the cover. "I want you to meet *Playgirl*'s 1979 Man of the Year. Ladies and gentlemen, welcome Howie Gordon!"

The *Donahue* theme song starts to play, and here comes Howie in the powder-blue three-piece suit and tie.

"Look at him!" Mama says. "Look. At. Him!"

"He doesn't usually dress like that," Amanda lisps through the fingers in her mouth.

"What do you expect? Silk pants?" I say. "This is *DONAHUE*." Howie's waving to the crowd. He's smiling. He shakes hands as he comes down the aisle! He's practically bouncing to the stage to stand beside Phil. The audience, almost entirely gray-haired ladies, claps politely and smiles, some bashful, some disapproving. I know them all so well, the ladies from the JCC and the mah jong club. They're no different in Chicago. "I should be there," I say.

The show cuts to commercial—three things we discovered denture wearers hate about denture adhesives—and then we're back. And Carly's there.

"Carly," Phil says to her in his let's-be-honest way.

"Yes?" she giggles softly, smiling that bright moonbeam smile. The puffy eyes are gone. She looks happy.

"I'm not going to wait long to ask you this question: I mean how . . . what . . . what's it like to be married to a man who's in his altogether on every magazine rack in the country?"

Carly, smiling ear-to-ear, answers easily. "It's kinda nice."

"Howie . . ." Phil says, stopping and starting dramatically, "so, what's it . . . well . . . congratulations, you're the Man of the Year."

"Thank you," Howie just beams. He's there. He's famous. "THANK you!" he says again, like it's about time someone said something nice, instead of asking how weird it is. Or vulgar. Or wrong.

"They voted for you, huh?"

"Yes!" he nods and beams.

"So, what do you do when you're not having your picture taken?"

"I'm an actor, primarily."

"So, this is a nice bit of hype for you. I guess it's legal and . . ."

"Legal? Why did he ask that? Is Howie illegal?" Amanda asks, alarmed.

"No, he's not illegal. Listen," Mama says.

"It's a great role," Howie says, unleashing that trademark smile. "A sex symbol is a nice role to play and I have a year to try to perfect it. As long as you're going to be a symbol for something, sex isn't a bad thing to be a symbol for."

"Yeahhh . . ." Phil ponders this, takes a question from the audience.

"I'd like to know who does the voting," asks someone we can't see.

"*Playgirl* readers," Howie says. "Yourselves."

Phil takes a few more questions, then decides to widen the conversation after a bit.

"Dianne Grosskopf is here," he says, "and she is executive editor of *Playgirl*. You are the youngest executive editor of a leading magazine, are you not?"

"That's right," says a pretty woman in the front row.

"Are you the final judge and jury on this . . . ?" Phil gestures to Howie.

"Yes, I am," she laughs.

"How'd you get that job?" Donahue begins, then changes tack because the question sounds condescending. "In other words, do you review photos as well as candidates?"

"I'm the one," she laughs again. "I'm the dirty lady."

"I'm sorry," Phil tries to explain himself, "but I've got this mental picture. You know, the old cliché story of the guy, the movie mogul, that walks up to the little waitress at Schwab's Delicatessen and says 'you're gonna be a star!' You do that for men, don't you?"

"Little waitress . . ." Mama murmurs. "Feh."

Dianne nods in response, explains the *Playgirl* process a bit, then brings it back to Howie. "Howie became Man of the Year," she continues, smiling his way, "because his charisma came right through on the camera. His centerfold was one of our most successful because women could identify with him. His personality came across and it's very difficult—men are not as comfortable posing naked as women who pose for *Playboy*."

A woman who looks like a hippie version of Grandma Charlotte—bigger hair, bigger glasses—says, "I've never seen a centerfold and I don't know if I want to. But they look great with clothes on."

Phil offers to show her but then says, "I don't want to make you see it if you really don't want to."

"I really don't want to," Hippie Grandma laughs, "but I do like them with clothes on!"

A pretty blonde stands up and says, "I'm a nurse, so I look at bodies all the time in surgery. And we keep a poster of *Playgirl* in the locker room to remind us that there are decent ones around." The crowd erupts, and Howie cheers her on.

"I took off my clothes and got photographed," Howie explains to the audience, which has gradually begun to melt in the palm of his hand, just like people always do. Just like I did. "OK, that's a bit strange. Any time you're dealing with the beast of sexuality you arouse a lot of feelings, positive and negative. But I don't feel bad about what I've done, and I work at not getting involved in other people's disapproval."

But Phil isn't letting him off that easily.

"Hmmm . . ." he thinks aloud. "Women for a long time had to deal with the pressure that goes with not looking like those airbrushed people in *Playboy* . . ." Barbi Benton. Debra Jo Fondren. Susan Lynn Kiger. Jill DeVries. ". . . and some women have really resented the whole implication that bigger is better . . ." The audience titters. "If you took a profile of American women, most of them don't fall into that kind of D-cup thirty-eight . . . Maybe men are buying into that same game of centimeters and maybe that's worrying about the wrong thing?"

"I feel like that man with the white hair doesn't like him," Amanda says sadly to Mama.

"Some people don't feel comfortable with nudity," Mama answers her. "That's OK. That's what Howie's saying. You don't have to look if you don't like it."

"They're hung up," I tell them, seeing it all now. So 1950s! So McCarthyesque! "Repressed. Puritans."

Mama laughs. "What do you know about being repressed?" She's being soft but the comment chars.

"If adults spent more time worrying about nuclear death and less time worrying about naked boobs, we'd all be better off," I recommend.

"I agree with that," Mama nods, eyes on Howie.

"Then why don't you pose naked in a magazine?" Amanda snipes.

An older southern lady stands up and says she grew up around brothers and isn't intimidated by the human body and loves sex, but the male genitals are ugly and nothing will change her mind about that.

"Have you seen my centerfold?" Howie shouts from the stage. "Maybe that will be a first step!"

"Well, I've seen some of these magazines," the lady snaps. "I don't know if it was *Playboy* or *Playgirl* or what. But some of the things I've seen on the news racks today, they turn my stomach. They're revolting."

"You know, maybe we should take a break," Mama says, standing to turn off the TV.

Amanda, David, and I shout in unison, "NO!"

The debate heats up, Phil Donahue defending women, men, anyone who might be objectified by the "adult industry."

It's one thing if the Serpico guy gives us crap at the Bunghole, but another thing altogether when Phil Donahue and his audience of little old ladies do it on national TV. Howie holds his own, never backing down, making eloquent points whenever he's given a chance. And in the end, we still feel it's a victory. He gave it to the Man.

"Well, kids," Mama says when they roll the credits, "you just got your first taste of the rest of America. Let's be glad we live in a place that's a little more tolerant."

"Salem?" I ask, incredulous.

"Let's start with 31 Chestnut," she replies.

Howie returns to Boston to guest on WCVB's *Good Day!* *Playgirl* has him flying in and out the same day to make an appearance in Ontario, so we don't get to see him, but Mama lets us stay home from school again for the noontime broadcast.

Uncle Rick comes over after work for a drink and says he had to convince the men lunching at the bar across the street from the Sylvania plant to switch on *Good Day!*—a show they'd never watch. But when it aired, Howie interrupted John Willis right in the middle of the interview to face the camera and say, "I just want to give a big hello to Rick and all the Sylvania guys at the Sports Haven Bar in Salem. I know you'd rather be watching *McHale's Navy* than seeing this hippie who got naked for a magazine, but you're the best and so is Salem!" The guys went ballistic. And John Willis, for the first time in his career, went silent.

The tour rolls on and Howie sends postcards from the road.

"Shook hands with the Prime Minister of Canada!"

"Did event with two *Penthouse* Pets in Warren, OH, at a van show. I got no $$$ but did get good pair of car speakers."

"Met *Playboy's* Miss August in Hartford. Issue's not out yet but I predict she will beat all comers. Look for her: Dorothy Stratten."

Who's the Stupid Idiot Now?

School ends with a whimper. Salem sheds its chilly cloak and quickly becomes a furnace. Come August, Papa packs us in the car for a summer on Mount Desert Island in Maine, where Howie and Carly will meet us for a much-needed reunion. Amanda and I distract ourselves by searching the side of the road for punny signs of worship: THE WORLD'S GOT YOU DOWN, BUT THE SON ALSO RISES. GOD IS AT THE END OF YOUR ROPE. WHAT IS MISSING FROM CH___CH? U R. SALVATION GUARANTEED OR YOUR SINS CHEERFULLY REFUNDED.

"Wait until you see the place we're staying," Papa shouts from the front seat. "You don't get to be in a place like this unless you're born into a place like this. But you're about to be reborn, *kinder-lekh*."

We take a dirt road up a hill to the house the owners have dubbed The Studio. It's the smaller of the two houses on the estate, but it's big enough to sleep all of us, including Howie and Carly, when they get here, and the four Freedmans, who I wish weren't coming. Although it's sprawling for a studio, the house is musty and old and not at all the kind of place I would like to be born. But it does have one thing going for it: a freestanding log cabin out back, up the hill. Miraculously, Papa lets me claim it.

I retreat to my new Fortress of Musty Solitude and fill it with familiar odds, ends, and jujus:

- Super Friends sleeping bag, stuffing spilling out, frayed red interior skin as soft as can be.
- RadioShack Realistic SCR-1 complete portable music system ("record your own tapes 'off-the-air,' in stereo, any time!").
- A three-pack of Concertapes low-noise, high-quality blank cassettes for recording stuff off the radio.
- Three tapes I bought from the Record Exchange before we left (*Damn the Torpedoes, Born to Run, A New World Record* [ELO]) and one from RadioShack (*Top Hits of the '70s, Volume I,* including "Black Magic Woman," "Hold Your Head Up," "Brandy," "Baby Don't Get Hooked on Me," and "Come and Get Your Love").
- Atjeh's bowls, balls, and bones.
- New issues of *Vampirella, Doc Savage, Morbius the Living Vampire,* and *Playboy.* This last I swiped from Gramps's downstairs bathroom before we left. As Howie promised, Miss August '79 is something different—pure and dirty, blonde hair, brunette pubes, gloss-red pinup lips, Little Annie Fanny boobs, and lonely eyes, missing something (you) while also possessing something (you).
- Bucky Kerchak, the stuffed monkey I got and named so long ago now, given name for Captain America's side-kick, surname for the Mangani king and slayer of Tarzan's father, John Clayton Sr. Evil though he is, without Kerchak there is no Tarzan. Anonymous though he may be, without Bucky Barnes, Cap is just a boring bunch of mus-

cles and a shield. You're the superlative sidekick, chum. Deputy of Destiny.

- Dusty baggie of clumped pot leaves, stems, and seeds I've saved from weeks of pinching, plus water bong, rolling papers, and turquoise feather roach clip.

Atjeh sleeps inside my Super Friends sleeping bag with me, protected from the kind of late-night trouble that might get her evicted from the family for good. Every morning my chest is gouged. This morning she scrambles against me, thick tongue licking my cheek, reeking of the garlic calamari I pawned off on her under the table at dinner last night. I reach up lazily to grab her face and hug her closer. She tries to take a bite out of Bucky Kerchak and I pull the little stuffed monkey away from her.

Howie and Carly still haven't arrived, so I seek out Papa and he takes me for a drive along the coast to the edge of Echo Lake. He talks a lot about when I was born. What the world was like then, how things have changed, how big I seem to him now.

"I still want to be able to pick you up and put you on my shoulders," he says thoughtfully. I used to sit there, above the crowds at Fort Sewall summer concerts, holding onto his ears, watching the performers, the expanse of Marblehead Harbor sparkling behind them, for as long as I wanted.

We park in a small lot and quickly disappear into the woods. I move slowly, tired and still chilled, but Papa coaxes me forward. "The quicker you move the quicker you'll warm up. Then you'll really be ready for a swim."

I watch my feet as we move at a steady clip through the woods of Acadia National Park. The trail is quiet, no backpackers or dog walkers to be seen, just beaver-felled trees and the red-white flash of a milk snake flitting under a rotten log.

"Crystal clear waters at twelve o'clock," Papa says as we emerge from the woods. The lake is huge with massive stone slabs at the edge, angled like Evel Knievel ramps just begging for a jump. "Ready for a swim?"

He sheds his T-shirt, runs up a particularly tall granite ramp, and disappears into the rippling mirror image of the cloudless sky.

Papa's energy is infectious, and I strip my own shirt and kick off my sneakers. I can smell my pits—a relatively recent phenomenon, one of many. The water in the lake is cold, but nothing like the icy Atlantic that hugs the island. I surface quickly, bobbing and spinning slowly in place.

I take five deep breaths, prepping for a deep dive. On the sixth I go under, head first, and open my eyes. The secrets of the lake are all there, like hidden ruins. Below, I see Papa emerge from behind a huge erect slab in the darkest part of the lake, his white body catching the sun. He swims toward me and waves. I wave back.

As we surface Papa laughs, wiping the lake water from his mustache. I feel like I haven't seen him for so long.

"God this feels good," he sputters.

We swim for close to an hour, and I can't stop. Even as my body grows cold I feel an inexpressible tug from the crystal water. No one else comes. The moment is just me and my long-lost father, diving, rising, diving again.

"Look," Papa whispers, pointing above us as we float on the warmer surface.

Over our heads a tiny bird hangs motionless on the wind, its wings a gray blur, its belly emerald green. It darts left. Hangs. Right. Hangs. Turns and jets away toward a patch of tall purple flowers in the meadow.

"Hummingbird," he tells me.

"Wicked."

"That's one word for it. Ready to go?"

"Not yet," I answer.

"Me neither." So we dive under the water again, back to our own new world.

.   .   .

We walk back in silence, my heart still beating with the thrill of the lake, my skin cool and alive with new feelings. The muddy path has hardened to dirt mixed with the powder of a million leaves trod, crumbled, and battered by Maine—its rugged weather and countless hikers who have come before us.

"Well, it's summer now," Papa says. He stops, kneels, and pulls an aluminum canteen from his knapsack. "Screwed the cap on too tight," he grunts. "Great." He twists again.

"Can I try?"

"I got it. Hold on. Oof. Little bastard's gonna hold a grudge."

"I can do it."

"Go ahead," he snuffs, a note of exasperation atop the invitation. I put my palm over the cap, hold the canteen to my chest, and twist. "See? It's not going . . ."

I feel my breath release with the cap, a little splash of water reaches up to my chin.

He chuckles, gazes up at the leafy quilt over our heads. A hot breeze nudges the branches and a few rays of radiant light break through and scatter along the floor of the forest. "Or maybe I'm just getting older? Hm? I know you are." We start back, Papa trailing behind this time, talking as much to himself as to me. "How the hell did that happen? When did *I* get old?"

"You're not old," I call over my shoulder as I jump across the last wet bull's-eye of what had been a broad puddle.

"Oh?"

"No. You're only thirty-eight. There's a kid in my class whose dad is fifty-two!"

"His dad had him when he was forty? Huh. That's like if I decided to have a fourth kid next year."

"Would you?"

"Not on your life. I mean, I love my children. You know that.

But this is work." Pause. "I mean, the best kind of work there is. I wouldn't trade it for anything in the world. I'd never trade you."

"Is that an option?"

"No! Of course not. That's not what I meant. I only meant that three is enough. Three is great. I love my three children and that's a good number, a good group for spreading my love around to. Don't want to spread it too thin."

"And Mama," I say.

"What about Mama?"

"Three children *and* Mama. To spread your love around to."

"Of course, Mama. You, your brother and sister, and Mama. And like I said, you're getting older . . . We're almost at the end."

"The end of what?"

"Of the trail. I mean, the point where the trail splits ahead. Keep a lookout."

I Can Handle One More

Howie and Carly arrive, naturally sparkling but also subdued. They're full of countless stories from the victory tour, encounters with stars and sycophants, yet there is a feeling of deep exhaustion at their core. For the first time, I can see a slight hint of effort behind their affection. Unconditional love, conditioned by new demands on a previously unencumbered life.

We flip through their latest photographs together after dinner, and I am reminded of that first night, almost a year ago, when scenes from their exotic existence together unfolded on an illuminated sheet tacked to the wall.

"I wish I could have gone with you," I tell them.

"It was something to see," Howie replies. "Ain't easy being handsome for a living."

"What about the wardrobe?" I ask. "Did you get it yet?"

"Not yet, gringo. Still waiting on that prize. But how about this velour jacket? Scored it at the big flea market in Berkeley." He turns around to show the Japanese dragon embroidered in the soft black material on the back.

We ooh and ahh and keep looking at pictures until Amanda stands up suddenly.

"It was better with you here," she says. "There, I mean. With us. You should stay with us."

"Oh, we missed the Coves!" Carly tells us. "You are our numero uno *familia segundo*."

"A-fucking-men," Howie testifies.

I look to my parents, Mama teary, Papa nodding approvingly. I'm grateful they've made this happen, again. And here in a musty summer house six hours north of Salem I am aware, for perhaps the first time, that where we are is less important than who we are with.

Steve, Enid, and their kids arrive a few days later, adding a new layer of chaos. The adults pad around in their Docksiders, sample the wines Steve collected on his recent vineyard tours, take turns cooking odd foods: salmon pâté balls stuffed in avocado holes; greasy green beans with chunks of garlic; blueberry ginger cookies; chicken with burnt skin; scallion pork dumplings, burnt in the pan. They drink, play Yahtzee and shoo us away.

Howie is the center of everyone's attention. "What's Phil Donahue like?" "Who did you meet in Hollywood?" I scoff. Where were *they* when we were posting fliers and lobbying voters?

I finally manage to get him away from the group and show him my cabin.

"It's a score!" he says. "Bachelor pad extraordinaire!"

"I like having a place to myself," I confirm. "Separate."

Howie lays on the bed, stares at the ceiling, and runs his hands through his hair. "Kind of like your Secure Position?"

"It is," I say, not having made that connection but in total agreement.

"I've been thinking about that notion," he tells me. "All this time on the road, I've been thinking about where *my* secure position is." I want to suggest Chestnut Street but I know that's not where he's going. "I'm thinking it might not be LA. I'm not getting the good vibe there. But that's where the work is. I don't know, we'll see. But if I'm honest, it's Berkeley. I'm home there." I nod, knowing and resigned. "You need to come out. California! You haven't been there since . . . when?"

"Since I was five."

"It's time, amigo. It's time. You'll see. The people are decent, nature is everywhere, and the girls are cute as can be. We'll eat tacos, walk the Golden Gate, and hit the naked beach near Pacifica!"

"Can I stay with you?" I ask, ready to fly.

"As long as you want. Any time you want. Just ask the folks." He sits up and puts an arm around me. "You have a second home there."

"It'll be my ninth, but that's OK," I tell him. "I can handle one more."

These moments with Howie are fewer than I would like, but I have a new distraction to occupy my time and thoughts. The nanny working for the family in the mansion up the hill grabs my attention by the throat. I've seen her coming and going on the path, little kids in tow, all blonde hair and white teeth, but we've yet to meet in person. That hasn't stopped me from making her virtual acquaintance in the privacy of my sleeping bag. As Penny made me forget myself and Gretchen made me forget Penny, so the summer goddess on the hill has possessed me anew. I forget what is missing and obsess about what might be.

Then one night, Yahweh decides to show mercy. He brings the vision to my cabin door in tight jeans and white Izod concealing a body built for a centerfold.

"Hi, I'm Sarah. From LA," she tells me.

"California?"

"Maine."

"LA's in California . . ."

"Lewiston-Auburn, silly. We call it LA." She walks over to my RadioShack Realistic SCR-1 and presses EJECT. "*Damn the Torpedoes*? I don't know this one," she says, holding the white Tom Petty cassette. "Do you like James Taylor?"

"Sure," I say, nodding. I like anything right now.

"Maybe I'll bring some by . . ."

"Sarah!" A gruff command from the top of the hill, plainly urgent.

"I have to go," she says, suddenly scared and already out the door. "Maybe we can hang out after my kids go to bed?"

I look for her over the next few days but she never shows. I sneak up to the mansion on the hill a few times, even knock once, but no one answers.

"What are you doing up there?" Papa says when he sees me ambling back down the dirt road one morning. He's wearing a red T-shirt with gold deco lettering: MARRIED.

"Nothing. Just looking around."

"For the babysitter?"

"Who?"

"I saw her. Give me a little more credit than that. I don't blame you. But I think they went sailing for a few days."

"Oh," I frown.

"I want you to take your brother and sister down to the dock," he says.

"Babysit?! It's vacation," I whine, but he flashes Papa eyes and I know I've lost.

I'm the only one who knows how to put a worm on a hook, and I do so dutifully. "I don't want to fish," Amanda sighs. "Me, too," David echoes. "I don't want to."

"Just fish," I tell them. Just shut up and fish.

My experience fishing has taught me that this activity is typically 99 percent waiting and, if you're lucky, 1 percent fish. But Mount Desert Island isn't typical. This is a place where hummingbirds visit you while you swim and summer goddesses appear at your door. So I shouldn't be surprised when a silvery school erupts beneath us. Suddenly, it's impossible *not* to catch a fish. Just drop a line and pull. It's thrilling. Magical. Until it becomes the scene of an epic fish massacre. After five minutes of hooking and landing we are inundated with dozens of flopping fish. Back at the house Papa informs us that our gift of thirty-seven slayed pollock is all but worthless.

"The only thing mushier than grilled pollock is oatmeal. Maybe we can make a stew."

He does, and it is disgusting. I go to bed hungry.

Sarah finally returns around eleven thirty. The lantern is still burning, as it has been each night before, but I fell asleep a while ago. "Are you awake?" she whispers, closing the heavy log door against the settling cold.

"Yup," I assure her, rubbing my eyes.

"OK if I come in?" I nod eagerly, sitting up and trying to get my bearings. "It smells kind of fishy in here." I shrug. "I brought some music. Where's your player?" she asks, pulling a white cassette from her back pocket. *Mud Slide Slim and the Blue Horizon.* I pop it into my little deck.

We position ourselves on the bed and start to kiss, as if we'd been discussing it all along. It actually seems like it's the only thing *to* do. Getting to know one another in any other way would be mere nuisance. Whatever we do here, no one will know anyway.

Atjeh starts whimpering from underneath the creaking springs of my bed and I kick her out of the cabin. She claws at the door for the next ten minutes and then finally quiets down.

I wrap my arms around Sarah, rubbing her back as we rub

tongues. When I reach for the clasp of her bra she leads my hands around to her chest, putting her covered breasts into the palms of my hands. I feel like an archaeologist who just discovered two precious golden eggs, and I clasp them reverently. She moans softly in my ear and I start to fill my pj's, thumbs circling the padded center of her bra cups in search of nipples. Sarah grinds her Dorothy Stratten body against me but when I try to slip my hand under the polo shirt she forces it down between her legs. I feel the heat below the denim, a vague dampness, and my blood surges down, evacuating all my extremities save one.

We're gonna do it. We're gonna do it.

I probe with my mouth more deeply into hers. She tastes like Jolly Ranchers—pure, fruity, so different from Gretchen's menthol smokes and Tab residue. I press the heel of my palm against her tilting crotch, searching for some elusive release, then slip my fingers up toward the waistband of her jeans. She grabs my wrist and moves my hand back up to her breasts, coos again in my ear.

"I should go," she says but then she kisses me again and we are back at it. *Mud Slide Slim* plays through another three times. Somewhere around the middle of the fourth round of "Hey Mister, That's Me Up on the Jukebox," I unsnap her jeans and raise the elastic band of her panties with shuddering knuckles. I can see paradise by the dashboard light.

We're gonna do it. We're gonna do it.

Sarah bites my earlobe, her voice raw and impossibly sexual. "I'll get in trouble if they know I left the kids alone in the house."

"You left them?"

"Yeah, the parents won't be back until after one. They always stay out that late. And they drink a lot, so they come home and don't notice much. They just make a lot of noise and then flop into bed in their clothes."

"You can stay with me."

"You're different than the LA guys. Sweet." She rubs my thigh the way you scrub a floor. "I'll come back again. I like you." We kiss once more, long, and then she walks out the door. "Keep the tape," she says. "And think of me when you listen to it."

The one thing I *don't* need is to hear "Love Has Brought Me Around" again. I huddle under my sleeping bag, trying for a solo performance, but my crotch kills and I can't seem to do much with it.

"Blue balls," Papa tells me in the morning when I explain what kept me up all night.

"What?"

"Was it the au pair from up the hill?"

"I hung out with her for a little bit."

"You mean made out?" he prods.

"Do I need to go to the doctor?"

"Nope. You need to go back up to your cabin and finish what you started."

"But she went home."

"That's not what I mean," he says, sipping his coffee loudly. "Do you have any *Playboys* up there?" I shrug. "Well, go and use them. Everything's backed up in your pipes. You need to clear the system. It won't feel better until you do." I don't know how to respond. "Go on," he nudges. "Better than getting a VD shot, right? That's what ends up happening if you go all the way."

"It does?!"

"With the wrong girl. We'll talk about it later. Go."

The summer days are chaotic, noisy, unplanned. Adults fly in different directions, making exotic foods, disappearing without warning, yelling about Ronald Reagan and welfare reform, whispering about cocaine and cancer. The kids lose themselves in puzzles, arguments, and the woods.

I call Uli every morning to let him know how far I didn't get with Sarah the night before. "That's so basil," he says each time, breezing past the failures and focusing on the details. "What color are her panties? Is her bra padded or lacy?"

Atjeh absorbs the wild spirit of Maine, nipping and barking relentlessly. David stomps around the house in flippers and mask, shouting "I love you, Papa!" through a snorkel. At dinner, Atjeh gnaws the snorkel in half.

"It's not easy defending this dog," Papa says. "But look at those eyes."

Howie retreats to his room with Carly more than ever.

We are all together in the studio, but something is keeping us apart. Papa says it's just the summer way, "Time to do your own thing."

We are banished each evening at seemingly random times, and I return to my cabin to console myself with Sarah's utter, amazing, forever foreplay that is never consummated. Human beings can't possibly be meant to withstand this kind of abuse! Papa said, "When you can, you're going to LOVE it," but I can't and I don't. Strangely, I find myself missing Gretchen. She may not be as pretty or well-endowed as Sarah, but she's easy to be with in ways I never considered.

Amanda, David, Rebecca, and Matty are banging at the cabin door, then bursting in, filling the space with their noise and bustle.

"Howie's making pancakes," Amanda trills.

"Can I read this comic, Lou?" Matty asks from the corner.

"Come have pancakes!" David says. "He's making them shaped like flying saucers!"

"Get out!"

The kids touch everything on their way out, a begrudging pancake train of brats.

"Pollock stew?" Howie calls when I finally show.

"Blech. How come you're up?"

"Rough night around here," he says softly, flipping a UFO burnt side up. "Rough night. I don't like sickness."

I nod, flashing on the late-night echo of Enid's horrible bark.

"So we haven't talked about our next move, hombre." Howie shakes his head, clearing his mind and changing the subject. "Burt does *Cosmo*, he gets *Smokey and the Bandit*. I do Man of the Year, but I'm not Paul Michael Glaser just yet."

"Burt didn't actually show everybody his penis," Carly says, shuffling into the kitchen, bleary but beautiful.

"That should make me a bigger star!"

"Not based on size," says Papa, his perm sagging and askew, cup of coffee in one hand, newspaper in the other.

"I didn't get into this line of work so people could forever comment on the length of my dick!"

"Should have thought of that sooner." Papa fake sighs, pats me on the head.

"I think you should go back on *Donahue*," I say. "All they talked about was whether or not it's right to have naked guys in magazines. They should do another one, talk about the new masculinity."

"Big word," Papa says.

"Amen, *niño*. I can't complain about being on a national TV show, but shit . . ."

"What about that other show?"

"Which? *Merv*?"

"Yeah, *Merv*."

"I actually got the call: 'Do you want to do the *Merv Griffin Show*?' At least, that's what I thought they were asking. But I don't have Hollywood ears or something, because what they actually said was: 'Do you want to do Merv?' See? I hear, 'Do you want to be on the *Merv Griffin Show*,' a big fucking afternoon television show. So I said hell yeah, and they said, 'Well, if you want to do *Merv*, you've got to *do* Merv.' And I go WHAT? And they said it again. 'You gotta DO Merv. You gotta suck his dick.' And I said, I don't think so. I don't think I want to do Merv."

"Howie?" Mama says.

"Princess!"

"Are you talking with my son about sucking Merv Griffin's penis?"

"Well, this isn't a case of *actual* dick sucking. It's a cautionary tale. The temptations of stardom and those who prey on the tempted . . ."

The warm pancake smell turns from amber to acrid as we realize all at once that no one is watching the pan.

I escape the after-breakfast banter and lie flat on Howie and Carly's sheets. I think I smell their waking sex, imagine how it looked, stretch my body, escaping into their warm world. My hand hits a hard object under the pillow and I pull out Howie's journal.

I feel my heart stop with the idea, already morphing into action, that I am going to read the latest installment. Not that this is off-limits. He always says it's an open book. But as my own journal gets more and more private, the idea of reading his feels increasingly treacherous. I close the door silently and sit against it.

He has underlined the title for this entry: "Alive in the Middle of a Post Card."

Mid-morning in Maine where Americans vacation with "Summer Drinks" rules. That means get your own. The day is filled with constant rapid fire organizing and moving, kiddie shuffling and doggie dodging. A lot of people in a little house. I've kept pace by imbibing intense drugs and bouncing off the wall. Today, I've had it up to here and come out of bed grouchy because screaming little Rebecca and Dave have broken into my dreams with absolutely repulsive kidlet squeals. Carly takes a birth control pill and we both feel the relief inherent that our present "vacation" is only a temporary plight.

I am sick of children and the wolf-coyote "Dog" that pretty much is a 90% source of irritation and 10% pure awe.

Food is King here and governs the flow of everyday TRAFFIC. I am yet to submerge myself into anything but food, kids, drugs, and ponds. I think it's time to clean some cobwebs out and pay attention to restful things.

I fling the book onto the bed and take this in. When he says he is sick of children, I know he means the little kids, not me. And I am sick of them, too. It explains why he and Carly are around less than ever, taking off when they can, sleeping until after we've all left for the pond. Why Papa takes long runs alone on the carriage trails every day and Mama bakes treats, picks berries, goes antiquing. She ends every day with a swim in the pond. Steve and Enid stay close to home, leaving the kids to wander. Matty gets lost in the woods for real and we have to call the police. A state trooper picks him up a mile down the road around dusk. Everyone cries, scolds, eats more pollock stew. The more scallions you sprinkle on top, the easier it is to swallow.

New Year's Eve in August

All these days are disappearing. There's never enough time with Sarah and she still won't touch my business. Never enough time with Howie and he still hasn't really explained how our partnership will proceed once he flies back to Berkeley. I keep trying to formalize both relationships but the next thing I know Mama's putting a plate of Elvis sandwiches in front of me, arm around my shoulder, kiss on my *keppie*, reminding me that "Tonight's our last night. Birthday night, and all together."

"All that's missing is Dick Clark," Howie says, pecking Mama on the top of her head as he walks by. "But I'll take the Hunan Princess over him any day."

Mama blushes and Papa says, "Hey! You've got plenty. Keep your hands off my one." He points to his MARRIED T-shirt, but he doesn't move any closer to Mama.

The adults dress up in the evening, fill baskets with food and drink, then go up to have a pre-party cocktail with Sarah's boss, the jerk on the hill. Carly sews two pairs of white drawstrings for my parents and presents them to Mama and Papa as a going-away, wasn't-this-a-wonderful-year? gift. They immediately slip into the loose pants and model for the group. Papa tops his off with a navy blue sweater dotted by sailboats. It's uncharacteristically preppie, but something on Mount Desert Island is rubbing off on him. Mama wears a matching white snap jacket with Nehru collar. Uncharacteristically hip, but then, she's let her hair down more than usual this summer.

"Do we have to spend time with that inbred blueblood?" Howie asks?

"Gotta kiss the ring," Papa slaps him on the back by way of encouragement.

"Listen," Steve, the wine connoisseur, says to Howie. "I'll bet you ten bucks this guy's going to have a wine cellar to kill for, but it will be filled with crap. So when he serves you his pricey vinegar, I'll give you the signal and you tell him 'it lacks a certain varietal character' and he'll know the hippies know more than he does about grapes."

"It's a plan," Howie agrees.

When they return we are all given something to carry down to the dock for the end-of-everything party. Papa's peppering me with more queries than I can answer. "Nice way to celebrate your birthday, tonight, isn't it? New Year's Eve in August? All together? Hard to say good-bye. But a good summer, don't you think? Memorable summer? What was your favorite part? I've got a few favorites. Favorite parts. But I want to know yours. Yours first," he urges as we make our way along the wooded trail.

I look at him curiously, wondering why the hell he's talking a mile a minute. "Yeah, I wish we could stay forever . . ."

"Not realistic. Everybody's got to work. But work is good for you. Builds character. Not to say that a bit of vacation doesn't, too. This has been good for everyone, I think. Gives you time to think. Relax. Remember what's important in life."

"I think it's important to—"

"Also reminds you what you can do without. Why are we living? What's it all for? Need to sort that out, make decisions, act. You can't wait forever for life to just turn out the way you want it to. You have to grab it. Don't abide boredom, Louis. Understand what I'm saying? Don't let it rule your life. That, and anyone else's expectations. They don't matter in the end, and if you follow the desires of others you never realize your own. You need to make a move. Take a stand. Don't apologize. See?" He catches a breath in the midst of the stream of words. I stare blankly at him now. "What? Am I talking too much? It's not me. Sorry. See . . ." he slows, pulls me out of the group trundling down the fragrant, wooded hill. "We had a bit of a party with our wealthy friend up the hill."

"OK."

"How did that Sarah end up treating you? Chastity buckle loosening at all?"

"What?"

"I just mean, did you get a little more relief? You can't expect too much at this age, but at the same time it's not fair to have to suffer."

Howie appears alongside us. "That guy's a dick," he says to Papa.

"Who?" Papa asks over his shoulder, his cautious shuffling down the hill turning to a flat-out run.

"Richie Rich Cokehead."

"Did you tell him it lacked a varietal character?" I asked.

"NO. I was all ready to show that snoot. But every bottle that came out Steve just kept shaking his head, giving me the ix-nay. And then the flush fucker pulls out the Château Lafite Rothschild and even I know it's slam dunk. The rich keep on keeping on, Hutch."

"You'll be rich by next year," I assure him.

Everyone flops down in the center of the dock. David snuggles against Mama, who stares off to the edge of the harbor.

Steve and Enid arrive a few minutes later, moving slowly. She holds her head kerchief against the breeze and settles down next to Mama. Steve wraps a flannel blanket around her, though it's one of the warmest nights we've had.

"Start with the '61 Château d'Yquem," Steve says.

Papa passes glasses around to the group, pours apple juice for the kids. "Here's to friends," he says as the sun drops. "Thank you for being with us through thick and thin. We love having you here."

"And here's to the Man of the Year," Mama adds.

"You mean me?" Papa mugs.

"I mean Mr. Gordon. Thank you for spending this year with us. The two of you . . . you're family . . ." She chokes painfully on the word, smiles sadly. "Family now. And no one wants to lose family . . ." And then she starts to cry, in front of us all. I feel it, too.

"Oh, my sweet Hunan Princess," Carly says, hugging Mama tightly. "It's just the end of the chapter, not the book."

"Can we look on the bright side and toast to the other man of the year here?" Howie's voice rises over the soft weeping all around us. "This marvelous boychik is thirteen today. That's man stuff. And I know there's no bar mitzvah here but we can do a little ritual ourselves, right?" He looks at me seriously: "You are circumcised, though, aren't you?" He doesn't wait for an answer. "Good. Because that's what my dad would call a *shanda for the goyim*. And it's the least fun of all the mystical Jewish rituals we have. I'd much rather put you on a chair and carry you around while we dance the hora than pull out my shearing scissors."

"Maybe later," Papa says. "Let's try the pâté first."

"Pâté, shmâté. This is our boy," Howie presses on, adopting a Russian accent, "joining the legion of strong-like-bull men! But also joining the human race with his heart and his generosity intact. You are a special someone, Louis Cove. And we love you. L'chaim!" he shouts, and everyone raises a glass and repeats, "L'chaim"— to life.

Uncomfortable with the attention, I lie back on the dock. The sun is tucked halfway into its horizon, turning the sky-screen blue, then indigo, then orchid. Going for beta. Leaving alpha behind.

I look back over my shoulder at the group: Mama stretched out, lying back on her elbows and looking out at the harbor. Matty, Amanda, and David rooting around in the bags of potato chips and Fritos. Enid huddled close to Steve, trying to stay warm in her robe even though the rest of us are in T-shirts. Howie and Carly kissing. Papa serving cheese and stuffed olives, pouring drinks, gracefully sliding along the dock in his Docksiders. Sarah promised she'd be here . . .

I turn back to the water, stare deep into its cold, clear depth. I can see the bottom, maybe ten feet below. A crab shoots out from under the dock, senses me, and disappears. As the world darkens I see sparkles below suspended like stars shimmering, winking on and off unexpectedly, and the display sucks my breath away. Fallout from Three Mile Island, I wonder? No. Too beautiful. My heartbeat rises and I turn again, ready to tell everyone about the magic dust bringing the sea to life—a million stars shimmering right below us—but then think better of it, wanting to keep the secret to myself a few minutes longer. It is so alive and inside me, the same feeling I had when I was in my cabin at four in the morning, with Sarah all over my skin and in my mouth.

"How about some fireworks?" Papa asks. "Our neighbor on the hill gave me some. And he's bringing more."

"There are fireworks down here," I say.

"What do you mean?" Amanda asks, sliding alongside me. Everybody moves in my direction and the dock swings around to compensate for the shift. "Oh, look. There really are fireworks in the water!"

"Poseidon's lighting up his candles for you, my man," Howie declares, arms open, accepting me as I wrap against him. "Happy birthday!"

"Happy birthday," Papa echoes. I turn to look at him, seeing me in the arms of another man, and my heart heaves with guilt. I break from Howie, smelling of wine and sea, to hug my father. And he hugs me back, hard. His love as strong as ever.

Just then, Sarah appears on the dock in cutoff shorts and a white T-shirt knotted above her waist. "Happy birthday," she whispers and kisses me on the cheek. The whole dock hoots in approval.

"This is literally the most magical place on earth," Carly says, staring into the dazzle of the phosphorescent water. And then she begins to sing that song again:

> *Love of my life I am crying,*
> *I am not dying,*
> *I am dancing.*

Sarah pulls me to her. "I wish I could go home with you. Your family . . . they're not like other families. *Definitely* not like mine. I want to be part of this one. Part of yours."

It's OK, I think. *It's actually OK.*

Mama and Enid join Carly and sing.

> *Dancing along in the madness,*
> *There is no sadness,*
> *Only the song of the soul.*

And then, just like on the record, we all leap into the chorus, exchanging partners, spinning until the dock is spinning with us, louder and louder beneath the last bit of life left in the sky.

> *And we'll sing this song,*
> *Why don't you sing along?*
> *Then we can sing for a long, long time.*

Why don't you sing this song?
Then we can sing along,
Then we can sing for a long, long time!

Out of the corner of my eye I see the rich guy from the mansion on the hill. He has appeared silently at the shoreline, a cigar clamped between his teeth and two live roman candles under each arm, unleashing a spray of blazing magnesium red fireballs over the blackening water.

"Happy New Year!" someone shouts. "Here come the '80s!"

Apologies to the
Emotional Barometer

Time slips, unmemorable in the absence of our friends. Our house always seems big, but with Howie and Carly long gone it's colossal. And hollow. This time they are gone for good, Mama is locked away in the basement framing prints or running errands, and Papa, who usually fills any available space, suddenly isn't. The spontaneous soirees are no more. I should be grateful for the calm. I should be.

Aged out of the Alternative School, I move on to something new. That polychromatic room with a single, empathic teacher and a—finally—familiar set of faces, has been replaced by a complex of fluorescent industrial hallways and cells that host besieged teachers and druggies who smoke Parliaments and listen to AC/DC, Foreigner, and REO Shitwagon. Combine a hospital, a prison, twenty Charlene Smutches for every Uli and Penny and you get my new high school. I feel like Mac McMurphy, locked in the Cuckoo's Nest, praying for Chief to mash the mercy pillow on my face and let it end.

Sarah's house in "LA" is 129 impossible miles from mine. Uli,

Gretchen, and Penny have scattered to other schools. I'm starting fresh, where fresh is a door closing behind me, not a window opening onto a new world. Fresh is time and place doing that familiar shuffle beneath my feet. Frozen never sounded so good.

It's a September school night but Mama announces that she's going out on her own for the evening. A first. Papa says he doesn't feel like cooking, also a first. He suggests Victoria Station for popovers and prime rib. "Plus you can ride in my new Celica," he says as we head out the door. I like the new sports car he's purchased. We never had two cars before. I wonder if he'd let me sit in his lap and try it? Walking out the door, Amanda looks left, right, then says, "I keep looking for the minibus. I wish it would come back."

I invite Uli, who I haven't seen in a few weeks, and we punch and wrestle in the back of the silver hatchback.

"Tell me about your day," Papa asks when the Victoria Station waitress delivers our entrees. "Worst part, best part."

"Worst part was . . . ummm . . . I can't say." I take a bite of my Reuben, extra Russian dressing squeezing out the sides and greasing my chin. "And the best part? Watching *Rabid* on cable after school."

"*Rabid* was on cable? During the day?"

"Yup."

He sighs briefly, and then says, "But what's this about the worst part? You can't say? That's not how this works. So *say*." He wags a finger at me and then uses that same finger to smooth one side and then the other of his mustache. I fidget. "You're trying to stall. Tell us the truth."

"I got in trouble."

"At school?"

I nod.

"For what?"

"I gave a girl a copy of *Delta of Venus*."

"Anaïs Nin," Papa explains to Amanda and Uli. "She was a lover of Henry Miller's. One of the greats." And to me he says,

"Well, at least it's quality. But you're not supposed to bring that stuff to school, Einstein."

"That's what I learned at school today."

Uli laughs. He knows I spent all of last night smoking pot and reading the book, which was on the shelf in the TV room alongside Isaac Bashevis Singer and Philip Roth. He knows I jerked off five times, about once every three chapters. But at least I'm on to the sophisticated stuff from the bookshelf instead of the bathroom or under the bed.

"And you thought this girl . . ." Papa nudges.

"Veronica."

"OK. Veronica was the right kid to share this book with?"

"She gave me something so I wanted to give her something." I touch absentmindedly at the serpentine talisman hanging from a chain around my neck.

"Fair enough. Moving on. Uli? Best part?"

"Ummm . . . My mom bought me a new derailleur for my bike?"

"A new derailleur, eh? What do you have now? Bianchi?"

"Peugeot."

"Good choice. Not a Bianchi, but you know your stuff. And worst?"

"When Lou gave Veronica that book instead of me."

Papa slaps his knee. "Ha! Extra points for honesty. You get dessert. Amanda? Best and worst?"

"I don't have a best or a worst. Everything was the same," she says.

Papa squints doubtfully, rips a popover in half and butters it. "But I have a question for you," Amanda continues.

Papa clears his throat. "OK. Well, the worst part of *my* day had to do with a new welfare policy that's seriously making me reconsider my faith in government . . ."

"It isn't about your best or worst," Amanda interrupts.

Papa scowls at the affront. "But we're *doing* best and worst."

"I'm not." Amanda, still a few months shy of eleven, sounds so unlike herself I can't help but look her way. What is that sound? Not angry. Not hysterical or whining. Just flat. There isn't really anything to her voice. Just an out-of-place monotone from the slight girl with the straight brown hair and the ugly new bionic glasses.

"Alright then," Papa recalibrates because he's heard the same unfamiliar tone. "Fire away."

Amanda brings her hands from her lap to the table and folds them neatly in front of her. She looks plainly at Papa and says, "Do you remember how you always said that you and Mama would never get divorced?"

My father clears his throat. "I remember." Papa's voice is different, too, now. Uncharacteristically soft. He takes a sip of beer and licks at the foam in his mustache.

"How come they have three kinds of carrot cake here?" I ask, feeling a sudden urge to change the subject. "Since when do they make cakes with vegetables? That's disgusting."

Amanda ignores me. She is staring at my father like he's a painting on a wall in a museum. "Can you still say that?" she asks him. "That you'll never get divorced?"

We all look at him now. He doesn't answer but his face turns deep red. He purses his lips, sips his beer, looks for the waitress then looks back at his ten-year-old daughter who has addressed him with astonishing directness.

"No," he finally says, simply. "No. I can't."

He says the words, then holds his mouth very tightly and swallows visibly, but there is more to be said and it is right on the tip of his tongue, pressing at the inside of his teeth to get out.

And then Papa starts to cry.

Resignation and disappointment spread gently across my sister's face and she nods knowingly. Then she starts crying, too. And for the next two unbearable minutes, they both sit there crying, loudly, embarrassingly, openly.

"What's going on?" Uli whispers to me as my father finally gets up and goes around the table to hold my sister.

"I don't know," I say, and I don't want to know. So Uli and I get up and go to the bar section with the tabletop Missile Command and shoot down planes and stop falling bombs and empty sugar packets into our mouths.

Three weeks go by. Nothing is said. Whatever caused the eruption seems to have subsided. I never ask, and Papa never mentions it again.

And then one day he calls to me from the second floor.

"Louis! Come down for a sec! Mom and I want to talk to you."

I'm reading about Red Ronin, a rampaging robot originally constructed to destroy Godzilla, who's now after the Avengers with a bitchin' solar blade. "Can't right now!" And for a moment there is no reply. I've done it. I've avoided the conversation I don't ever want to have.

Papa arrives silently at my door, eyes the water bong I left by the bean bag chair.

"You're high?"

"No." Iron Man's getting the shit kicked out of him by a shuddering yellow-green blast of plasmatic energy erupting from Ronin's shield. His arms cross awkwardly, legs fly back behind him in a paralytic superhero ballet. I imagine Tony Stark, trapped inside, sweat against iron, listening to his breath echo in the helmet. So claustrophobic. Can't escape.

"Son. Honey. You need to come down now. We have to talk about something."

I toss the comic on the lower bunk, swing down to the floor, and follow him down the hall, around the banister, down the stairs, and into his room. My sister and brother are there on the bed with my mother. No one says anything. I lie down, facing away from the family, spot an ancient bunny pellet among the dust bunnies under Mama's dresser.

As unusual as we are, this part turns out to be surprisingly by-the-book, my parents reciting the script you'd expect: "We've got something to say" . . . "difficult" . . . "sad news" . . . "divorce."

Amanda wails at the word. My mother breaks at the sound. David is lost. I lie still, silent. The questions come next, all from my sister: "Can't you do something? Try harder! You promised. Who's staying? Who's going? Where will we live? What about school?"

Now David cries, because Mama and Amanda are crying. And Papa is crying again. The ugliest sight of all. They are an emotional hurricane on the bed, wet and bellowing. I can't stand it. *This is where we are. Message received. Let's move on.*

"Don't you want to say anything?" they ask me.

I look at my sister. "I'm sorry I made you clean up your own puke that time I was babysitting you," I say, recalling her on her knees, swirling sick with a wet towel. She starts to cry again and I go to my room.

Mom comes up first, knocks lightly at the door, asks if she can come in, goes away when I say "no."

Papa next, no knock, just calls my name, says "If you want to talk . . ."

Only when Amanda calls meekly for me do I unlatch the door. She stands there, skinny and shivering in a worn flower nightgown, swollen eyes searching my face. She's unsure of what to expect. Will I tease her? Punish her? Send her away feeling worse than when she knocked? Looking at her sad little frame, I am suddenly soft.

"How did you know?" I ask.

She shakes her head slowly, staring at the bleached square in the center of the floor where Bunny Yabba used to live.

"I didn't," she whispers, tears running silently down each side of her face. "I just asked. Maybe that's why . . ."

"That's not why."

"But maybe if I never asked. Maybe if I never said anything . . . ?" My sister's body folds in on itself and she chokes on the grief squeezing out.

"It's their fault," I touch her bare shoulder. She shakes her head again. "It's *their* fault, not yours." She collapses against my chest and I hug her, weakly at first, then more tightly as the heat of her tears soaks through my shirt.

The signs have been all around me but I failed to see them. I wasn't looking. I was looking for naked girls. Water bongs. Howie. I didn't listen to the most highly attuned emotional barometer in the family. She saw this coming a mile away, didn't she? Suddenly all her crazy whining and crankiness passes through a universal translator and comes out as: *Hey! I see what you're doing! You're fucking up and breaking us! Stop!*

"You're the only one who was paying attention," I admit out loud. "I should have known, but I didn't. I'm the oldest. That was my job." This makes her cry harder and I stop talking.

Eventually she quiets and I walk her down the hall and tuck her into bed. She looks longingly at me before she closes her eyes and I shrug. "Remember the time we discovered sparks under the covers on Christmas Eve?" She nods. "Shouldn't have been a magical night. We're Jews. But they were there, right?" Nods again. It was just static. I know now, but we didn't know then. She still doesn't. Better that way. "Remember the glowy things under the dock in Maine?"

"Uh huh."

"Magic things. The awesome alrightness of being. Think about them while you fall asleep."

.   .   .

I lock my door, stuff a towel against the crack, pack the wooden bowl, turn off the lights, light two candles and sandalwood incense, spread a fuzzy orange blanket on the floor. The weed loosens the sad wrinkles of my brain. I climb out the window onto the ledge, gulp reflexively at the bite in the air, jump down onto the gravel-covered roof, and make my way up the steep slate gable to the highest point of the house. I'm four stories up, sitting on that knife-edge, surrounded by a black glass sky, under a rotten crescent moon. From here I can see the dark silhouette of the backyard, the emptying limbs of the trees, the warm light from the fancy house next door. The leaves bring back the memory of *North Shore Sundays*, whipping all around.

Pulling my knees to my chest I rock gently at the top of the house, feeling the family below me.

NICE WORK, YAHWEH! KEEP IT UP!

It's a choice now. Break or be broken. I can slide back down to my room or just let go and fall back the other way. It will feel the same until it doesn't, and then it will feel like thirty feet of thin air, and then it will feel like the brick Chestnut Street sidewalk, or maybe the wrought-iron fence in the front yard if I'm really unlucky.

I choose neither, shimmy along the metal stripping at the peak until I'm side by side with the chimney. Balanced precariously on a small brick ledge that pokes from its side is a bottle of Southern Comfort that Uli and I mixed with apple cider a few weeks ago. Disgusting then, worse now. But the sweet-hot bitter flood takes me further away.

I finish the bottle, slide back to the gravel roof. I can't say how long I was out there, but Here's Johnny! with Dr. Joyce Brothers and David Bowie. I pull a box of Franken Berry out from under the bed and eat a few fistfuls while Johnny does the monologue.

Bowie appears, red James Dean jacket, white T-shirt. The crowd goes nuts and Johnny says, "After all this, he'd better be good." Bowie sings "Life on Mars." *Take a look at the lawman beating up the wrong guy*. Best song I've ever heard.

I try to keep my eyes open during the commercials but before I know it it's morning and I'm hungover and Mama is calling up the stairs. I might hate her. For waking me up. For letting this happen. I fall back asleep. She calls again. I slap water on my face, grab a bagel, and walk all the fucking way to school.

The Smell I'm Tasting

It takes just three days for my mother to leave home for good. She takes Amanda, tries to convince me to join her. She found an apartment in Brookline, a town next to Boston, but I refuse. You can't make me switch schools *again*, I tell her. So Papa, David, and I form an unlikely roommate alliance, but after weeks of endless crying, David ships off for the new land. Still, I stay.

This city I rejected, where everything goes to die, where they celebrate the dark and the dead, is where I now want to stay and live, even as everything that is good dies around me.

> *It is no matter that the place is joyless for him; that he is weary of the old wooden houses, the mud and dust, the dead level of site and sentiment, the chill east wind, and the chillest of social atmospheres;—all these, and whatever faults besides he may see or imagine, are nothing to the purpose. The spell survives, and just as powerfully as if the natal spot were an earthly paradise.*

Good old Hawthorne. Knows this place well.

Papa and I begin a new life as men in this cavern of a house. I never imagined it could be more empty. But it is. David's room, Amanda's room, Howie and Carly's room, all vacated and left behind closed doors. My bare feet echo through the hall of the abandoned third floor. Howie's naked pink lady with the acrylic nipples still points to the guest room but the guests are gone.

Atjeh goes, too. But not to Brookline. To live "on a farm," Papa says. "We've got to take care of each other now."

Perversely, I've gotten what I wanted all these years: Papa, all to myself. As furious as I am, I take comfort that we are bound together by the rending. At home in the ashes of the last. We'll eat our meals together. Listen to Duane Ingalls Glasscock on BCN every Saturday morning. Maybe we'll even smoke pot together.

I start sleeping on the floor of the TV room next to Papa's room, drifting off to *Twilight Zone* reruns and repeat viewings of *The Exorcist*, convinced if I watch it enough times I won't be scared anymore. Take that, Man of the Year.

I try to explain the story to Papa but he's disgusted. "*Feh*. Why do you keep watching that kind of shit?"

"You took me to see *Jaws* when I was eight. What's the difference?"

"Well, we didn't watch it in bed, for one thing." He eyes the silver chain around my neck, a snake that's dangling against my greenhorn chest hairs. "Where'd you get that?" he asks curiously.

"Punk rock girl at school. I told you."

"Girls giving boys necklaces. It's all coming full circle. Good for you. She's a punker?"

"Yeah. Veronica. She has bleach-blonde hair and wears these crazy clothes. The whole school hates her but they just can't see past the window dressing. She's the cutest girl in the school."

"Good. Good for you. Sounds different from Sarah, yes?"

"Is Lenny Bruce's real name Leonard Schneider?"

Papa laughs. "So it is. And what ever happened to Gretchen? I never see her anymore."

I shrug. Gretchen is just too rough around the edges, and I don't need any more rough in my life right now. She tried a couple of times, but I just didn't answer the call.

"It's good to try different things. Experiment. I never did. The fifties weren't so good for that. You dated a few, maybe kissed a few, got married early." He quiets again. Then, "Listen. Speaking of. I have a bit of news. House business. Do you remember Mrs. Heffernan?" We've had many guests at our table but Papa's colleague from work is memorable. Well, maybe not on her own, but who could forget when her husband sneezed all over himself at dinner? He laughed at someone's joke and let loose a herculean butterscotch and olive gusher all over his sweater. Enough to fill a shot glass. Uli was so mad he missed it.

"You mean Mrs. Booger McBoogerwitz?"

"That's not nice. Not how you should remember her."

"Kind of hard to forget. And you tell that story *all* the time."

"Fair enough. Anyway, coincidentally, she and her husband are also getting divorced."

"Because of the snot?"

"Don't be a smart-ass," he says, but he smirks in a way that suggests the snot might have been part of it. "It's a difficult time for her," he says, regaining his footing, "and she has no place to live. So she's going to stay with us for a while."

"With us?" I'm incensed, and I don't know the half of it yet.

"It's the least we can do."

In a fit of desperation I call Grandma Wini.

"I don't think they're ever going to get the family back together again," I weep into the phone.

"I know, my love," she says, weeping back at me on the other end of the line. "I know. I can't take it. I can't stand it. This is the most terrible thing that has ever happened to me." Pause. "And I know it's the most terrible thing to happen to you. You don't deserve this." Then starkly more sober: "No, you don't deserve it."

"Can you talk to him? Can you make him try to get the family back together again?"

"Oh I can't, I can't," she wails, losing the momentary resolve. "It's not my place. He's a grown man. And you know your father."

But what do I know about my father, really? Only what he wants me to know. That, and what he can't successfully hide.

Danielle Heffernan arrives with a few bags and a guitar and takes Amanda's old room at the end of the hall. She wears tweed business suits during the day but at night she loses her formal edge. Strawberry blonde hair frames her freckle-sprayed face, demure little nose, and her apologetic smile. She could be one of the girls at Salem State College. And her seemingly genuine interest in me adds some light to empty old 31.

"Tell me about *The Silver Surfer*," she says, picking up a new book-length special edition.

"This one's by Stan Lee," I explain. "He created all the best. I think it's going to be a collector's item so I keep it in plastic."

"I'll be careful," she assures me, slipping the book gingerly from its protective envelope. "Wow. 'The Ultimate Cosmic Experience'? That's quite a claim. Is he actually surfing in space?"

"Lou," Papa intrudes. "I want to talk to you about something."

"Hold on," Danielle says. "We were in the middle of a conversation."

"Guys . . . Danielle . . . Can we just . . ." Papa's exasperation is annoying. "Can we return to the real world for a second?"

"Let's not and say we did," says Frank, standing in the open doorway to the TV room.

"Jesus!" Papa springs up. "Can you knock before you barge in next time?"

"Since when?" Frank asks. "Does Jack Tripper make Larry Dallas knock? No. Oh . . . Hi, Chrissy."

"Danielle," Papa reminds him.

"I know, I know. But it's such a swingin' pad around here now. Very free. Very '80s."

"Four's a crowd," Papa huffs.

"Hint taken. I just came over to say that I'll be away for the weekend and was hoping you could water my plants."

"Done. But I thought you got a roommate."

"Off in his old Corvette with his new girlfriend. Another one scraped off the bar at the Pig's Eye, I'd imagine. So I thank you for the neighborly kindness . . . And you'll walk my dog?" Frank adds.

"You don't have a dog," Papa and I say in unison.

"Just testing. You're good. Arrivederci, people."

"Hey Frank," I jump up to follow. "Can I borrow some records?"

"Sure, *ragazzino*. I just bought *In cars, daduhm, da dum daduhm*."

"Wait, Lou . . ." Papa calls behind me, but I am down the hall and through the swinging door that leads to Frank's apartment. I don't enjoy his serious talks anymore.

I return to my room with the Gary Numan album and a copy of *Diamond Dogs*. I felt fine all day but as I lay the record on the turntable I feel exhausted and my mood turns black. The Aladdin

Sane–era Bowie glares at me, now half dog, neutered by airbrush and disturbingly exposed. It's apocalyptic and depressing.

I look at the clock. Seven p.m. I wake up at eleven, the needle still bumping back and forth at the end of the vinyl. I stop the clicking, head back to my bunk, then turn and run to the cold black pitch of the bathroom and puke the day's meals in three torrential heaves. My face, my body, all my skin drips with sweat. I peel off the clothes I fell asleep in, find a dry pair of pajamas, trade the boggy sleeping bag on the top bunk for the guest bag on the bottom, and slip inside, shivering wildly.

When I wake again Danielle is standing beside the bunk, her head level with mine.

"You feel hot," she says, stroking my greasy hair.

"I got sick last night," I say, feeling like Amanda, so pitiful after she barfed her eggs.

"I noticed," she whispers softly. "You managed to leave a bit behind on the bathroom floor. I went skating in the dark in there." I turn my head to spare her from the smell I'm tasting. "I told your father that you should stay home from school today. I'll hang out and keep you company." I nod, press my face into the flattened pillow, grateful for the advance work she has done on my behalf. "Take off your shirt."

"Hm?" I ask, craning my neck to see her.

"I brought some alcohol up. It will help cool this fever." I follow her instruction, feeling awkward at the exposure. I lay weakly on my stomach, try to hide my chest, new nipple hairs and blackheads sprouting between my pecs. "Come down to the lower bunk here." The isopropyl pours cold and rubbery on my back—a violent sensation that makes me jump. If she were my mother I would be screaming, refusing further treatment. But I just hold my breath, curl in on myself, and wait for her warm hands to work the alcohol off.

Like Carly, Danielle brings an open affection into the house that's been missing. But Danielle is a different breed: conservative in dress, Catholic in faith, Irish in descent, and totally alien to me. I *should* be turned off by the conventional, doting way in which she treats me. I *should* be wishing for my mother to be nursing me back to health. But Danielle attends to me with a sense of focus I haven't known before. No other kids compete for her care. The idea that I have a physical or educational need that would go unattended is anathema to her. And beyond this sense of obligation, she seems genuinely interested. In me. *Reading a book? Let's discuss. Want to learn guitar? I can teach you a Beatles song. Sick? Stay home. I'll take care of you.* In a way, I feel more like a child than I have for a very, very long time.

"Oh, you're so tense!" she laments kindly. "How does a boy get so tense? It doesn't seem right."

"I have a lot on my mind."

"Of course you do. I know that. But you're"—pressing harder—"carrying"—harder—"it"—twisting my shoulder muscles—"in . . . your . . . back . . ." I scrunch my eyes at the exquisite pain and press deeper into the Wonder Bread mattress bunk, a complicated little feeling blooming between my legs.

I still have a fever when Papa comes home. He appears in my room with copies of *MAD Magazine, Spider-Man,* and *Fantastic Four.*

"You need anything?" he strokes my head awkwardly. "Want some tea?"

"No. Not right now." I'm glad he's making this effort but it should be Mama.

"OK. Shout if you need anything." And then, just before he's out the door: "By the way. I'm going to let Danielle start sleeping in my room. I think she'll be more . . . comfortable." Shivers replaced by the nuclear heat of a core breach. "OK? Amanda's room's too small, anyway."

Even if I could answer, I wouldn't know how. He's not asking for permission. He never does. That vacuum of silence in my room is the first moment of truth we have had in so long. Papa waits to see if I will bite, dig deeper, question his authority. I hold, hoping he might open, give, tell me what is really going on. How is it, really, that we are alone here? And who is this woman, really?

We should be able to talk, to have an honest conversation about what is happening to our family. We stayed behind because we are men, facing a hardship that should be surmountable if we stick together and share the weight. If we tell one another what risks we are facing. We could be Thunderbolt and Lightfoot. But we're not. I don't ask questions. He doesn't offer answers.

Valentine's Day comes and goes. I spend the evening with my bong and a pile of chalky heart candies I got from some girls at school.

"Where's Danielle?" I ask when my father comes home from work alone.

"Looking at an apartment," he says, stirring cottage cheese into my noodles.

"Is she moving out?"

He answers, not looking up from the bowl. "She's looking at an apartment."

"Where's she going?"

"Back Bay. It's a very fancy section of Boston. I'm getting my own apartment in Boston, too."

"But you said we're staying here," I blurt. "You promised."

"I know," he says, handing me my dinner. "But this will be easier. You'll like it."

"No."

"Yes. It's decided. We're going. Come be with me in Boston. It will be great. Danielle and I have fallen in love. It's a wonderful thing," he says softly, eyes damp and hopeful.

"This is the reason you and Mama aren't living together any-more. This was the reason all along."

"No. No. I promise you. This is just something that happened. I know this is a terrible time for you. It's a terrible time for me, too. But Danielle is a wonderful person. I think you can tell that by now. She's wonderful. Don't you think? Teaching you to play guitar. Taking care of us . . ."

"I don't care! That's not the point! You promised you'd never get divorced. And now you are. You promised we could stay in Salem. And now you're saying we can't. Why should I trust any-thing you say anymore? *Any*thing?"

I look him in the eye now. So hard, but I don't look away. His face reddens, mouth twists below the handlebars of his mustache. "Because," he says. "I'm your father."

"Not good enough anymore," I tell him, no longer angry, just empty. "I thought it was. It *should* be. But you don't deserve the title if you don't act like one."

"Listen to me." He adopts a tone that suggests he's trying to slow us both down, but looking in his eyes I can see him searching. He's trying to find the right answer. He doesn't have it this time.

"No. I don't want to listen. I always listen to you. Now listen to *me*: You did this. You did this. And you're not even sorry."

"No," he says softly. "I'm not."

His eyes search mine, hurt but resolved, and I realize he is fi-nally telling the truth. This family, the way it has been, it isn't what he really wanted. All the people he surrounded us with here? Frank? The Cuban Cutter? Glovey Butler? Even Howie and Carly? They were his way of filling gaps we couldn't possibly patch for him. Happiness gaps. Or unhappiness gaps, smoothed over with colors and characters and cocktail times. We were never enough. He needed to assemble an entire cast to move the play forward and get himself from Act to Act.

Staring at him I see now that he's found his leading lady. He can stop being the director and start being the star in his perfect little life performance. What we all wish for, maybe, just not for our dads. Dads are supposed to support our dramatic productions, not the other way around.

Hawthorne, that old Salem scribe, said happiness "in this world, when it comes, comes incidentally. Make it the object of pursuit, and it leads us a wild-goose chase, and is never attained. Follow some other object, and very possibly we may find that we have caught happiness without dreaming of it."

Papa didn't follow Hawthorne. He followed his all-American, God-given right to the pursuit of his happiness, and he caught it, without dreaming it.

Why, then, would he ever say he was sorry?

They're gone within a week. The house is on the market for just a few days before there is an offer. The new owners agree to keep Frank on as a tenant and he agrees to take me in. I feel a fleeting sense of triumph. I've beaten back the tide of the family tsunami, exited Papa's lame midlife crisis and set my own course.

But as Frank helps me lay my threadbare sleeping bag on the nappy couch in the downstairs foyer of his apartment I feel a surge of panic and, then, a ferocious anger. I barely hear Frank's offers of kindness over the whoosh of bad feeling. When he excuses himself I pull my journal, school kit, and Bucky Kerchak out of the travel bag Papa gave me before he left ("every man needs a good rucksack for his adventures") and sneak through the second-floor swinging door into the house that, just yesterday, was mine.

31 Chestnut is void of sound, furniture, everything but packing boxes. I walk through the space where the pool table once was. Through the strange gap left behind where the dining room table

had once been. Where Howie unfolded his centerfold and Carly smiled through puffy eyes. Where Mama fed us cottage cheese and noodles and Papa taught us how to know you're alive and how to fight a girl.

Where we danced.

Nothing on the second floor. Nothing on the third. The movers came and went while I was at school. I am as empty as my home has become.

Howie and Carly's room is the coldest, exposed in the front corner to February wind. In the glare of the bathroom light Mama's recipe painted on the shower wall is a false offering to a family that no longer eats here. Howie's zucchini potato pancake bird looks on, angrily. They'll paint over all of this, whoever they are.

No. I'm not empty. I am fury. I am hate.

I walk to the end of the hall, nearly black with dusk, open the door to the tall linen closet, and climb the shelves to the highest one, just inches from the ceiling. There, I set Bucky against the back wall, leaving him as best I can in a standing position. As soon as he seems stable, I balance against the top of the closet, lock my feet onto the wooden shims that hold the shelves, and brace with my belly as I scribble on the last page of my journal.

When it is done, I tear the page free, place it over Bucky's face, and thrust the sharp tip of my compass through the paper, through Bucky's head, and into the forgiving cedar behind it. Leaning back, I stare at him, impaled, dead eyes veiled by the greeting I have left behind for the new residents of my old house:

GET OUT!

They'll find this one day. They'll be frightened and they'll leave and I'll sneak back in again. I just need to stay with Frank long enough, make sure he doesn't do anything gay to me, and then I'll have the house all to myself.

Giving Tongue

"Hey, hey . . ." Frank says gently. He is rubbing my back.

Was I screaming in my sleep? "It's time to wake up. You overslept." I bolt upright on the sofa, the feeling of his hand still crawling on my skin. How long has he been sitting here? How much of me has he touched? All these months sleeping on his couch and I still haven't convinced myself he doesn't want me to be his boyfriend, though he's never done a single thing to make me think he wants anything except to be a surrogate dad.

"There's coffee here," he points to a mug on the ottoman. "You can have whatever you want for breakfast. I'm off to work." He smiles, looks at me searchingly, frowns. "Are you OK?"

I nod, still trying to catch my breath. A sound comes from upstairs, on the other side of the house. My side. I grunt.

Frank pulls on a jacket and stops at the door. He looks up, listens, shakes his head with resignation. "I'm sorry," he says. I nod in return but can't speak. So many things are unspeakable now. "Hang in there," he says. "It will come back around. What feels like a bullet in your brain today will be like a splinter in your finger tomorrow. You can count on that. I promise."

I smile to show I appreciate his sympathy, then I slip back under the blanket and wait for all the sounds to subside.

The school year proceeds according to a strict formula: blazing intoxication at night and perpetual agitation during the day. The former, a reasonably effective antidote for the latter, keeps me out of school a lot. And it generates a new sense of paranoia that keeps me housebound and cable-tethered. Uli and I drift apart. Veronica remains too beautiful to seriously pursue. Mama calls often but I'm rarely around. Frank dutifully takes messages. I can read the longing behind the words and it keeps me from returning her calls. Papa checks in once a week and seems angry that I haven't come over to his dark side. He doesn't try hard to persuade me, he just lets me know, in his silent way, that he's there when I'm ready to embrace him. I don't speak to Howie and Carly nearly as often, but they're so much better at bridging the distance with just a few carefully chosen, blatantly honest words. "This is shit. We love you. Be strong." I'd rather go to California and live with them than succumb to either of my parents' new realities. While Howie and Carly aren't offering that much, they do invite me to spend the summer there if I can find my way out. I promise them I will.

For now, Frank is turning out to be the most stable force in my universe. He knows I'm smoking and tabbing mesc but he doesn't judge, he just reminds me to be careful and makes me promise to come to him if I take one too many tokes over the line. He wakes me every morning for school with those gentle back rubs which I now realize are more innocent than my baby brother. Frank is, in fact, playing house. He has a little boy to take care of—his *ragazzino*—and he takes exquisite pleasure in the responsibility. I stop fearing his touch and find a rare comfort when he pulls me softly from my steady bloom of bad dreams. For a few months, Frank is the selfless parent the world will never give him the chance to truly be.

When the school year ends he drives me to Logan Airport. Mama has granted my one birthday wish: a round-trip ticket to Berkeley. In truth, I would have been fine with one-way but I knew to ask would be to break her heart that much more.

Frank hugs me good-bye, pats my cheek, tells me to be good. "I'll send your stuff to your mom's," he says. "It's going to be lonely on Chestnut Street."

"I may be back," I offer, but he shakes his head.

"You're always welcome, but you've got people waiting on you."

"If they really wanted me, they would have tried harder," I tell him, shouldering my travel bag.

Frank smiles sadly and pats my cheek again. "Maybe they need to know you really want them?"

I have to wait until the lady in the seat next to me falls asleep before I can pull the June issue of *Playboy* out of my backpack on the plane to San Francisco. It's Dorothy Stratten's Playmate of the Year pictorial. She's on the cover, white dress just *this* close to falling off. As with Howie, the choice feels inevitable. She must have had *some* campaign manager.

The ride over the Midwest is bumpy but eventually the seat-belt light goes off and I take Dorothy to the lavatory for a mile-high whack. Back in my seat, I fall asleep in five minutes, head against the window on the other side of the clouds.

Howie picks me up at the airport, arms waving and hugging, lifting me off my feet. We've hardly spoken for months, but time has lost its power to separate us.

"Jesus! You're big now." I try to lift him to show just how much.

We drive to Berkeley in a gold '71 Camaro, windows down to vent the smoke from a bit of a joint and a few cigarettes. Howie offers me some of the former, which I decline, and none of the latter.

"What happened to the minibus?"

"Felt the need for speed," he smiles. "You OK?" he asks before we get to the cottage. I nod. "This thing with your folks, it's a big piece of shit."

I nod again.

At the house, Carly wraps me up like a burrito, signature-tight, in her soft arms. She lays out an assortment of food but the only thing that appeals is a bowl of grapes. I flop onto their bed, the only communal space in this tiny two-room cottage, and pick at the fruit. My ears have yet to pop.

Traveling across the country hasn't erased, as I hoped it might, the feeling that things are irrevocably changed. The levity I expect in their presence is tempered by muffled questions: How's Mama doing? Does David understand what's going on?

The window is open and the lively smell of eucalyptus fills the room—so different from the smell of fireplace ash and chestnut mold. Howie's pot smells different, too—pungent and emerald, not like the crumbly brown 'lumbo back home. I grab a baggie from the night table and pluck out a bud. It's sticky, crystally, and lush like everything here, but almost too alive. The flourishing world of California brings my internal gray to stark relief.

"My stomach hurts," I say, though it's more than that. I just feel bad. Indeterminately bad. Full of bad. Sunday morning bad. And it is Sunday morning, kind of. The early morning flight that took me to San Francisco took me backward in time. Brunch time. But the Sunday paper here isn't gray, it's pink. And there's mango instead of lox.

"Want some tea?" Carly asks somewhere outside my ear muffle. I shake my head, reach for another grape. They're sweet, wet on my dried-out tongue. I can't stop eating them.

"Can I turn on the TV?"

"If you want," Howie says. He looks at Carly with sad eyes I don't miss and then plops down alongside me.

Star Trek is on. Kirk splits into two: a weak, whiny Kirk and a violent, aggressive Kirk. When it ends, another comes on. Spock goes home to Vulcan for a mating ritual.

"It's a marathon," I say happily when a commercial promises twenty-four straight hours of *Trek*. I down handfuls of grapes like popcorn for the next five hours, disappearing into a world of impassive orange and purple skies and alien papier-mâché landscapes.

My stomach only gets worse, and I start to feel a contact high from the weed Howie's been smoking beside me.

"You want to go for a walk?" he asks.

I nod. We turn off the TV, run the Camaro to Shorebird Park, and walk out along the fishing pier. Howie limps slightly and I give him a quizzical look. "Knee," he says. "It's fucked up."

California is relentlessly sunny but the wind blowing off the water gives me a chill.

"I'm going to be in a movie," Howie says. "It starts filming next week."

"Really?" I perk up. Howie smiles, a movie-star smile. I knew it. He's going to be a star. Jeff Bridges in *King Kong*, pulling Jessica Lange out of the ocean and saving her over and over again. "What's the movie? What's it called? Can I come watch you film it?"

"It's called *The Candy Stripers*," he says. "And no, you can't."

I sleep on a pullout couch in the front room, separated from Howie and Carly by a set of flimsy French doors and the sheer curtains that cover their panes. The wall above my head is filled with books.

I browse the titles before I fall asleep, settling on a little orange paperback about sex among inmates in prison.

I don't sleep well.

"Listen," Howie says as he passes me a breakfast joint. "I just sent a letter to Dorothy."

"*Wizard of Oz* Dorothy?"

"Dorothy Stratten, Hutch. I just wrote and said 'Hey, you're the Playmate of the Year. I'm Man of the Year. Let's get together and do some stuff.' Makes sense. Right?"

"She's going to be in a roller disco movie with Scott Baio," I recall, handing the smoking stub back to him.

"See? There you go. Why does it need to be Chachi? He's a kid. It should be me. Me and Dorothy on the silver screen. Sex symbols. It could be a musical. A disco musical about a band. And our music could be so intoxicating that it frees everyone up. Drops the hangups. And people fall in love every time they hear it. And we can call it *Sex Cymbals*. With a *C*. Like that? I like that. I like that! I'm going to write that. And I'm writing you in, too, hombre. You can be our guitarist. Fuck Scott Baio."

"Do I get to meet Dorothy?"

"Does Kurt Russell make a shitty Elvis?"

"Yes?"

"Yes."

"Well, you're already going to be in a movie."

"Not that kind of movie," he says, oddly low. "Robert Blake did *In Cold Blood*, not *Behind the Green Door*, you know? You don't get to be Baretta by playing Doctor Bishop. I know that now. I'm not even using my real name because everyone in LA says it could hurt my chances of doing the straight movie/TV thing."

"What name are you using?"

"Marc Howard."

"That's a good one."

"Look, last year I made five bucks an hour busting concrete.

Tomorrow they're paying two hundred for a half day to get my dick sucked in a closet by a nurse."

"And you're feeling bad? That's so dumb!"

"Hey, what the fuck do you know? It sounds like a good deal, but so did winning Man of the Year."

"So, you didn't get all the money Dorothy did," I admit. "Or the movie contract. Or the Corvette . . ."

"Keep it going, chief."

"What about the complete wardrobe? You still get a complete wardrobe for winning."

"Yeah, they promised me a complete wardrobe. LA-style? You could be talking anything. I was thinking five to twenty-five thousand dollars easily. But they just make promises. I spent days and days chasing them down. They were going to give me ten cents a copy for every boner poster of me they sold. So, good, I said, let's sell a million of them! But then eighty percent of their advertisers threatened to quit if they ever showed another man sprouting wood." He shakes his head. "Somehow my penis has become the line between erotica and pornography. I was their first guy with a hard-on and I'll probably be the last. And I haven't seen a dime. I got fifty posters."

"And the wardrobe?"

"Right. I need to stop smoking this shit for a little while." He taps out the joint, runs his hands through his hair, and presses on. "Yes. The wardrobe I finally got, after me nagging and nagging them, refusing to go away, writing nasty letters and being an asshole, as much as I could be without alienating them completely. Then, finally, I get a call from Linda Desiante, the publisher's secretary. I call her The Tongue 'cause she tells me the secrets of how to maneuver the shit, you know? I keep running into LA people who are just soooo fucking savvy. They're players in The Game. And they just look at me like a Berkeley rube. They just laugh. I come down in my flea market clothes and Carly's handmade pants. LA never got the revolution. Ever. They hate everything about it. Rags and torn jeans—that's high fashion in this world." He points out the window, his frustration painful for me to watch. "In LA . . . they don't even let you in the room. I can't get a table at a restaurant. They just hate it, 'cause they can't make any money off it. LA doesn't understand the revolution because the revolution is about sharing. We have enough here. *Here*. But LA is all about greed. The two never fit together and it's why I'm never going to make a home there. But I respect this woman, Linda. The Tongue is the queen of that empire. She laughs, too. She knows the story. But she likes me, so she tells me how to behave."

I'm having a hard time following. Partly because I still don't know what happened to the wardrobe, partly because I am way too high way too early in the morning, but mostly because this isn't Howie. Since when does he care about how people view him or how they *think* he should behave?

"So what happened to your fucking wardrobe?!" I yell, shocking him out of that place I don't want to see him go.

"OK, Jesus. I'm just telling you. There's a backstory here."

"The backstory is starting to sound like a sob story," I mumble, not intending to be mean.

His look confirms I've gone too far. But this is not what I came to California to find.

"I just need to know what happened to the wardrobe," I say. "OK? Please."

"Sure. When it came time to finally give me the wardrobe they were going to write me a check. The Tongue says 'How much do you want.' So I say five hundred. And she shakes her head and points her thumb higher. And I say, a thousand? She points higher again and I say fifteen hundred? And she says OK. She's the one who quietly let me know that I was an idiot and I had no idea what I was doing. I got fifteen hundred bucks, skipped the clothes, and bought a top-of-the-line Betamax camcorder. And I didn't do Merv."

"Good."

"I also went out and bought a tongue," he adds, and I choke on my milk. "A cow's tongue. Not sliced—a whole cow's tongue. It must have weighed, like, five pounds? Ten pounds? I had the butcher wrap it and I gave it to her. She was unwrapping it in her office and she screamed. Screamed! It was the only time I was able to leave her speechless. It was a great moment in my life. And maybe in her life, too. I know one thing: she'll never forget it. She knew all about LA, but she didn't know everything."

I howl and he laughs with me—not just high and merry, but that smile that takes joy in the other. That smile that is love.

Bobbling at the Joints

The naked beach past Pacifica, finally.

Howie and I smoke mind-bending weed in the Camaro, all the way to Shangri-la, stumble down the treacherous dune of Devil's Slide, and strip. I haven't been naked *on* a beach since I was four, but it doesn't feel free the way it did back then. I'm beyond high, relatively pubeless, and there's not a Playmate in sight. The only naked women here look like copper raisins carrying prunes.

What's more, the water is just as cold as Maine. No one told me that!

I turn onto my stomach and scan the mass of old flesh but it's hard to see past the group of naked Mexican men who form a circle on the beach between us and the water. They drink beer and bray, clearing the area.

One of the men catches me staring, sees my bloodshot eyes dart away, and calls out to me. I look back and he begins to pour beer, in a slow and frothing yellow stream, all over his dick, shrieking with laughter and calling to me in Spanish. He points to his wet joint, then to me, then squeals and rolls on his back. I don't know what he means but it totally freaks me out.

"Ignore the peanut gallery," Howie advises me. "Everyone has their own way of dealing with nudity. Some do it better than others."

Here's my way: I don't get up for the rest of the day and by bedtime my ass is so charred I want to cry. Carly rubs a thick layer of Noxzema on my butt cheeks—an experience that almost makes the burn worth it, but I can't help feeling like she's going to put a diaper on me next.

I spent the day on my stomach and now I have to sleep that way. Every time I roll over the sting wakes me, and the greasy slide turning back over in my jammies feels like I pooped.

I'm never going to a naked beach again.

"Aren't you going to be late?" Carly, drowsy with sleep, luscious.

"Fuck!" says Howie, rushing to the mirror one more time. He's smiling but he looks queasy.

"Break a leg," I say.

"This is what you *want*," Carly says. "Go get it." He nods and flies out the door, leaving dark feathers of exhaust and engine grumble behind.

"Well, this is just us. Let's make something of it, bambino."

We spend the day wandering together through the Exploratorium, the Palace of Fine Arts, and the lagoon, weaving between tiny field trippers and their teachers. As amazing as it is, I'm more excited for the tacos Carly has promised to make. I've never eaten Mexican food outside of Mexico.

"How's your tush?" Carly smiles. She hands me a hard corn shell and we sit on the edge of her bed and eat dinner.

"Fine," I frown, recalling her humiliating application of cold cream on my ass and the greasy sleep that followed last night. "How do you think Howie's doing?"

"I'm sure he's doing . . . great? I don't know. It's a little hard to talk about."

I imagine being on a movie set with Howie, watching him have sex with a real actress. How do they pick who has sex with whom? Does he get to do it with more than one woman? Carly hasn't said much, but she seems at peace. I don't know how. My mother cries every time we talk, and that's because her husband had sex with another woman last *year*. (Well, and ever since.) But I know this can't add up in the end. How can she not go back to being all puffy eyed? Howie's sleeping with an actor, I rationalize. They're getting paid. He'll be a bigger star because of it. Not just a magazine, *Phil Donahue* one-afternoon-stand star, but a movie star. Who cares what kind of movie it is? It's a *movie*. The comfort Carly exudes gives me the courage to ask.

"Do you care? About the kind of movie he's making, I mean."

"I care that he's happy," she says, as clear and as quick as a thunderclap, and I believe her. I don't think she wants anything more in this world than to be with him and see him happy. It's a major miracle: Howie found the perfect woman—the one who lets him be himself. And all the signs suggest that, despite the pain he may cause her, he is the perfect man for her.

"Did you know that Howie came *this close* to becoming a rabbi instead of being in this movie?"

I gag on a tortilla chip.

"He applied to the Hebrew Union College to become a rabbi. He likes history, you know. But they told him that in order to get into the rabbinic program you have to spend two years in Jerusalem studying Aramaic. So he chose *Candy Stripers*."

"Oh, well, that makes sense. Rabbi Gordon. Dr. Bishop. So similar."

"Either way, a Jewish mother should be proud!" We giggle,

scoop salsa, recline. Without meaning to, Carly breaks the mood. "Speaking of Jewish mothers, how's yours doing?"

I straighten, wrap the remainder of my tacos for later. "Bad. I don't know. I haven't seen her much. I don't like Brookline. When I go she's always crying. She gets mad even more than she used to."

"Poor Hunan Princess. She needs some loving." She pauses, looks at me deeply. "And so do you. Do you have a girlfriend?"

"Maybe."

"Penny?"

I shake my head.

"Gretchen!" She seems excited by that one. "No? Not Sarah?"

"No," I tell her. "New one. She's blonde. Kind of new wave. She wears triangle earrings and blue leather boots."

"Pretty?"

"Really really pretty. Almost . . ."

"Too pretty?"

"Yeah. I don't know how that's possible, but it's true. She's so pretty I get nervous. When she walks down the hall at school all the kids yell "Punk! Punk!" But she's not even really punk. She likes Blondie and The Cars, not the Dead Kennedys."

"Shiksa fever. I've seen it before. You want to play with the fire but you don't want to get burned." She musses my hair. "Know what I mean?"

"No."

"Some people make you hot and that's good. You want that. But your partner—the one you are really meant to be with—that one needs to be the one you can tell everything to." Her gaze drifts to the front door, as if Howie has just appeared. "They still have to make you hot, of course. You can't go without that. But there has to be trust and honesty. Otherwise you carry around secrets and secrets are like rocks in your backpack. The more you have, the heavier your load. You keep trying to drag it around with you, everywhere you go, until one day you just drop it all. And *that's* the shit. But if you stick to the people you can bare your soul to, and you return the favor, then your pack never gets too heavy."

I mull it and it strikes me as true. The secrets in my family dropped all at once—they were heavy. My parents were unhappy. My father was unfaithful. So capable of succumbing to their own drama, they could barely parent anymore. They were only capable of leaving me behind.

Carly intuits my destination: the dark rabbit hole. "Come on," she says. "Let's watch a little TV." She runs a Betamax tape of her and Howie on *Pittsburgh 2Day*, his hometown talk show.

The interview follows the same general pattern as *Donahue* did, but it's even more awkward because the hosts are just local TV boobs. "What's it like to pose naked? How do you feel about your husband being a sex symbol? What's your diet like?" And then, there's a surprise.

"We have some very special people in the audience," host number one, Patrice King, says from the crowd.

"You betcha!" Howie calls.

"These are Howie's parents! Would you stand please? Mr. and Mrs. Gordon!"

"Look at Howie's dad," Carly says. "Buttoning up his sports jacket and adjusting his belly?"

Howie's parents look really old. His mom, in pink sweater and red polka-dot blouse, follows his dad, standing beside him. She's holding Mr. Gordon's trench coat and hat against her chest. He takes them from her and hangs the coat over his left arm, hat in hand.

"Mr. Gordon, I have to ask you. How did you feel when you heard your son was going to be a centerfold in *Playgirl*?"

"To tell you the truth, honey, I was really uptight." The audience laughs. A guy in the back wearing sunglasses nods and smiles. You can hear Howie hooting above them all.

"Honey!" Carly giggles.

"You want to know something? Much more than my wife was."

"Oh, really?" Patrice asks.

"Yup, that's an absolute fact. But I tell you, knowing my son, he always does the unexpected."

"The *opposite*," says Mrs. Gordon.

"The opposite of what you want him to do. You know? That's Howie." The camera bounces back to Howie and Carly on stage. They're smiling, genuinely, but it's less superstar, more tender. "The thing that surprised me . . . about this whole thing. Our friends, our relatives, our neighbors—at first I was afraid to show my face." TV Howie's face falls just a bit, unsure where his father is going. "But I was surprised how well they took it. They got a real charge out of it. It added a little spice to their life. So everything turned out real good." He smiles genuinely, his own superstar smile, and Patrice holds his arm comfortingly.

"They seem nice," I say just as the real Howie bursts through the front door.

"I need the bedroom," he says curtly. "Can you guys go in the other room?"

"OK," Carly nudges me off her bed. "But can you give us a hint about your day?"

"Intense." He slams the french doors behind us. We shrug at one another and curl up on the couch.

"Were you reading this?" Carly asks, holding up the bright orange paperback that begins with a guy's first-person account of being raped in a prison cell. "Oy. Your mom's going to kill me."

Through the curtains I can make out Howie hunched over the desk that is nestled against the window of his room. Is he hitting the desk with his fists? Shaking it? Just typing furiously. It lasts a long time. And then, as suddenly as it began, it ends. Howie flings open the door, wild eyed, surrounded by stanky smoke. "Carly?"

"Yes . . . ?" Carly says slowly.

"Yes. Hi. I need you." He beckons her with a hand as he turns back to the desk. "And *niño*," he calls over his shoulder, "take a walk around the block."

"What?" I ask.

"Howie!" Carly lays a calming hand on his shoulder.

"Sorry. I mean, can you go grab me a pack of smokes? There's money on the table in there. And you can get yourself something, too."

"Howie," Carly soothes. "How about *talking* to us a little bit."

"I will. I will." He comes and stands at the door, looking to me imploringly. "Just help me out, hermano?"

"No prob." I grab the bills from the table, slip out the front door into a cooling night, find my way out to Martin Luther King Jr. Way, browse the comic books at the convenience store, and pick up *Spectacular Spider-Man* #40. Headline: "THIS, THEN, IS THE TRAGEDY." And below, five Spideys flailing in a tumultuous timeline—from regular Spidey to Spidey with a lizard face, ready to strike, eyes bloodred, fangs bared, scaled arms, pointed claws, thick tail wrapping treacherously around his legs. In a blue box above his head it says: "TO BEGIN AS MAN . . ." And in a red box by his lizard feet: ". . . AND END AS **MONSTER!**"

I read by streetlight on the slow walk back to the cottage, the unfamiliar exile from my friends' private lives making me lonelier than ever. I tiptoe up the stairs and enter through my darkened room. Howie's desk lamp softly filters through the sheer French door curtains and they are there, glowing, on the bed. My breath catches. Behind the sheer folds, Carly's legs are spread, ass in the air, Howie on top of her, thrusting. Her feet are bare. Her toes grip and release. Blood pulses in my skull.

This is it: the one thing they have yet to share with me. But the vision of Carly's heels rattles me, as if I am seeing something not meant to be seen, neither titillating nor seductive. I try to will her feet down to the bed. Wish silently for them to switch positions. It doesn't happen. They just keep fucking like this, Carly pushing herself up and against Howie. Howie slamming down with the same ferocity he brought to the typewriter.

My head feels like Carly's feet: flopping, bobbling at the joints, wagging loosely with the forces that pound against it. I feel guilty at the sight of her soles, dark from our barefoot walk in the park.

I go back outside. This is the porch where they got married, I realize. Those pictures. The smiles. The group watching them in their nakedness, steaming water fusing them together. It is a fond memory still: shocking then, romantic now, after everything I've seen since.

I return to Spidey under the yellow bulb of the porch light, ears turned toward the night sounds of insects in the yard and away from the night sounds coming from the bedroom. I flip to the final page, which concludes with a cliffhanger promising that, very soon, Spider-Man must face "The Macabre Menace of Meteor Man."

Lights flick out in the houses around me. Howie and Carly's bedroom lamp still glows.

I pee in the bushes, return to the porch, and flip back to the cover of issue #40. Five Spideys, all in pain, fighting the transformation to lizard. I read it again, from the start.

This, then, is the tragedy.

One Day I Will

Nothing moves this morning. I can't remember my dreams but when I wake I expect to be surrounded by rubble, the ceiling ripped off or caved in, cars tossed around the yard like Tonka Toys. Instead, a soft breeze eases through the window. I can smell the world and I wonder how cold it is back home, wherever that is. California, alien with its scents and prolific sun, is too bright for witches and ghosts. Howie and Carly are still asleep in a tight knot on the other side of the curtain. Together.

The phone rings until the machine picks up.

"Hi everyone, it's Phyllis. It's Mom." My stomach backs up to my spine. "I just wanted to say hi. Hi and I miss you all. And Lou, I miss you so much. Your brother and sister miss you and we can't wait for you to come home." Wherever that is. "So just call back. We'll see you soon."

I lie looking at the ceiling for a time, wondering what will happen when I do go back. Mama's apartment in Brookline, so small and unfamiliar, loud with the old C-line trolley cars clanging along Beacon Street.

Papa's new place—a basement apartment on Marlborough Street in the Back Bay—is worse: two tiny bedrooms side by side at the end of a narrow hall that opens onto a living room/dining room/galley kitchen framed at the end by a door of wrought iron. On the other side of the bars there's a small brick sitting area walled off from the Dumpsters and the fancy cars parked at senseless angles alongside one another. The apartment has two windows, one in each bedroom, also protected by black bars. In Salem the wrought iron was decorative. But we're not in Salem anymore.

"Huevos?" Howie opens the french doors, smiling in Carly's nightgown.

We eat together while Carly showers and scoots out of the house to a meeting.

"So?" I ask, watching him dump salsa on his eggs.

"Yup?"

"That's gross."

"I beg to differ. But we've already agreed to disagree when it comes to palate, haven't we? And I'm a hungry motherfucker." He spoons even more salsa on the plate.

"Are you going to tell me about it?"

Howie nods, chewing and swallowing, slurping coffee. "It's complicated," he begins slowly. "It's a new kind of experience. Didn't go exactly as I imagined." I shrug a casual acknowledgment, as if I understand what he's talking about. As if I have some kind of experience that can relate to this. "It's one thing to pose for a camera, by yourself, when you're the center of attention and you're the focus. It's arousing in a nice way. But when you're fucking a woman, your attention is turned toward her and toward yourself. Then there are these cameras and people and they're telling you how to move and what position to get into and when to come . . ."

"Sounds tough." I snort.

"Tougher than you think. They pay you for two things: to stay hard and to come when they tell you. And to look pretty. I did a decent job of looking pretty. But the other stuff was harder. I have this beautiful woman and she's dressed like a nurse in a hot little white uniform with the pink pinstripes and she's sucking me off . . . and I can't make it happen. Look: I can do sit-ups for my body, memorize all my lines, but I can't guarantee that I'll have a bone in my boner come game time."

"So you . . . ?"

"Lost it."

"No."

"And I got hives."

"No. Really? No!"

"*Sí.*"

"So you . . . you didn't do it?"

"No, I did it. It just took *forever*. And the funny thing is, the only way I could make it work was to *not* be Marc Howard the porn star. I actually had to be Howie Gordon, the fat Jewish kid from Pittsburgh again." His eyes meet mine and find utter confusion. "I had to go back to when I was that guy—that guy who was nervous and hot for the hottest girl in my class. And I had to work for that gift because I was fat and when I finally got with Mary Beth Scanlon . . ."

"The shiksa goddess?"

He laughs, my favorite laugh of his, as if the world just got unexpectedly brighter. "Did I tell you that?" he asks, grinning at me.

I raise my eyebrows, smile back. "On the roof. Magical mystery tour of fantabulousness and first vagina you ever touched."

"Well, yeah. Alright, compadre. That's it. Me and the shiksa goddess. You know, I thought I wanted to have this experience of getting blown by a porn star, but in the end the thing that got me hard and kept me up and made me come was the one thing I could always count on, my fantasy of fantasies, Mary Beth Scanlon and her hot little mouth. We never did it. I could never get her to go all the way. So every time I have sex, I'm thinking about her a little, about *what if*? What if this were her? That was so much sexier than the professional on her knees trying to fluff me back to life and get a wrap. And in the end, it was *me* that got me off. Me and Mary Beth. And that's how it ended. And they gave me a check for two hundred dollars and I went home."

"It does sound like fun. I mean, not all the people watching, but . . ."

"Well, they asked me to do another one. So we'll see if it gets better. But enough with the one-way confessional. What about you? You writing in that book I gave you? Laying down some truth?"

I get my journal and let him read at random, anxious but ultimately feeling safe in his hands. He finds the dream entry.

"I think the part about suffocating in the spongy wetness is scary as hell," he says, rubbing his face. "Did you really have that dream?"

I nod. "I dream about food a lot," I say, realizing it for the first time. "That one, about landing in the cabbage. Then this one." I read him a different piece, about being in a restaurant, starving, but only finding carrot cake on the menu.

"Hmmm . . . Suffocating in food. Nourishment and sustenance turning against you . . . You really have something there, Sigmund."

"I just don't know why everything—including my dessert—has to be made with vegetables."

"I hear that. But you're in the wrong town, compadre. Ever hear of Chez Panisse?" I shake my head again. "Big on veggies."

"Well they can suck my panisse."

"Good! Now you're freeing the muse. What else you got?"

I jump ahead a few pages. I know where I'm going, I just don't know if I can read it aloud.

"This one's a little . . ."

"This one's the one I want to hear," Howie says gently, as if he already knows what's burning on the page.

I start to read.

"'One of the hardest things for me to admit . . .'" My voice cracks a bit and I start again.

"'One of the hardest things for me to admit to myself I will now try to admit to you. Pause-think-be kind. At the moment my father finds sexual release with a woman named Danielle Heffernan. To my knowledge my father had been doing this only weeks after my mother had moved. He told me that this was true. He told me that there was no connection to their separation with this. My father has outright lied to me. I will never again believe him under any circumstances. I will never forgive him.'"

I look up at Howie. His eyes drive into mine, hard. He doesn't say anything but he is willing me on and I want to be strong for him.

"'His is a sad case. He uses his affair to purposely hurt my mother and I will not see her deliberately hurt by any man. My father is in deep trouble when it comes to associating with me. He neglects me, he pushes me past any fair expectations, and in no way repays me. His is the illusion that my hurting him is the most terrible thing I could do. He may be right but hurting me is worse. He has to understand. I am old enough to understand a situation but too young to do anything about it. Why my life has come down to so few words is a question unanswered because there are so many words but my hands have failed to yet write them. But one day. One day I will.'"

I close the book and we sit in silence. Howie doesn't take his eyes from mine but he doesn't say anything, either. He nods almost imperceptibly, shifts in his seat, pushes away the huevos detritus, and sighs. My face contracts with the wave of salt water I am trying to hold back. I need him to say something.

His face is sad, arms crossed. All his fiery intensity has fallen in on itself, crushed under its own great weight like a star going black.

"Come here," he says suddenly, his voice so soft, but still it fills the room. He opens his arms and I am sucked into them, his gravity pulling me away from my own desperate singularity. And as I tear from my decaying space in the universe I feel the months of withheld tears rain down against his chest and I am choking to stay above it all, gasping not to talk but just to breathe.

Surrender Dorothy

My last day comes too quickly. I wake up extra early, anticipating the flight. "Premature evacuation," says Howie, shaking his head.

I open the door of my room to the outside. One more whiff of warm air and lemon. The *Chronicle* is on the stoop. I sit down, unfold it. They found the *Titanic*. Carter's new strategy to take down Reagan. A $1.8 million Brinks robbery right here in San Francisco. But none of it matters. Dorothy Stratten's photo is on the front page.

For a moment this seems like good news. Coming to town? Meeting the Man of the Year? But, no. The headline says something different:

"PLAYMATE OF THE YEAR" MURDERED

The police found her and her estranged husband, Paul Snider, dead in his apartment. Both nude, lying there for at least a day, Snider with a twelve-gauge shotgun underneath him. Lieutenant Dan Cook said the motive was "that he was despondent over the breakup of the marriage."

I didn't even know she was married.

There's something about newsprint that doesn't do her photo justice. Dorothy should be glossy and in color, not a victim of rough black-and-white offset.

"It makes me sick," Howie says when I show him, and he is visibly disturbed. "This is the message coming all over again to watch out for one another. Love one another. Because you never know when it's going to slam shut. And you get whacked."

"I guess I was the better campaign manager?" I muster, despite the dark news.

"I think that's what they call damning with faint praise, hombre. But yes. The best I could ask for."

The drive to San Francisco International is cold and foggy, not how I imagined summer in California. Howie and Carly recharged some of what was lost in me, but there is, I am realizing, no way to retrieve the way things used to be. Their space is too small, and their lives are no longer as free. Dorothy dying is the capper—driving home the point, more than my fractured family seems ever to have done, that what we dream of and strive for is not necessarily what it seems.

But there's a plane waiting and a ticket in my pocket.

"Did you know about my dad?" I ask Howie, staring through the window at the fog hugging Yerba Buena.

"What about him?"

"About Danielle?"

"I knew that." He doesn't offer more.

I press. "When did you find out? Did you know it was happening before they got divorced?

"Does it matter what I know?"

I bristle at the question he uses to answer my question.

"Come on. You always say live life honestly. Be honest now," I stammer. "Why protect me? Nobody cared before. If I smoked pot. If I disappeared for two days. If I saw you all naked or snorting coke or telling secrets you shouldn't be telling in front of kids. I saw Carly giving you a blowjob in a slideshow just after I turned twelve. You showed me that! You showed me everything!"

I can't hold the rage. I need to open the car door and fling myself out—to be run over by an eighteen-wheeler before I come to a stop. My cheeks already feel bloody with road rash.

As if he senses my desperation, Howie stops the Camaro hard on the shoulder of the 101, pointing at my door.

"Get out."

He meets me around the passenger side, grabs my shoulders, and forces me down toward the ground. I won't cry this time.

"Listen. I'll always be honest with you, OK? That's my rule and I'm not gonna be the one to break it. But before I am, I want to tell you something. Can you listen to me?"

I look away, the blazing, heavy metal traffic so close.

"Can you listen to me?" he asks again above the roar.

I look away.

"Listen to me!" Howie yells, his voice so sharp it cuts the fog I'm trapped in. He's never yelled at me before. But I hear him now.

"There's something I want to share with you."

I nod again, unable to answer.

"When I was twenty-three or twenty-four my parents came out here to California. They heard that I moved out to a commune and that meant Charlie Manson to them. So they wanted to see what was going on and make sure I was OK. And while they were here I was getting Rolfed and doing all this counterculture kind of crap. I said to my dad when we got left alone, 'You know, I don't know anything about you. I want to know your story. I want to be friends. I want to know about your life.'"

"I don't want to be friends with my dad," I interrupt. "Ever."

"Hey, shut up for a second. Just listen." He holds my shoulders with his strong hands, trying to hold me back from the road. "I told my dad I wanted to know *his* story, OK? I wanted to be a man and know the man. So he obliged. He started telling me what I *thought* I wanted to know. And it's all about this hooker he was seeing on the side."

I am back with him at this unexpected turn. The metal-rubber-asphalt din hushes. He feels me come back and his hands loosen. "And it got to the point where his lips were moving and he was talking but I wasn't hearing him anymore, because inside I had become my mother. And the voices inside my head were going *You fucking son of a bitch. How dare you . . . Does mother know you're fucking a whore?!* And the truth was he was actually going to see this hooker with my mother's brother. The two of them would go and see her together. I mean, I went blind thinking about it. But I finally came out of that trance and said *'Dad! Dad! Dad! Stop! I was wrong. I can't do this. Let's just go back. You be my dad, I'll be your son, and I . . .'* Ugh. It was awful." He shakes his head. "So I learned a life lesson there. And later I heard about a line in the Bible: *'Thou shalt not gaze upon thy father's nakedness.'* Because if you pull down your dad's pants, if you stare at your dad's dick, it's going to make you crazy."

A million wheels return to focus, along with a sound like a squadron of TIE fighters, bearing down for attack. Howie's grip tightens again.

"I share that with you because there are things you really don't want to know about your dad. And you've crossed that line more than most because of the divorce. Because somehow in living through this, you've been given permission to see your parents as people, not parents. That's different. You have a Dad. A capital-*D* Dad. And you know Peter. Peter has a sex life. I didn't want to know that stuff about my dad. I couldn't handle it.

"Just sit on this for today. Think about what I said on the plane going home. When you get home, go to sleep. And when you wake up in the morning, if you still want to talk about it, call me and I'll tell you anything you want to know."

I cry when the plane takes off and I cry when I walk in the door of Mama's new apartment, but I don't let her see. Amanda and David are asleep.

"Did you have a good time?"

"I love California."

"I do, too. And I love Howie and Carly. How are they? We should call them and tell them you're back safely."

"You can," I say.

She wants to stay up and talk but I tell her I'm too tired and I go to bed, even though it's just seven in the evening by my circadian clock.

I don't call Howie the next day, or the day after that. I consider what he said—how ironic it is that the guy whose dick I have stared at more times than I can count is telling me not to stare at my father's dick. I want to maintain the anger I felt in the car on the way to the airport. I want to be angry at him now, and maybe deflect the anger I am feeling for Papa. But anger is hard for me to sustain. For better or worse, this is me—hungry enough to keep searching for the edible side of the rotten apple.

When Mama takes me to buy new clothes I don't complain. When she shows me how to find the right T line on the map that will get me to my new school, I listen attentively. When she asks me to babysit for Amanda and David so she can go out to the single parent group meeting at Runkle School, I say no problem.

"I'm so glad you're finally here," she says.

"I am, too," I assure her.

She hugs me. "I need a man around the house!" I nod silently.

"I was reading a mystery novel last night and it spooked me." I nod again. "But now you're here."

I take Amanda and David to the Star Market on the T and buy all the fixings for tacos, then I make them like Carly does, crumbling the beef in a cast-iron skillet and sprinkling chopped onion and tomato on top. I heat a Table Talk pie in the oven. I get cherry, even though I really want apple. Amanda and David like cherry.

Papa calls after dinner. "Danielle and I want you to know: you can come live with us as soon as you're ready. We'll help you get back on your feet."

"I'm OK," I tell him.

"You could use some adult supervision," he says, and when I don't reply: "Danielle says she wants to get back to the guitar lessons."

"Maybe," I tell him.

"How was California?" he changes tack.

"I love it."

"What's not to love? And Howie?"

"Making movies. Being Howie."

"He can't be anyone else, that's for sure."

I wish you could. Remember sitting on the stoop? Swimming in the lake? Hugging me on the dock on my birthday like no one around us mattered. I never wanted to be so far away from you.

"I love you, Lou," he says.

"I love you, too," I tell him. And I do. Gazing upon it all, I still do.

The next morning I wake up and spend a good part of the morning in Mama's bathroom, sick to my stomach. My ass has started to peel from the nude beach burn: the long strips of skin a last memento of California wildness. There's a copy of *Bostonia* maga-zine next to the toilet and when I'm feeling less queasy I take the psych questionnaire inside, then write the results in my journal: "Says that I am under too much stress and that I need professional medical help. Cosmic bummer."

Howie's bent and frayed *Scarlet Letter* has been added to the books Mama picked to put on a small shelf in my room. I splay on the bed and flip through it back to front. The word "Salem" jumps out instantly from the appendix:

> The novel was immediately popular, allowing Haw-thorne to move away from Salem with this good rid-dance: "I detest this town so much that I hate to go into the streets or to have the people see me. Anywhere else, I shall at once be entirely another man."

The T clangs by outside on Beacon Street as I lie there, Chest-nut Street still alive in my mind. No. This is where Hawthorne was wrong. I hated Salem, but then I latched on to it. And I held on because that was the only anchor I was offered. Wishing the eighth home to be the final, the stable one. But my obsession with place has turned out to be a red herring. New York. Salem. Cali-fornia. They were only as nourishing as the people who shared the space and time. Howie is right: if we're all going to get whacked, what matters is who is standing beside you when the universe speaks your name. And it matters that you stand with them.

Howie calls. It's been a week since we said good-bye.

"What's the word, compadre?" he asks, three thousand miles removed.

"What's up with you?"

"Starting a new film tomorrow. *The Dong Show*. I play Chuck Bare-Ass."

"I'm starting a new school tomorrow."

"I know. You ready?"

"Yup." An abbreviation for a universe of information. I can't find the words to explain to him just how ready I am. How ready he has made me. And how scared I am.

"Hey. You know, you never called me back."

"Yeah, well, you were right."

"It's not about right or wrong, little brother. It's about how deep you want to swim. You don't have to go all the way."

"I'm not going to. I'm going my way."

"That's the way you were meant to go," he says softly.

"Thanks," I tell him. "I think I got it."

"OK, then. I love you. You know that? We love you. You're the man."

Author's Note

The Family Endures

How lucky I am to love, and be loved by, this amazing cast of characters I call family.

Amanda lives in Western Massachusetts with her husband, Matt, and her son, Zachary. She is a woman of rare sensitivity and compassion who has devoted her career to helping children in crisis.

David is a DJ living in Los Angeles with his wife, Jen. He spins records around the world, regularly mixing the retro sounds we grew up to with twenty-first century beats. He has little memory of the events that occur in this book, but he does remember Bunny Yabba fondly.

My father and Danielle married in 1984. They took me in when things were at their worst, helped me finish high school, and taught me, by example, the skills I would need to have a career of impact and meaning. They also gave me two beautiful sisters, Antonia and Dirrane, and cofounded a welfare-to-work company together which they continue to run. In 2009 they were featured in a Discovery Channel series called The Science of Sex Appeal in which their longstanding relationship was put to hormonal and neurological tests. They passed.

My mother nearly died in 1993 from a sudden liver infection. Her then-boyfriend Rich, a loving and curmudgeonly anti-Papa, stayed faithfully by her side through the transplant and recovery and they were married in 1996. She recently took on a consulting assignment to develop banking software. The woman who wielded a sledgehammer with grace has smashed more than her share of walls post–Chestnut Street.

Carly continues to help others as a therapist in California, providing support to adolescent women and their families, couples seeking help with sexual issues or the psychological aspects of infertility, and people struggling with health care providers. Her ability to express and inspire joy is an enduring gift to this world.

Howie retired from porn in the mid-'80s when HIV/AIDS swept in, after appearing in more than a hundred X-rated films and videos. He won the porn industry's equivalent of an Oscar at the first ever AVN awards in 1984, taking home not one but two trophies for best actor and best supporting actor in the same year. He still keeps journals and, in 2013, published *Hindsight: True Love & Mischief in the Golden Age of Porn*, a memoir about his storied career. His iconoclasm, artistry, and honesty continue to influence my understanding of what it means to be a good human being, and a good man.

Howie and Carly are still married. They have three kids and two grandkids. Aside from Uncle Rick and Aunt Leslie, they are the only couple we know to have survived the Great Divorce Wave of the 1980s. If you're a romantic, you may think it's some kind of miracle. If you're a cynic, a case of make-believe. But it's just them: honest and in love.

I met and fell in love with my wife, Dana, on a cold November night in a Northampton ice cream shop in 1993. She was one week from moving out of town and I don't like ice cream. But certain things are meant to be. Dana's direct and honest way was instantly familiar, and an instant relief. We married in 1998 and Sam and Sylvie joined us shortly thereafter.

Howie and Carly returned to New England for a visit last autumn. They only stayed for a few days this time around, and it wasn't nearly enough. A little older and slower than in 1978, they are no less capable of inspiring delight and imagination in every generation of the Cove family.

Howie and me, back in Berkeley, California, 2014

Acknowledging Memoir, Memory, and the Many Supporters of *Man of the Year*

The risk in taking a snapshot of a brief, dramatic period is that it will be seen as representative of an entire life, and that the people who populate the story—the way they behaved, their blunders, heroism, bad decisions, honest mistakes—will be frozen in time. The moments I recall in this book were defining ones for me, but they constitute just one chapter in a lifelong tale. This chapter begins with the last, best year in the life of my nuclear family, as well as the events that led to its painful implosion. By the end, everyone was struggling to do the right thing.

Conversations here are remembered, transcribed from my earliest journals, and informed by interviews I conducted over a two-year period with all the major players (and some of the minor ones, too). Events are sometimes conflated to provide a more efficient narrative, or because they have converged over time in the fickle glue of gray matter. With few exceptions, I have changed the names and obscured certain details of people who appear in these pages to protect their privacy.

The most important thing for the reader to know is this: there wouldn't be a story to tell—and I certainly wouldn't be capable of telling it—if my family hadn't found a way through the challenging times. The support of my parents, my siblings, and Howie and Carly Gordon during the writing of this book and all the years leading up to it is what has given me the strength to be disciplined, to remain true to myself, and to my desire to write this story.

Family and creativity are the two most precious gems in my life, even though they occasionally threaten to collide. Holding the whole of this life is never easy, but loving one another deeply and listening closely to the other gives us all a fighting chance. I hope that I have shown you all the same grace and understanding that you have shown me throughout my life.

For everyone else who helped along the way, portraying you in this book is simple.

This book became a reality over dinner in Los Angeles, after a stop in Berkeley to visit with my old friends. The brilliant and inquisitive Jessica Elbaum asked me what I was writing these days. Although I had not yet begun, this was the story I told her. Her enthusiasm and encouragement have persisted, and if you like this book you have Jess to thank.

I received substantial creative support from Sarah Larson, Mary Cronin, Tammy Greenwood, and Jane Cavolina—literary lights, all.

Women and men of the year include Lisa Nelson, Catherine Newman, Sarah Hedrick, Naomi Shulman, Matthew Glassman, Tom Timmins, Jeb Brody, Courtney Kivowitz, Dana Adam Shapiro, Joshuah Bearman, Steve Bodow, Shoshana Berger, Ben Gundersheimer, Scott Goodstein, Damon Lindelof, Aaron Lansky, Brooke Berman, AJ Jacobs, Jill Soloway, Larry Smith, Christopher Noxon, Davy Rothbart, Lauren Redniss, Ira Silverberg, Emily Spivack, Susan McPherson, Ross Martin, Betsy Amster, Ina Stern, Jane Friedman, Tina Pohlman, Alex Grossman, and Colby Smith. Thank you for seeing something worthwhile here, and thank you for supporting me.

I want to extend a special thanks to Joshua Foer, *Man of the Year* enthusiast and true believer.

When we first spoke, I told Alex Jacobs that I had devoted my career to championing the creative work of others and now I was looking for someone to champion mine. He promised that I would get more than some*one* in this process, I would get the support of the entire team at Elyse Cheney Literary Associates.

I can happily report that they *are* the champions.

Alex: no one could wish for a better campaign manager. Happily, I also found a friend.

What's more, I have had the good fortune to be adopted by the Flatiron Books family: Colin Dickerman, Bob Miller, Marlena Bittner, and James Melia. From the moment we met, I've asked myself just one thing: *Where have you been all my life?* It doesn't get better.

Above all, Dana. I often reference Emerson's claim that "The man is only half himself, the other half is his expression." But you are my true other half, and my expression loses its meaning without you. You made the time and space for this work, but all along I have understood that my time and space is empty without you, Sam, and Sylvie. Thank you.

Lou Cove
Amherst, MA
2016